A DEVOTIONAL GUIDE

FOR

_____

DATE

_____

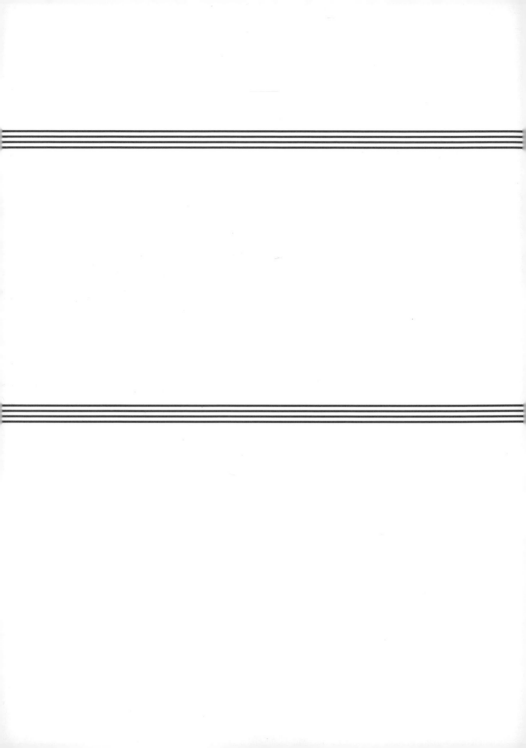

365 Days *of* Total Heart Health

Transform Your Physical and Spiritual Life

By Ed & Jo Beth Young

With Physical Health Tips by

Dr. Mike Duncan (Cardiovascular Surgeon)

and Dr. Rick Leachman (Cardiologist) of the Texas Heart Institute,

and Physical Fitness Expert Kristy Brown

Published by J. Countryman®, a division of Thomas Nelson, Inc., Nashville, Tennessee 37214

Unless otherwise noted, all Scripture quotations are from the *New King James Version*® of the Bible (NKJV). ©1979, 1980, 1982, 1992, Thomas Nelson, Inc., Publisher. All rights reserved.
Scriptures with the notation (NCV) are from the *New Century Version*® of the Bible. Copyright © 1987, 1988, 1991 by Thomas Nelson, Inc. All rights reserved.
Scriptures with the notation (KJV) are from the *King James Version* of the Bible.
Scriptures with the notation (NASB) are from the *New American Standard Bible* © 1960, 1962, 1963, 1971, 1972, 1973, 1975, and 1977 by the Lockman Foundation, and are used by permission.

Compiled and written by Wallace Henley.

Author is represented by the literary agency of WordServe Literary Group, 2235 Ashwood Place, Highlands Ranch, Colorado 80129.

Designed by the DesignWorks Group; cover, David Uttley; interior, Robin Black
              www.thedesignworksgroup.com

Project Editor: Kathy Baker

ISBN 1–4041–0209–4

Printed and bound in China

I will praise You, O LORD,
with my whole heart;
I will tell of all Your marvelous works.

PSALM 9:1

*"What does the L*ORD *your God require of you,*

*but to fear the L*ORD *your God,*

to walk in all His ways and to love Him,

*to serve the L*ORD *your God with*

all your heart

and with all your soul."

DEUTERONOMY 10:12

Introduction

YOU CAN HAVE A HEALTHY HEART LIFESTYLE in ninety days! That's the blessing that awaits when you embrace a Total Heart Health lifestyle, one that realizes that a healthy *physical* heart is as important as a healthy *spiritual* heart. But it's not enough to just reach Total Heart Health—you have to maintain your heart. This daily devotional will help you stay focused and motivated all year long. Every day you'll find three things:

A devotional reading emphasizing the heart
A health tip for your spiritual heart
A health tip for your physical heart

The authors of this book are so committed to Total Heart Health at our church, Second Baptist Church of Houston, that we have a worship center, a fully equipped fitness center, and a café serving healthy meals—all under the same roof. We can say with confidence that if you implement the principles presented in the *Total Heart Health* resources, it will change your life. We are living proof, as are hundreds of men and women in our church and community who have adopted the Total Heart Health lifestyle.

Are you ready for a healthier heart? Then let's get started!

January

We are the stewards,
not the possessors, of health.
Caring for our bodies is a way
of honoring and loving God.

♥ The Day Is Here!

PSALM 118:24
This is the day the LORD has made;
We will rejoice and be glad in it.

FULFILLING LOFTY NEW YEAR'S RESOLUTIONS begins when we say, "*This* is the day . . ."

We promise ourselves a day will come when we will lop off destructive habits, renew the mind, transform behavior, start a healthy diet, begin an exercise program, deal with our stresses, be kind to our kids, romance our spouse, and quit kicking the dog.

And, oh yes, on that day, we will launch into spiritual renewal, developing intimate personal communion with God and spending time in His word.

SPIRITUAL HEART FOCUS
Set a goal to spend quality personal time with God each day this year.

But then we procrastinate. Waistlines bulge, blood pressures spurt up, family quality shrinks, and spiritual vitality sags. The dreams and hopes at the start of a new year are pots of gold at rainbow–ends where we never arrive.

But the way to renewal begins when we declare, "*This* is the day . . ." God has created this as a day of beginning. Seize it, and walk in it toward *Total Heart Health*.

PHYSICAL HEART FOCUS

Weigh yourself and check your Body Mass Index (BMI). Commit yourself to building a new dietary and physical fitness behavior this year that will be heart–healthy. Tomorrow we will talk about how you accomplish the goal.

❤ The Fullness of Days

GALATIANS 4:4, 5

When the fullness of the time had come, God sent forth His Son, born of a woman, born under the law, to redeem those who were under the law, that we might receive the adoption as sons.

BUCKETS OVERFLOW beginning with a single drop. History's events were the drops of destiny, filling the bucket of time until it overflowed in its culminating event, the coming of Jesus Christ. The process you launch toward total heart health begins with the droplet of one day. But as you persist, the vessel of your days gets full and overflows. New heart–healthy habits become your lifestyle. What has been sheer discipline becomes delight.

> **SPIRITUAL HEART FOCUS**
> Launch out today on a 21–day commitment to change your daily routine to include at least 30 minutes per day in personal meditation on Scripture, prayer, and worship.

In the Bible, forty years symbolizes a generation. The old has passed away and the new generation has emerged. Some people say it takes twenty–one days to shatter an old habit and forty days to cement a new behavior. And in ninety days, the new often becomes one's lifestyle.

Jesus says those who endure to the end will be saved (Matthew 10:22). This is true not only for our eternal salvation, but for the fullness of total heart health as well.

PHYSICAL HEART FOCUS

Make today the first in a 21–day effort to spend a half–hour daily in physical exercise, and practice good dietary habits throughout the day. Consult your personal physician about diet and exercise, especially if you have persistent health problems.

❤ Making the Most of Your Time

EPHESIANS 5:15–17

See then that you walk circumspectly, not as fools but as wise, redeeming the time, because the days are evil. Therefore do not be unwise, but understand what the will of the Lord is.

To MAKE THE MOST OF YOUR TIME for total heart health, devote thirty minutes each day to strengthening the spiritual heart, the foundation of a healthy, balanced life. Doing this at the beginning of the day, as Jesus did, gives order to the remainder. Giving another thirty minutes to the physical heart through exercise makes the most of your time regarding bodily health.

The concentrated periods paint the portrait of the whole day. The spiritual heart radiates through continual conversation with God. The physical heart glistens through good diet and other healthy practices throughout the day.

At day's end, you look back satisfied, knowing you have made the best use of your time.

SPIRITUAL HEART FOCUS
For your personal time with the Lord, choose a place and time free of distractions and focus on Him alone.

PHYSICAL HEART FOCUS

Determine not to let interruptions keep you from your daily workout, and refuse temptations to gobble down unhealthy fast food.

❤ The Core of Total Heart Health

MARK 12:28–31

Then one of the scribes came, and having heard them reasoning together, perceiving that He had answered them well, asked Him, "Which is the first commandment of all?" Jesus answered him, "The first of all the commandments is: 'Hear, O Israel, the LORD our God, the LORD is one. And you shall love the LORD your God with all your heart, with all your soul, with all your mind, and with all your strength.' This is the first commandment. And the second, like it, is this: 'You shall love your neighbor as yourself.' There is no other commandment greater than these."

FREDERIC–AUGUSTE BARTHOLDI FACED two challenges in designing the Statue of Liberty: how to hold together 100 tons of copper plate and how to make a structure strong enough to resist fierce winds. The answer was a 94–foot–high skeleton of wrought iron at the core. It's so strong that Lady Liberty sways only three inches in a 50–mile-per-hour wind.

> **SPIRITUAL HEART FOCUS**
> Meditate on what it means to love God, other people, and yourself with healthy love.

Jesus revealed the skeletal core of God's intention for human beings. There are three elements to this "heart of the heart": total love for God, dynamic love of your neighbor, and healthy self–love.

This is the core of total heart health. Building your life on Jesus' foundational principles provides you the vitality and strength to withstand the fiercest winds of adversity and trial.

PHYSICAL HEART FOCUS

Take your lunch to work or school. Then you can control what you eat and how many calories you consume.

♥ Loving God with the Total Heart

ROMANS 12:2

And do not be conformed to this world, but be transformed by the renewing of your mind, that you may prove what is that good and acceptable and perfect will of God.

SOME RESEARCHERS NOW SUGGEST that the brain may be hardwired to respond to God, but even if it is, we must be transformed to love Him. Jesus says we are to love God with all our heart. Sin fragmented human personality. Flesh and spirit are often at war with one another. Through Christ's sanctifying work, human personality undergoes a process of reintegration and harmonization.

Some theorists still support the fragmentation theory, separating the physical heart from the spiritual heart. New scientific discoveries are overturning this dualism.

SPIRITUAL
HEART FOCUS
Commit yourself to God to being a good steward of both your spiritual and physical heart.

We cannot have total heart health if we focus only on the biological heart and ignore the spiritual. But true spirituality means accepting the stewardship of the physical heart God has given us as well.

This is what it means to love God with the totality of heart.

PHYSICAL HEART FOCUS
Success motivates you to continue, so set realistic exercise goals that fit your lifestyle.

♥ Loving God with All Your Soul

MARK 12:30

"'And you shall love the LORD your God with all your heart, with all your soul, with all your mind, and with all your strength.' This is the first commandment."

THE SOUL IS THE "HEART" of personality. Loving God with all your soul means centering thoughts on God, governing emotions by His character, and setting the will on the Lord and His Kingdom interests.

A daily spiritual exercise helps me* express love for God at the soul level. I pray using the acronym SELF. It works like this:

S = Surrender. I surrender myself to God in prayer, acknowledging His Lordship over my whole personality.

E = Empty. I ask the Lord to examine my heart and to help me empty myself of anything that is out of line with His character or that would block communion with Him.

SPIRITUAL
HEART FOCUS
Try praying through
the SELF acronym.

L = Lift. I "lift" praise, worship, and thanksgiving to God.

F = Fill. I ask the Lord to fill me with His Holy Spirit.

Loving God with all your soul keeps you from falling into the fundamental idolatry: the worship of self or your own personality.

PHYSICAL HEART FOCUS

Substitute fresh strawberries or orange slices in place of out–of–season tomatoes in your green salad.

*All first-person references in this book are by Ed Young.

♥ Loving God with All Your Mind

MARK 12:30

"'And you shall love the LORD your God with all your heart,
with all your soul, with all your mind, and with all your strength.'
This is the first commandment."

AS A PERSON "THINKETH in his heart, so is he," says Proverbs 23:7 (KJV). The mind is the "heart" of thought.

To love God with all your mind, you must control speculations, which are scenarios dreamed up to rationalize behaviors or to explain experience (2 Corinthians 10:5). They are often unhealthy, and they can separate us from the truth that will set us free (John 8:32).

SPIRITUAL HEART FOCUS
Change your leisure and entertainment habits from watching movies and programs that depict violence and project nonbiblical sexual values.

Loving God with all your mind means ridding the soul of "every lofty thing raised up against the knowledge of God" (2 Corinthians 10:5 NASB). Literally, these are mental barriers blocking God's truth. We must constantly take our thoughts "captive to the obedience of Christ" by aligning our wills to conform to the mind of Jesus Christ.

What goes on in the "heart" of thought can determine the health of the physical heart.

PHYSICAL HEART FOCUS
Regular medical checkups are a must for early diagnosis and prevention of heart disease.

❤ Loving God with All Your Strength

MARK 12:30

"'And you shall love the Lᴏʀᴅ your God with all your heart, with all your soul, with all your mind, and with all your strength.' This is the first commandment."

"Wʜᴇɴ I ʀᴜɴ, I ꜰᴇᴇʟ Gᴏᴅ's ᴘʟᴇᴀsᴜʀᴇ," said Olympic champion Eric Liddell in the film *Chariots of Fire,* capturing what it means to love God with all one's strength.

"Strength" refers to your ability and might. Loving God with all your strength also means being a good steward of your physical health.

Years ago, I had 90 percent blockage in one of my arteries until angioplasty cleared my blood vessels. I realized physical health is a gift from God, and caring for our bodies is a way of honoring and loving Him.

We are the stewards, not the possessors, of health. After my heart episode, I changed my diet and exercise habits.

As you are a good steward of your physical heart, you also will sense the pleasure of God in physical as well as spiritual endeavors.

SPIRITUAL HEART FOCUS
Thank God for your physical strength. Even if you're weak, thank Him for the strength you do have.

PHYSICAL HEART FOCUS

Use the stairs in your home or at work as an exercise machine. If you don't have stairs, visit a fitness store and invest in a stair–stepper.

❤ Loving Your Neighbor

MARK 12:31

"And the second, like it, is this: 'You shall love your neighbor as yourself.' There is no other commandment greater than these."

TOTAL HEART HEALTH NECESSITATES healthy social relationships.

The word for "neighbor" appearing in Mark 12:31 means "near." Jesus says we are to love those we bump up against each day. This includes family, colleagues, schoolmates, fellow church members, cashiers, restaurant staffs, and hosts of others.

We are to love them unconditionally. When we love people without strings attached, our stress is greatly reduced, because so much tension arises as people fail to meet our expectations or respond in ways we hadn't anticipated.

Loving people unconditionally means we are free to love them in a healthy manner.

> **SPIRITUAL HEART FOCUS**
> What do you do to bless and encourage people? Make a list and pray for opportunities to bless others.

PHYSICAL HEART FOCUS

Remember, you add weight when you take in more calories than you burn off each day.

❤ Loving Yourself

MARK 12:31

"And the second, like it, is this: 'You shall love your neighbor as yourself.'
There is no other commandment greater than these."

JESUS CALLS FOR SELF–DENIAL, not self–hate.

As in most attitudes and practices, there is a perverted self–love and a healthy self–love. Healthy self–love is knowing and loving your true self. Paul terms himself the "chief" of sinners (1 Timothy 1:15), but Paul also encouraged people to "imitate me" (1 Corinthians 4:16; 11:1).

Healthy self–love recognizes personality as the arena of God's transforming work. When you love yourself the right way, you are cherishing and celebrating the person God made you to be.

In Greek mythology, the problem with Narcissus was that he fell in love with his own reflection—the projection of his image. Healthy self–love is loving what God loves in your personality, not what you have made of yourself. It's unhealthy to idolize the self, but good to esteem yourself as the creation and instrument of God.

> SPIRITUAL
> HEART FOCUS
> Give God thanks that you are made in His image, and thank Him for the unique gifts and talents He's placed in your life.

PHYSICAL HEART FOCUS

Proper self–esteem regarding your physical body means eating right, getting to your ideal weight, and regularly participating in moderate exercise.

❤ The Clean Heart

PSALM 51:10

Create in me a clean heart, O God, And renew a steadfast spirit within me.

PHYSICAL HEART IMPURITY has internal and external causes. Internally, genetics affect heart health, such as an inherited tendency to have high cholesterol. So, too, "in sin my mother conceived me" (Psalm 51:5) is a description of our spiritual heart impurity.

External physical harm may come through oxidants formed as oxygen in the bloodstream interacts with harmful chemicals in the environment. Spiritually, the world's fallen culture corrupts the heart.

SPIRITUAL HEART FOCUS

Your weak spots are the places the devil can control. List in your journal your weak spots, along with specific goals for gaining the Lord's strength in those areas.

"Create" in Psalm 51:10 is the same word used in Genesis for God's creation of the world. The Psalmist is praying for a heart as pure as the world in the first day of creation.

The great joy and hope of life in Christ is the knowledge that the God who spoke worlds into being can form a new heart in His child.

PHYSICAL HEART FOCUS

Avoid all tobacco use. Tobacco is perhaps the most potent and pervasive external toxin affecting the physical heart.

♥ Diagnosing the Defiling Heart

MATTHEW 15:16–20

So Jesus said, . . . "those things which proceed out of the mouth come from the heart, and they defile a man. For out of the heart proceed evil thoughts, murders, adulteries, fornications, thefts, false witness, blasphemies. These are the things which defile a man, but to eat with unwashed hands does not defile a man."

"YOUR CHEATIN' HEART will tell on you," both Hank Williams Sr. and Jr. have crooned. The condition of the heart reveals the whole person.

A sick physical heart affects the body's vitality, and a sick spiritual heart, says Jesus, defiles one's total existence. Physical heart disease is the world's leading cause of death, but the top problem of all humanity is spiritual heart disease.

Good diagnosis is vital for treating the sick physical heart. Stethoscopes and electrocardiogram machines are blessings. Diagnosis also is critical for healing the spiritual heart and the defilement it brings to the whole person. The Great Diagnostician of the defiled spiritual heart is the Bible, God's Word. It probes deep, down to "the division of soul and spirit, and of joints and marrow" (Hebrews 4:12).

Allow the Word of God to diagnose your spiritual heart's condition, because diagnosis is the first step in healing.

> **SPIRITUAL HEART FOCUS**
> Submit yourself to the Holy Spirit for a spiritual "heart appraisal." Write down what you hear and record goals and objectives to deal with problems.

PHYSICAL HEART FOCUS

Treat blood pressure or cholesterol problems aggressively. Heed your physician's advice. Check your blood pressure and cholesterol.

❤ The Heart Examination

PSALM 139:23–24

Search me, O God, and know my heart;
Try me, and know my anxieties;
And see if there is any wicked way in me,
And lead me in the way everlasting.

THE GREAT PHYSICIAN EXAMINES the heart through the Great Diagnostician, the Word.

In Hebrew, "search" means to examine intimately, with fine, penetrating detail. A cardiologist will look for the smallest ripple in a strip of test paper from an electrocardiogram and listen for the faintest fluctuation in the heart's rhythm. The expert physician will probe for heart problems by examining the whole body.

SPIRITUAL HEART FOCUS
If you have anxious thoughts consider the possibility you lack confidence that God can take care of the matter. Ask Him to increase your faith.

When God searches the heart, He searches the total person. God examines the mind for anxious thoughts that cause conflict and doubt within us. The Great Physician, using the Great Diagnostician, searches our external behaviors, bringing to light those practices and habits that hurt us and others.

The heart examination leading to life that is vital in the present and enduring in eternity occurs as we daily allow God, through His Holy Spirit, to search us and know us.

PHYSICAL HEART FOCUS

People in their 20s and 30s need regular medical checkups, because it's vital to detect problems early and prevent those for which you may have tendencies.

❤ It's All About the Blood

LEVITICUS 17:14

"For [blood] is the life of all flesh. Its blood sustains its life. . . ."

LONG BEFORE WILLIAM HARVEY IDENTIFIED the circulatory system, God revealed that every organ in the body is energized by the blood pumped by the heart.

A woman in our church witnessed a kidney transplant. At first the new kidney looked pale and anemic, but once the surgeons attached it to the blood vessels, the organ surged with life, glowing with a healthy pinkish tint.

Anyone redeemed by Christ and indwelt by His Spirit should manifest spiritual energy and vigor. These qualities hinge on how fully Christ's life, brought by the Holy Spirit, flows in that person.

If you have received Jesus Christ as your Savior, you have been cleansed by His blood. *Bios* is the New Testament Greek word describing your material body, and *Zoe* is the Greek term used most often to designate God's quality of life. By receiving Christ's blood, you have received the very *Zoe* of God, which is life eternal!

SPIRITUAL HEART FOCUS

Ask God to clear out all obstructions to the flow of His precious Life in you and to manifest the brightness of His Presence in and through you.

PHYSICAL HEART FOCUS

Are you confused about good and bad cholesterol? LDL is bad because it can make your life "Lousy," and HDL is good because it can contribute to a "Healthy" body.

❤ The Depository of Truth

PROVERBS 4:20–22

My son, give attention to my words;
Incline your ear to my sayings.
Do not let them depart from your eyes;
Keep them in the midst of your heart;
For they are life to those who find them,
And health to all their flesh.

FORT KNOX CONTAINS GOLDEN BRICKS weighing a total of almost 150 million ounces—the bulk of the United States' wealth in gold.

The human heart is a vault holding the wealth of God's knowledge. A heart empty of God's truth is as devoid of purpose as Fort Knox without its gold.

Empty vaults are nothing more than musty caverns, useless until they're filled with treasure. Using a heart as a storage space for trash is like using the Fort Knox vault as a waste dump.

If the gold in Fort Knox was stolen, it would impact the U.S. economy and generate a financial shockwave across the world. When God and His truth are missing from the human heart, there is a negative effect on the well-being of the total person and of every life that person touches.

> **SPIRITUAL HEART FOCUS**
> Ask God's forgiveness for allowing your heart to be the storage space for worthless things rather than His truth–treasures.

PHYSICAL HEART FOCUS

Regular exercise boosts the good (HDL) cholesterol in your body.

♥ The Springs of Life

PROVERBS 4:23

Keep your heart with all diligence,
For out of it spring the issues of life.

OUR SPIRITUAL HEART DEFINES our character.

"Jericho" means "fragrant," and people found the city a pleasant place to live. But at one point, the quality of life in the whole region declined because the headwaters of the stream providing vitality to the area went bad. At the request of the men of the city, Elisha poured salt on the source of the water and purified the stream (2 Kings 2:19–22).

Just as it is vital to constantly monitor water quality, we also must watch over the wellspring of the spiritual heart. Moral pollution at the headwaters of personality spreads spiritual disease to the total person, reducing the quality of living and bringing the threat of death.

SPIRITUAL HEART FOCUS
Worship God as the ultimate wellspring of all that is pure and good.

PHYSICAL HEART FOCUS

Substitute water for soft drinks or other beverages.

❤ The Projector

PROVERBS 27:19
As in water face reflects face,
So a man's heart reveals the man.

LONG AGO, MOVIEGOERS IN THE AMERICAN WEST watched silent movies with the same formula: a black–hatted fiend tries to eliminate the hero and save the innocent lass.

Once, a cowboy in the theater suddenly shouted, "We ain't gonna let him get away with that, are we?" He and his fellow viewers yanked their six guns and riddled the screen, firing at an enemy that wasn't there. To get rid of the bad guy, they should have aimed at the projector.

SPIRITUAL HEART FOCUS
Ask the Holy Spirit to show you where you are "shooting at the screen" with respect to issues in your life, confess the real sin to God, and receive His forgiveness.

Total heart health is not the result of aiming at symptoms, imagined or otherwise. Physically, an ashen face is not cured by cosmetics, but by dealing with the heart congestion that may be causing it. Spiritually, healing doesn't come by dabbling with the superficial manifestations of sin, but by going right to the core, the heart that needs Christ's transforming touch.

PHYSICAL HEART FOCUS
Save money and calories by planning all your meals for the week, then preparing a grocery list based on the plan.

❤ The Blessing of Critique

HEBREWS 4:12

For the word of God is living and powerful, and sharper
than any two-edged sword, piercing even to the division of soul
and spirit, and of joints and marrow, and is a discerner
of the thoughts and intents of the heart.

"JUDGMENT COMES FROM EXPERIENCE and great judgment comes from bad experience," said a senator forced to resign because of sexual misconduct.[1]

How much easier for us if we could gain judgment without having to pass through bad experiences.

In New Testament Greek, "judge" is *kritikos*, from which we get "criticize." Few enjoy criticism, but the word also means to note possible negative outcomes of our plans.

The thoughts and intentions of the heart are those discussions we have with ourselves, and those discussions result in purposes and actions. Everyone needs a wise, experienced counselor to whom they can say, "Before I carry out this plan I'd like you to review it and point out the flaws."

SPIRITUAL
HEART FOCUS
Think about a specific situation in which God's Word held you back from actions that might have been harmful to yourself or others, and give God thanks.

Our mental heart is contriving constantly. By allowing the Bible to critique the ideas and notions, we will have the benefit of great judgment without the pain of bad experience.

PHYSICAL HEART FOCUS
Check with your doctor along the way as you pursue a lifestyle of healthy eating and exercise.

❤ The Burned and Hammered Heart

JEREMIAH 23:29

"Is not My word like a fire?" says the LORD,
"And like a hammer that breaks the rock in pieces?"

ANCIENT METALLURGISTS HEATED GOLD or silver with extreme temperatures that burned away the dross and left the metal pure. Then with great skill they hammered it into a desired shape.

In the eighteenth century, a silversmith was viewed almost as a sculptor. In the fire the metal was purified, made pliable, and hammered into usefulness.

This is how God transforms the human heart. His purifying fire scorches away the impurity and leaves a life conformed to His character. Then comes the Divine Hammer, shattering the arrogance that resists His reforming actions and shaping the personality back into its intended design, which is the very image of God!

SPIRITUAL HEART FOCUS
Thank God for specific experiences that have been used in transforming your heart, and ask Him to continue to work in "forming Christ" in you (Galatians 4:19).

In the silversmith shop, this is a process of many steps. The metal is heated, pounded, reheated, hammered some more, then plunged into cooling water to harden the new shape. This also is God's style in forming our hearts into Christlikeness.

PHYSICAL HEART FOCUS
Digestion begins in your mouth, so chew your food slowly and thoroughly.

❤ The Ultimate 'Spin Zone'

JEREMIAH 17:9
"The heart is deceitful above all things,
And desperately wicked;
Who can know it?"

"FAIR AND BALANCED." "We report, you decide." "The most trusted news in America." "You are entering the 'no–spin zone.'" Despite the slogans, Americans still do not trust the media.

There is no spin as drastic, though, as that of the sinful human heart, which, according to Jeremiah 17:9, is "deceitful." Fraud is a felony in the eternal courts as well as earthly.

The spiritual heart is the ultimate spin zone. This is why the Bible describes it as "desperately wicked" or "sick."

But there is wonderful news. First, the deceptive heart can be transformed into the truthful heart by the power of Jesus Christ. That which is incurably sick can be healed by His might.

SPIRITUAL HEART FOCUS

Claim the promise that you will know the truth and be set free by it (John 8:32), and ask God to help you discern what is really going on in your spiritual heart.

Fitness guru Jim Fixx was defrauded by his heart and died of cardiac arrest because he didn't know what was happening inside. When we acknowledge the potential of the heart's deceit we've taken a giant step toward total heart health.

PHYSICAL HEART FOCUS

Weight loss and weight control require your active participation. They don't just happen.

♥ The Propaganda Machine

PROVERBS 12:20
Deceit is in the heart of those who devise evil,
But counselors of peace have joy.

GORDON "SWEDE" LAWSON, an American POW in Vietnam, reported that each captive's cell had a loudspeaker that blared communist propaganda at them.

There is no greater propaganda machine than the human heart under the deception of its rebellion against God.

SPIRITUAL HEART FOCUS
Thank God for manifesting truth in Jesus Christ, and commit yourself to being a disciple of Jesus Christ.

Two things are essential to overcome propaganda. First is the ability to recognize misinformation. The only way to recognize the false is to know the true. Second, to overcome the lies, one must be able to use the truth effectively to refute propaganda.

This is why it is important actually to be a *disciple* of Jesus Christ. A disciple is a learner. Jesus said, "I am the way, the *truth*, and the life" (John 14:6, emphasis added). To know Him is to know the truth and shut down the propaganda machine.

PHYSICAL HEART FOCUS
Know your family history relating to cardiovascular disease.

❤ Elements of the Big Con

1 JOHN 1:8–10

If we say that we have no sin, we deceive ourselves, and the truth is not in us. If we confess our sins, He is faithful and just to forgive us our sins and to cleanse us from all unrighteousness. If we say that we have not sinned, we make Him a liar, and His word is not in us.

BACK WHEN PEOPLE CARRIED CASH, "confidence men" bilked the unwary directly. Now, con artists often email promises to deposit millions of dollars into bank accounts whose holders are duped into providing the numbers.

John reveals the spiritual con perpetrated by the fallen heart. First is denial: "Sin? I'm not a sinner!" Second is rationalization, through which the person convinces himself he's not a sinner. Finally is projection, in which an individual claims the problem is with God, who *thinks* the individual is a sinner.

Jesus Christ gives us each a new heart, full of truth. Rather than denial, there is honest confrontation with the fallen nature through the confession of sin. Acknowledgement of our true condition and the need for God's forgiveness gets rid of rationalization. Accountability displaces projection as we admit the problem is within ourselves, not God or any other human being.

This all leads to a healthy, truth–giving heart rather than a deceitful heart.

> **SPIRITUAL HEART FOCUS**
> It's been 21 days since you committed yourself to new habits in your daily spiritual routine. Keep going now for another 19 days and you will reach the "milestone" of 40 days.

PHYSICAL HEART FOCUS
Twenty–one days ago you resolved to exercise daily for at least 30 minutes. Keep going for 19 days more, and the routine will begin to be part of your lifestyle.

❤ The Bitter Heart

PROVERBS 14:10
The heart knows its own bitterness,
And a stranger does not share its joy.

GENERAL WILLIAM HENRY CHASE WHITING spread disparaging rumors about General Robert E. Lee. But when Jefferson Davis asked about Whiting, Lee reportedly answered, "I think he is one of the most able men in the entire army." Lee said later, "It was my impression that the President wanted my opinion of General Whiting, not Whiting's opinion of me."

Bitterness is a poisonous root defiling all it touches, and the human heart is its soil. Robert E. Lee could have watered the root of bitterness by focusing on Whiting's accusations and slanders. Instead, he chose to snatch it out, refusing to let bitterness grow in his heart.

> **SPIRITUAL HEART FOCUS**
> When your heart wants to dwell on wrongs committed against you, thank God that He will use even those for His purposes in and through you. Then pray God's blessings on people who hurt you.

When we focus on the wrongs done us and the gossip spread about us, we cultivate the root of bitterness. However, when we bless those who curse us, as Jesus instructed, the poisonous root is plucked out.

The person who uproots animosity will experience the vitality of God's joy.

PHYSICAL HEART FOCUS

Don't allow the complexities of daily life to divert you from taking care of your heart.

❤ The Greedy Heart

ACTS 5:1–5

But a certain man named Ananias, with Sapphira his wife, sold a possession. And he kept back part of the proceeds, his wife also being aware of it, and brought a certain part and laid it at the apostles' feet. But Peter said, "Ananias, why has Satan filled your heart to lie to the Holy Spirit . . . You have not lied to men but to God." Then Ananias, hearing these words, fell down and breathed his last.

THE GREED IN ANANIAS AND SAPPHIRA kept them from placing their full gift at the apostles' feet. Because the heart symbolizes the core of being, this means greed was on the throne of this man and woman as individuals and as a couple. The cure for their greed was drastic: the hearts of greed stopped beating. Ananias and Sapphira both dropped dead when their true heart condition was exposed. You and I might not thud to the floor in physical death when we enthrone greed on our hearts, but coldness and insensitivity will shroud us.

SPIRITUAL HEART FOCUS
Confess any sin of greed that may be lurking in your heart, and receive God's gracious and abundant forgiveness.

Leona Helmsley, reportedly owner of prime New York real estate and a convicted tax evader, got herself tagged as one of America's greediest people. When her 40–year old son died in 1982, Helmsley reportedly sued for his estate, leaving his four adult children $432 each and his widow $2,171.[2]

Don't let greed make your heart cold as death.

PHYSICAL HEART FOCUS
Weight loss involves a two–front assault: Cut the calories and increase the exercise.

♥ The Lusting Heart

PROVERBS 6:25
Do not lust after her beauty in your heart,
Nor let her allure you with her eyelids.

SEXUAL TEMPTATION IS A WHISPER LOUD as an atomic blast.

Consider David viewing Bathsheba in her bath. He knows God's principles and truths about sexual morality, but the trumpet blasts of conscience are silenced under the whispers of his lusting heart. The man after God's own heart shushes the voice of God in him so he can focus on perversion and murder. The rest is torrid, terrible history.

The man who had been a strict judge of Israel is lenient with himself.

SPIRITUAL HEART FOCUS
Set your heart on intimacy with God above all else, and refuse anything that would disturb your deep communion with Him.

But God is able to overwhelm the whispers of the seductive heart. Nathan, God's prophet, captures David's indignation with a report of startling injustice. Then Nathan tells David he is the perpetrator of the injustice, and David's remorseful heart turns again toward God.

Beware the whispers of the lusting heart lest you find the stark truth in your face.

PHYSICAL HEART FOCUS

Healthy sex with your spouse is good cardiovascular exercise, but inappropriate sexual activity endangers your health.

❤ The Healing Power of Silence

PSALM 46:10

Be still, and know that I am God;
I will be exalted among the nations,
I will be exalted in the earth!

THE DECEITFUL HEART LOVES NOISE. Lies cloak themselves under chaos. Dins hide deception.

So we avoid silence. Elevator music, background TV noise, and radio chatter all litter our audio landscape. Silence is so rare, even in church, we get edgy with it.

But there are times when God escorts us into silence. There, in that quiet place, duplicity becomes obvious and truth heard.

"Be still," says God. In today's lingo we might say, "Cool it" or "Let it go." Knowing God in this sense is to know Him by observation and recognition. To observe is not only to see, but to hear as well.

The only way we can really hear God is to silence the cacophony in our hearts. We can let it all go, relax in His presence, listen intently, and then we will hear and find healing for our hearts.

SPIRITUAL HEART FOCUS

Ask God to help you shut out the noise that keeps you from hearing Him, and write down the meditations of your heart.

PHYSICAL HEART FOCUS

Take the stairs instead of the elevator, at least two flights up and down. You'll get good exercise and solitude as well, since most people will be on the elevator.

❤ When Your Heart Groans

ROMANS 8:26–27

Likewise the Spirit also helps in our weaknesses. For we do not know what we should pray for as we ought, but the Spirit Himself makes intercession for us with groanings which cannot be uttered. Now He who searches the hearts knows what the mind of the Spirit is, because He makes intercession for the saints according to the will of God.

STEPHEN CRANE WROTE:

There was a man with tongue of wood / Who essayed to sing,
And in truth it was lamentable. / But there was one who heard
The clip–clapper of this tongue of wood
And knew what the man / Wished to sing,
And with that the singer was content.

There are situations in which sentences won't form around the pain. The matter is too big for words, the contours too twisted for a neat prayer–package. All we can do is groan.

In such times, the Holy Spirit is investigating, sensing, even feeling (Hebrews 4:15) the inexpressible hurts and confusions at the core of our being. The Father experiences our pain through the probing touch of His Spirit, who translates our heartfelt groans into the language of Heaven. We know He knows, and we are no longer alone in our pain. This is contentment.

SPIRITUAL HEART FOCUS

Thank God for understanding your griefs, pains, and trials. Thank Him for listening to you through His Spirit even when you cannot speak. Submit your concerns to Him.

PHYSICAL HEART FOCUS

If you've failed in caring for your body, share that grief with God, then set realistic goals for improvement and plan to achieve them.

❤ The Sheltered Heart

PSALM 91:1–4

He who dwells in the secret place of the Most High
Shall abide under the shadow of the Almighty.
I will say of the LORD, "He is my refuge and my fortress;
My God, in Him I will trust."
Surely He shall deliver you from the snare of the fowler
And from the perilous pestilence
He shall cover you with His feathers,
And under His wings you shall take refuge;
His truth shall be your shield and buckler.

"HYPERVIGILANCE" STRESSES the heart.[3]

Some people are afraid to relax their guard for a moment. Hypervigilance leads to hypertension, and hypertension to an unhealthy heart.

In military camps, sentries are assigned so everyone else can sleep. In the same way, the person trusting in God knows the Great Sentry is always awake. Resting in God means abiding under His shadow, like a baby eagle nesting under its mother.

SPIRITUAL HEART FOCUS
Meditate on Jesus as the Good Shepherd, and consider the implications for yourself and for those whom you care about the most.

Those sheltered by God abide in Him. These people don't scamper under His wings only when they're in trouble; rather, their constant walk is in relationship to God. Through that intimate communion, such people have learned to trust Him wholeheartedly. Abiding in God means resting from the hypervigilance that strains the heart.

PHYSICAL HEART FOCUS
An overly restrictive diet can have dangerous health consequences.

♥ The Pulled Heart

LUKE 10:40–41

But Martha was distracted with much serving, and she approached Him and said, "Lord, do You not care that my sister has left me to serve alone? Therefore tell her to help me." And Jesus answered and said to her, "Martha, Martha, you are worried and troubled about many things."

IN THE CAROLINAS, where we once lived, a "pig pickin" featured pulled pork, in which chunks of succulent barbecued meat were pulled right off the bone.

Barbecue might be for pulling, but not the heart. "Worried," as Jesus characterized Martha, means to be pulled in two different directions. The bothered heart is assaulted by tumults of noise, trouble, and stress.

SPIRITUAL HEART FOCUS
Ask God to help you gain clarity in every issue of life and in every decision you make.

Most of us have felt the strain of an emotional heart pulled in conflicting directions. The assault of so many external voices and sounds keeps us from thinking clearly.

The answer to the pulled heart is in one of my favorite passages: "Trust in the LORD with all your heart, and lean not on your own understanding. In all your ways acknowledge Him, and He shall direct your paths" (Proverbs 3:5–6).

Straight, God–directed paths lead to clear decisions that relax the pull on the heart.

PHYSICAL HEART FOCUS

For a good back stretch, lie on the floor on your back and slowly stretch out your arms and legs, making your torso as long as you can.

❤ The Peaceful Heart

JOHN 14:1

"Let not your heart be troubled; you believe in God, believe also in Me."

THE DISTURBED HEART SENDS TSUNAMIS of anxiety crashing over the landscapes of our lives, turning them into fields of debris.

Jesus says the way to calm the turmoil is to believe. Passengers on a cruise ship in the Gulf of Mexico in 2003 thought they were skirting a hurricane, but the storm turned, and they awoke in the middle of the night in the tempest. Later the seasoned captain told passengers he had never been afraid, because he knew how much stress the ship could take.

Belief in God is resting in His limitless sufficiency. Belief in Jesus Christ is to throw all one's weight on the completeness of His redemption. No crisis is bigger than God. No storm can overturn the finished work of Christ's atonement.

The peaceful person is one who has linked the head–knowledge of God with heart–knowledge of Him. Fact and experience are joined. The troubled heart is calmed.

SPIRITUAL HEART FOCUS

Worship God as the changeless One. Thank Him for the peace He offers through Jesus Christ, and submit the tempests of your life to Him. Then ask Him to calm your storms.

PHYSICAL HEART FOCUS

Try to avoid fast foods and eating on the run. Most fast foods are loaded with trans fats, which are bad for your heart.

❤ Softening the Hard Heart

HEBREWS 3:7–8

Therefore, as the Holy Spirit says:
"Today, if you will hear His voice,
Do not harden your hearts as in the rebellion,
In the day of trial in the wilderness."

"DO YOU WANT A WATER SOFTENER?" the well–digger asked his customer.

"Why do I need a softener?" the farmer asked.

"The water around here is mighty hard," the digger replied. "The minerals in it build up hardened deposits around your plumbing." This summarizes the problem of the heart hardened toward God. The stain of a sinful lifestyle blemishes the personality made for beauty and usefulness. The deposits become crusty, impenetrable, and insensitive.

SPIRITUAL HEART FOCUS
Thank God for times He has softened your heart to be more responsive to Him.

Skleros is the Greek word for "hard." It refers to something dried out. In English, we borrow the term "sclerosis"—like arteriosclerosis, which refers to hardening of the arteries—to describe certain kinds of ailments. People who are hardened toward God suffer spiritual sclerosis.

The water–softening device, explained the well–digger, injects a salt compound into the well water. Allow the Lord today to inject in you the "salt" of His Word and faith to soften your heart.

PHYSICAL HEART FOCUS

When exercising, wear comfortable clothes that fit well and that are appropriate for your exercise plan for the day.

February

A heart of love
should be the quest of every
disciple of Jesus Christ.

♥ Healing the Spiritual Heart 'Murmur'

HEBREWS 3:7–9

Therefore, as the Holy Spirit says:
"Today, if you will hear His voice,
Do not harden your hearts as in the rebellion,
In the day of trial in the wilderness,
Where your fathers tested Me, tried Me,
And saw My works forty years."

THE CARDIOLOGIST HEARS A SWISHING NOISE in the patient's heart and calls it a "murmur." This usually means a structural problem with one of the heart's four valves. There's also a *spiritual* heart murmur. The Hebrews suffered this ailment in the wilderness. God gave them manna and they complained, so He gave them quail. They lamented their wandering, so God gave them a pillar of fire at night and a cloud–stack by day. They arrived at the Promised Land, but moaned that giants were there. Spiritual heart murmur is a complaining heart, characteristic of contemporary consumer religion. This heart follows God for what it can get out of Him. The cure is the grateful heart.

SPIRITUAL HEART FOCUS
Ask the Holy Spirit to reveal areas where you suffer from spiritual heart murmur, confess this condition as sin, and receive God's forgiveness.

When Jesus was challenged to feed five thousand and had only morsels of fish and bread, He didn't murmur over the insufficiency, but "gave thanks" (Mark 8:6). Gratitude cures your murmuring heart!

PHYSICAL HEART FOCUS

If you're told you have a heart murmur, further tests are needed to determine its significance.

❤ The Stone Heart

EZEKIEL 11:19

"Then I will give them one heart, and I will put a new spirit within them, and take the stony heart out of their flesh, and give them a heart of flesh."

DR. DENTON COOLEY COINED THE TERM "stone heart" to describe an irreversible heart condition following certain open-heart operations. There was no cure for stone heart, and it was always fatal.

When Jesus Christ transforms a life, He yanks out the stone heart and replaces it with sensitivity. "Flesh" is often thought of as a negative, but in Ezekiel 11:19 the word means "rosy" and "fresh."

A man's prize clock stopped ticking. He changed the weights, face, and hands, but nothing happened. All the while his little boy watched. Finally, the child said, "Daddy, I think the poor clock needs a new inside."[4]

Jesus Christ gives us a bright new face and hands ready for new works, but He does so by giving us a "new inside," a rosy, fresh heart.

> SPIRITUAL HEART FOCUS
> What "color" would your spiritual, emotional, and mental heart be, and what do you need to do to get it "in the pink"?

PHYSICAL HEART FOCUS
Look for new opportunities to exercise as part of your routine, like taking a new neighborhood route, or mall–walking.

❤ The Aloof Heart

HEBREWS 3:12

*Beware, brethren, lest there be in any of you an evil heart
of unbelief in departing from the living God.*

"SHE IS STANDOFFISH," A WOMAN SAID of a snobbish acquaintance.

The heart that falls away from God is one that stands apart from or is aloof from God. Unbelief is the cause. To reject faith in God is to say either He does not exist or that He is not worthy of one's trust. In both cases, this is spiritual snobbery.

SPIRITUAL
HEART FOCUS

Has there been a crisis when you blamed God and withdrew from Him? If so, confess the truth, receive His forgiveness, and love Him again.

That the aloof heart is described as "falling away" or "departing" infers that once the person believed in God, but lost that trust. The Israelites bounded through the dry bottom of the split sea, but skidded to a stop at the edge of the Jordan when spies reported there were giants on the other side.

Suddenly, those who walked with God through the desert became standoffish at the river.

The problem was that they believed the negative report of the spies more than they believed God.

Any time we doubt God's capability in a situation we will become standoffish toward Him.

PHYSICAL HEART FOCUS

The focus of fellowship with your friends should not be eating a meal, but simply enjoying each other's company.

❤ A Whole Heart

1 CHRONICLES 28:9

"As for you, my son Solomon, know the God of your father, and serve Him with a loyal heart and with a willing mind; for the LORD searches all hearts and understands all the intent of the thoughts. If you seek Him, He will be found by you; but if you forsake Him, He will cast you off forever."

PARENTS UNDERSTAND WHEN THEY DON'T HAVE their kids' full attention. "You will brush your teeth," says a mother. "Yes, ma'am," answers the youngster, merrily scouring her two front teeth only.

Such was the commitment level at one point in colonial America. Children born to church members were enrolled in membership, whether they had made a commitment to Christ or not, through the "halfway covenant."

In 1727, New Jersey pastor Theodore Frelinghuysen declared the only people who could take the Lord's Supper at the church he served were people whose changed lives showed they had received Jesus Christ. Controversy erupted, but so did revival.

A wholehearted person is one with no hidden agendas. There is no room for other gods because the wholehearted person's entire devotion is to the true and living God!

SPIRITUAL
HEART FOCUS
Write down in your journal some of the ways God has changed you and how He's still transforming you.

PHYSICAL HEART FOCUS

Each day you give wholehearted effort to your diet and exercise programs, the closer you are to your healthy lifestyle goals.

❤ A Willing Mind

1 CHRONICLES 28:9; MATTHEW 26:41

"As for you, my son Solomon, know the God of your father,
and serve Him with a loyal heart and with a willing mind; for the LORD
searches all hearts and understands all the intent of the thoughts. If you
seek Him, He will be found by you; but if you forsake Him, He will cast
you off forever.". . ."Watch and pray, lest you enter into temptation.
The spirit indeed is willing, but the flesh is weak."

ALL BILLY'S MOM ASKED OF HER college–bound son was that he attend church. Billy spent a weekend at a college pal's ranch. Sunday morning his buddy invited Billy on a daylong fishing trip. As they rode out on horseback, Billy heard a church bell, growing fainter with distance.

Suddenly, Billy turned to his friend. "Got to go back and go to church," he said.

SPIRITUAL HEART FOCUS
Commit to not letting your flesh pull you away from God's Spirit.

"Wait," answered Billy's pal, "we can all go next Sunday."

"Nope," Billy replied, "I've got to go back now, while I can still hear the bell!"

It wasn't easy for Billy to turn his horse and gallop away from his friends and the lake. But he had a willing heart, and that overcame the tug to get away from the bell.

People with willing hearts and minds can be trusted to answer the call and never want to get beyond its range.

PHYSICAL HEART FOCUS

When you eat, try to sense the feeling of being satisfied before you are stuffed.

❤ The Heart's Location

MATTHEW 6:19–21

"Do not lay up for yourselves treasures on earth, where moth and rust destroy and where thieves break in and steal; but lay up for yourselves treasures in heaven, where neither moth nor rust destroys and where thieves do not break in and steal. For where your treasure is, there your heart will be also."

WHEN DAVID LIVINGSTON DIED, his heart was buried in Africa where he served, though his body was laid to rest in his native England.

A physician about to operate on a human heart can peg its location in the chest cavity. Everyone knows where the physical heart is located. But Jesus says the address of the spiritual heart—the core of the human being—is wherever the person's treasure is. If one knows the Africa of David Livingston's expansive love, one can find the resting place of Livingston's heart.

Literally, your treasure is whatever you regard as having exceptional value. What you value determines the focus of your heart, and the focus of your heart reveals what you really value.

SPIRITUAL HEART FOCUS

Value Christ and His Kingdom above all else, and you will be blessed in all other areas of life (Matthew 6:33).

PHYSICAL HEART FOCUS
Don't skip breakfast.

❤ The Ignited Heart

LUKE 24:32

And they said to one another, "Did not our heart burn within us while He talked with us on the road, and while He opened the Scriptures to us?"

GREAT SORROW DOUSED ALL HOPE in the hearts of the men as they trekked from Jerusalem to Emmaus. They had just seen Jesus executed. Later, they recognized the accompanying Stranger as the Savior, and then He was gone. However, like a torch touched to kindling, His presence reignited their smoldering hearts. He moved on elsewhere, but the power of His influence remained.

SPIRITUAL HEART FOCUS
Meditate on the implications of the resurrection for hope in your own life, and ask God to ignite your heart with His hope.

My friend Jim DeLoach told of seeing an illustration of a burned–down shack. An old man stood looking at the charred chimney, all that remained. A tattered little boy clung to his leg, crying. The artist, Jim reported, wrote the old man's words along the bottom of the picture: "Hush child, God ain't dead!"[5]

The presence of Jesus is all it takes to ignite a heart that has lost its dreams. If He "ain't dead," neither is hope.

PHYSICAL HEART FOCUS
Weigh daily, or at least every few days, to reinforce your weight goals.

❤ Triumphant but Not Triumphalistic

LUKE 24:36-39

Now as they said these things, Jesus Himself stood in the midst of them, and said to them, "Peace to you." But they were terrified and frightened, and supposed they had seen a spirit. And He said to them, "Why are you troubled? And why do doubts arise in your hearts? Behold My hands and My feet, that it is I Myself. Handle Me and see, for a spirit does not have flesh and bones as you see I have."

WHEN THEY REALIZED JESUS was really alive, the Emmaus men dashed back to Jerusalem, to tell the other disciples of Jesus' triumph.

But shortly they would learn the difference between *triumph* and *triumphalism*. As they shared the news with the apostles, Jesus appeared before them all, presenting His scarred hands and feet. Therein lies the distinction.

Triumphalism says, airily, "There are no scars, no pain, no tears, no blood, no cross, just happiness and victory!" The triumphant heart knows that victory is coming, but at great cost. The heart of triumph sees both the joy of the empty tomb and the horror of Golgotha, yet still endures the cross for the "joy set before Him" (Hebrews 12:2).

SPIRITUAL HEART FOCUS

Don't deny suffering because of a triumphalistic attitude, but also don't allow the pain to obscure the reality of the gain.

Jesus calls you to hope based on reality, not dreaminess floating on fantasy. That's the difference between triumph and triumphalism.

PHYSICAL HEART FOCUS

Keep a daily journal of what you eat and drink, as well as the intensity and duration of exercise.

❤ The Established Heart

PROVERBS 4:4; 1 THESSALONIANS 3:13

He also taught me, and said to me:
"Let your heart retain my words; keep my commands, and live."

So that He may establish your hearts blameless in holiness before our God
and Father at the coming of our Lord Jesus Christ with all His saints.

THERE ARE VARIETIES of baseball umpires.

The orthodox umpire is an absolutist. If the ball comes across the plate between the armpits and knees it's a strike, unquestionably.

The modernist umpire says, "They are what I see." Balls and strikes are what he says they are, not what they really are.

SPIRITUAL HEART FOCUS
Seek God's forgiveness for times you've "called it" the way you have seen it rather than the way it is by His standards.

The postmodern umpire doesn't believe there is an absolute strike zone, nor that one can even know if a pitch is a strike or not. Since there is no absolute zone, and no way of knowing, if the postmodern ump wants it to be a strike he merely declares it so.

Spiritually, the person with a mature, resolved heart knows there are absolutes. God's Word sets the strike zone, and it does not vary. Such a person doesn't play the game of life in confusion, but plays in settled certainty about right and wrong.

PHYSICAL HEART FOCUS

A heart–healthy diet, combined with regular exercise and no smoking, can eliminate 80 percent of heart disease and 70 percent of certain cancers.[6]

❤ Yank the Plank

LUKE 6:41–42, 45

"And why do you look at the speck in your brother's eye, but do not perceive the plank in your own eye? Or how can you say to your brother, 'Brother, let me remove the speck that is in your eye,' when you yourself do not see the plank that is in your own eye? Hypocrite! First remove the plank from your own eye, and then you will see clearly to remove the speck that is in your brother's eye. A good man out of the good treasure of his heart brings forth good; and an evil man out of the evil treasure of his heart brings forth evil. For out of the abundance of the heart his mouth speaks."

WE ARE TO HAVE A DISCERNING HEART, but not a judgmental heart.

A few years ago, I had eye surgery so I could see better without glasses. On a follow-up visit, while waiting, I memorized the bottom line of the vision chart. When the doctor asked me to read it I proceeded to recite the bottom-line letters perfectly. "It's a miracle!" he declared. Then I had to tell him the truth. That meant I had to face the facts about my own capacity to see. My eyes were much better following the surgery, but still not strong enough to read that tiny type.

If we are going to discern and see clearly spiritually without being judgmental, we must face the fact that there's a huge log in our own eyes, and "yank the plank."

SPIRITUAL HEART FOCUS

It's now been 40 days since you embarked on a new daily spiritual routine of giving at least 30 minutes to Bible reading, prayer, and worship. Stay the course another 50 days and the new habit will be a lifestyle!

PHYSICAL HEART FOCUS

Check your weight and BMI. We hope you're discovering that what began as a discipline of daily exercise and good diet is now becoming more natural.

❤ The Simple Heart

2 CORINTHIANS 11:3

But I fear, lest somehow, as the serpent deceived Eve by his craftiness, so your minds may be corrupted from the simplicity that is in Christ.

THE MIND, SOMETIMES SYMBOLIZED in the Bible by the heart, is the center of reflection and awareness. The happiest people are those who have simplicity of heart. Literally, their consciousness is not layered with confusing, conflicting allegiances.

The devil tries to cheat, seduce, and delude people from this peaceful state of simplicity with complex questions, doubts, and theories, which Paul calls "fables" (1 Timothy 4:7).

SPIRITUAL HEART FOCUS

Thank God for speaking so plainly and simply in Jesus Christ and the written Word, and ask the Holy Spirit to guide you into a simple and pure devotion to Christ.

Prime among the enemy's strategies is to cast doubt regarding the nature of Christ, because He reveals God to human beings. Our culture has lost the simplicity of devotion to Christ. There's the cosmic Jesus of New Age "spirituality," the Hollywood Jesus, the humanitarian Jesus, the salesman Jesus.

But there is only one genuine Jesus. Knowing Him in simplicity leads us to the Father. Don't be tricked away from Him.

PHYSICAL HEART FOCUS

Avoid buffet-style restaurants when you're pursuing a weight-loss goal.

♥ The Untroubled Heart

JOHN 14:1

"Let not your heart be troubled; you believe in God, believe also in Me."

MY DAD WAS A TROUBLESHOOTER for the local power company. If the power went out anywhere in our region, my father would get things humming again.

"Troubleshooter" is a terrific job description, because trouble abounds in a fallen world.

Some people believe Christians will never have problems. That's shallow triumphalism, as we saw in the February 8 meditation. Others think Christians will have troubles but not be troubled by them. But Jesus is not calling us to stone–faced insensitivity.

What Jesus *is* saying is that our hearts can be untroubled when we recognize that He is fully God and on our side. We may wince in our pain and feel the stress of our problems, but if we believe in Jesus as He is, we will recognize that even though we have an adversary, the devil, we have an Advocate who is the only begotten Son of God, God over all!

> ### SPIRITUAL HEART FOCUS
> Think about a troubling situation you face now and the implications of Jesus as your friend and advocate in that situation.

PHYSICAL HEART FOCUS

Don't go it alone. Get a buddy also focusing on developing a heart–healthy lifestyle, work out together, share successes, and encourage one another.

❤ The Heart of Peace

COLOSSIANS 3:15
And let the peace of God rule in your hearts,
to which also you were called in one body; and be thankful.

THE SEA BENEATH THE CLIFF LEAPS with the ferocity of hungry wolves, the white–tipped surf resembling claws.

Odd vista for a painting called *Peace*.

But under the cliff's ledge the picture reveals a mother bird, sitting on a nest holding her babies. The storm rages, but they are sheltered away, in peace.

God's peace is not the absence of turbulence, but calm in the midst of it. Peace comes from being restored to intimate relationship with God. Peace is the fruit of the Holy Spirit who comes into the heart of the person who receives Jesus Christ.

Jesus didn't come to give us boredom, but drums. He didn't come to sit us on the guru's mountain above the fray, but to take us to Golgotha. The real miracle is giving us peace there, as the hammer pounds the nails into our hands.

Peace that remains in those moments is the only peace worth having.

> **SPIRITUAL HEART FOCUS**
> Do a "fruit inspection" of your life, assessing the development of love, joy, peace, patience, kindness, goodness, faithfulness, gentleness, and self–control. Jot in your journal ideas about how to nurture growth of this spiritual fruit.

PHYSICAL HEART FOCUS

For a refreshing change, choose a simple fruit dessert instead of a calorie–laden sweet.

❤ The Loving Heart

1 PETER 1:22

Since you have purified your souls in obeying the truth through the Spirit in sincere love of the brethren, love one another fervently with a pure heart.

THE EMPEROR CLAUDIUS CANCELLED WEDDINGS, believing he couldn't recruit soldiers because Roman men were too interested in their women. Saint Valentine, a Roman priest, married people secretly, in defiance of Claudius, and got his head lopped off. Now there's a day named for him.

Eventually, the idealized shape and color of the heart became the symbol for Saint Valentine's Day because people recognized true love is from the heart.

Jesus Christ revealed this by bringing into focus a rare Greek word for love. *Agape* designates love devoid of self–interest, love that is patient, kind, not boastful nor arrogant, never inappropriate in its expression, not prone to grudge–bearing, celebrating truth and wincing at wrong, putting up with all kinds of injustices against it, believing and hoping for the best always, and hanging in there no matter what (1 Corinthians 13:4–7).

Such a heart of love should be the quest of every disciple of Jesus Christ.

SPIRITUAL HEART FOCUS
Thank God the Son for loving you so much He took your penalty on the cross and for the Holy Spirit making you conscious of God's love. Ask God to help you express genuine love to others.

PHYSICAL HEART FOCUS

When it comes to a Valentine gift, be neither a "giver" nor "receiver" of a huge box of candy, especially if your Valentine is also on a heart–healthy diet.

♥ The Compassionate Heart

COLOSSIANS 3:12
*Therefore, as the elect of God, holy and beloved, put on
tender mercies, kindness, humility, meekness, longsuffering.*

JULIAN THE APOSTATE WAS A ROMAN RULER who wanted a return to
the old paganism instead of the Christianity embraced by Constantine.
But Julian couldn't refute the deeds of Christ's followers, and he
lamented, "The impious Galileans (Christians) relieve both their own
poor and ours. It is shameful that ours should be so
destitute of our assistance."[7]

SPIRITUAL HEART FOCUS
Think of the acts of compassion
people have extended you,
and give God thanks for them.
Ask Him to increase the
compassion in your heart and to
open opportunities for you
to serve people.

Christ's love in a person's heart results in
compassion. To try to stop works of
compassion from people transformed by
Christ is like trying to put a lid on Old
Faithful. The passion inevitably is going to
send the geyser spurting.

Compassion is an emotion, but, stirred by the
Holy Spirit, it is also deeds. Faithful is the way needy
people should view persons who have been given hearts of compassion by
Jesus Christ.

PHYSICAL HEART FOCUS
Your body can't operate without fuel. Fill it with the correct "octane," and then use
the fuel in serving other people.

❤ The Pure Heart

1 TIMOTHY 1:5

Now the purpose of the commandment is love from a pure heart, from a good conscience, and from sincere faith.

JACK WAS A BRUISER, BOOZER, and womanizer. Then he met Jesus Christ.

"Jack," I asked him several years after he had received Christ, "what's been the best thing about walking with Jesus?"

"I'm no longer afraid," he answered.

I was stunned: A rough–chiseled guy like Jack afraid?

"I'm no longer afraid of phone calls, of being found out, afraid somebody will figure out what's going on in my inner life, afraid of some husband confronting me about an affair with his wife."

I got the picture.

"When I came to faith in Christ and got my life cleaned up," Jack continued, "fear left my life. That's the most marvelous thing about following Christ."

"Perfect love," writes John, "casts out fear" (1 John 4:18). Jack experienced the love of Christ, who purified his heart and cleansed it of fear.

SPIRITUAL
HEART FOCUS
Talk to God about your secret fears, and ask for growth in the pure love that makes no room for fear.

PHYSICAL HEART FOCUS
Don't let the fear of failure keep you from setting and pursuing realistic dietary and exercise goals.

♥ The Heart's Delight

PSALM 37:4

Delight yourself also in the LORD,
And He shall give you the desires of your heart.

CHILDREN DELIGHT IN WHAT THEY HAVE, teenagers in what they do, and adults in what they are. So, an adult whose primary delight is in possessions or activities has an immature heart.

The mature heart does enjoy possessions and pleasant activities, but "delight" is a much deeper word than "enjoy." The "delightful" is that which is exquisitely delicate, something to be preserved, protected, and cherished. You treasure a priceless antique but enjoy a coffee mug.

SPIRITUAL HEART FOCUS

Worship God as the One who knows what you really want: to conform your desires to His will and work in your life so that He is your greatest delight.

"Desire" is a preference, something you want but can live without. Trivializers get priorities confused, treasuring what ought to be merely liked and liking what ought to be treasured. If one cherishes relationship with God as life's greatest treasure, the desires of life come with the package as God wills.

PHYSICAL HEART FOCUS

Think of your calorie intake as a checking account that you fill and "spend," by expending energy and calories through exercise.

❤ Washed Heart

JEREMIAH 4:14

O Jerusalem, wash your heart from wickedness,
That you may be saved.
How long shall your evil thoughts lodge within you?

"WHY DO I HAVE TO WASH MY HANDS all the time?" I asked my mother when I was a child. She knew about germs, but I didn't.

The same thing was true for the Jews. In ancient times, Orthodox Jews lived longer than most anybody. They followed hand–washing rituals, though they knew nothing of microscopic monsters hiding in their environment.

Washing one's heart is good spiritual hygiene. Evil is the germ that needs to get wiped away. Washing the heart is the spiritual equivalent of washing the hands. Two things are essential. First, you must have a strong cleansing agent. Spiritually, that's the blood of Christ, which is salvation. Second, you've got to have "water," and that's the Word of God (Ephesians 5:26).

> SPIRITUAL
> HEART FOCUS
> Thank the Holy Spirit for
> inspiring, preserving,
> and interpreting the "washing
> agent," which is the
> Word of God.

Receiving Christ and being immersed in His Word produces a washed, "germ–free" heart.

PHYSICAL HEART FOCUS
Salmon helps fight "bad cholesterol" (LDL), so add it to your menu regularly—but avoid the fattening sauces.

♥ Awakened Heart

SONG OF SOLOMON 5:2
I sleep, but my heart is awake . . .

IN PRE–COMPUTER DAYS I STRUGGLED with the tangled equations of physics. Then one day in the middle of that first semester, I had an awakening. "I see it now!" I told myself.

Similarly, there are times when our consciousness may be asleep, but our heart, the inner core of understanding, is wide awake. There comes a wonderful moment when our head awakes to what we know in our heart, and there is a completeness of understanding that impacts our behavior.

> **SPIRITUAL HEART FOCUS**
> Recall the moments of God–sparked awakening and discovery in your life, and write in your journal the things you learned, decisions you made, and the outcomes.

This is the way the Word of God transforms us. We read it, hear it preached and taught, and often don't understand it. But all along, that Word is being planted in us (James 1:21). Our hearts are awake, even though our minds are asleep.

Then the day comes when we cross over into a new level of spiritual maturity, and we shout, "I see it now!"

Perhaps today will be one of those moments for you.

PHYSICAL HEART FOCUS

The best exercise in the world is a hearty laugh, so give in to the urge to guffaw at every opportunity.

♥ Looking on the Heart

1 SAMUEL 16:7

But the LORD said to Samuel, "Do not look at his appearance or at his physical stature, because I have refused him. For the LORD does not see as man sees; for man looks at the outward appearance, but the LORD looks at the heart."

IT'S A GOOD THING FOR ALL OF US that God looks on the heart and not the outward appearance.

"Look," as used in today's scripture, means not only to see externally, but to perceive and understand. God knows what really drives our behaviors. When others see the pout, God sees the pain. Our "High Priest" is "touched with the *feeling* of all our infirmities" (Hebrews 4:15 KJV, emphasis added).

SPIRITUAL HEART FOCUS

Ask God to intensify your heart's passion for Him and to align your behavior with your heart–desire.

This doesn't excuse bad behaviors, but lets us know we have a Lord whose forgiveness is based on His understanding of why we did wrong. It also means when things don't come out like we intended, He sees and smiles on what we really intended, not the mess others may see.

All our relationships would be improved if we reacted, not on the basis of external behaviors, but on the concerns of the heart.

PHYSICAL HEART FOCUS

Never go to the grocery store on an empty stomach.

♥ The Heart's Focus

2 CHRONICLES 16:9

"For the eyes of the Lord run to and fro throughout the whole earth, to show Himself strong on behalf of those whose heart is loyal to Him. In this you have done foolishly; therefore from now on you shall have wars."

WHAT CATCHES YOUR EYE?

Earlier in this book I wrote that my dad was a power company troubleshooter. When we walked through town, he saw every pole and transformer.

I have been a pastor all my professional life. On trips, I see steeples and church buildings. That's where my heart is.

What catches your eye reveals the focus of your heart.

God is a heart–watcher. His eyes latch their gaze onto the heart totally friendly, open, and yielded to Him.

> SPIRITUAL
> HEART FOCUS
> Embrace Christ as the
> Giver of grace and mercy,
> and enjoy being in
> His presence.

Some try to hide from God's probing look, but those who are heart–friendly toward God welcome His gaze, knowing the Father watches them to support them in their quest to walk in His ways. Literally, God's intent is to "show Himself strong" on behalf of such people.

If you love God, you don't have to run from His eyes, even if you fall. He gazes at your friendly heart, and only wants to pick you up and carry you.

PHYSICAL HEART FOCUS

Drink a tall glass of water before each meal, and it will help you eat less and feel more satisfied.

❤ The Expectant Heart

PSALM 33:20–21

Our soul waits for the LORD;
He is our help and our shield.
For our heart shall rejoice in Him,
Because we have trusted in His holy name.

LEONID BREZHNEV'S WIDOW STARTLED the grim communist guards by making the sign of the cross on the chest of the deceased—who had been leader of the Soviet Union, an officially atheistic nation.

Gary Thomas wrote, "There in the citadel of secular, atheistic power, the wife of the man who had run it all hoped that her husband was wrong," and that Jesus "might yet have mercy on her husband."[8]

The soul, symbolized by the heart, has an expectancy of God's ultimate intervention. One atheist declared he was fighting despair with expectancy. "I know I shall die in hope," said Jean–Paul Sartre, a month before his death. Sadly, though, Sartre said, "hope needs a foundation."[9]

The person whose heart's expectancy is based on faith in the living God rejoices, because he or she has a firm foundation for the heart's expectancy.

SPIRITUAL HEART FOCUS
Jot in your journal the things you would expect from the hands of the loving, merciful God.

PHYSICAL HEART FOCUS

Boost your sandwich with lots of lettuce and veggies, and get a bigger crunch and fewer calories.

♥ The Ready Heart

PSALM 78:5–8

For He established a testimony in Jacob,
And appointed a law in Israel,
Which He commanded our fathers,
> *That they should make them known to their children;*
> *That the generation to come might know them,*
> *The children who would be born,*
> *That they may arise and declare them to*
> *their children,*
> *That they may set their hope in God,*
> *And not forget the works of God,*
> *But keep His commandments;*
> *And may not be like their fathers. . .*
> *A generation that did not set its heart aright.*

SPIRITUAL HEART FOCUS

Ask the Holy Spirit to reveal elements that keep your heart from being ready to spring into action at God's command. Confess these things as sin, and receive Christ's forgiveness. Ask God to give you a heart of readiness.

AN ATHLETE'S HEART WEAKENED by hard partying is not ready for the big game. A soldier whose heart is tangled in burdens can't focus on the battle (2 Timothy 2:4).

Jesus often teaches about preparedness. In a parable He talks about virgins not prepared for the bridegroom's arrival (Matthew 25:6–13), and He warns about followers not ready to set out on mission because of unresolved affairs (Matthew 8:21).

Our hearts must be ready to respond because, as Psalm 78 shows, other generations depend on it. What keeps your heart from being ready to leap into action?

PHYSICAL HEART FOCUS

Go to an online calorie counter, look at meals you anticipate today, and record the calories in advance. Many diet and cookbooks will offer calorie charts as well.

❤ The Heart's Outlook

EPHESIANS 1:18–19

The eyes of your understanding being enlightened; that you may know what is the hope of His calling, what are the riches of the glory of His inheritance in the saints, and what is the exceeding greatness of His power toward us who believe, according to the working of His mighty power.

YOUR OUTLOOK DETERMINES YOUR OUTCOME.

Your outlook springs from your heart. The enlightened heart sparkles with hope.

Abraham looked up at the stars and saw God. Lot looked up and saw Sodom. Lot lost everything when Sodom burned down, but by faith Abraham inherited a city made by God, eternal in the heavens (2 Corinthians 5:1). Abraham had an enlightened outlook, but Lot's vista was dim.

SPIRITUAL HEART FOCUS
Can you see the gold in the rock? Meditate on Romans 8:28–29, and record your thoughts on how God used past crises to shape and encourage you now.

Two prospectors sought a vein of gold deep in a dark mine. One searched with a candle, while the other had a brilliant lamp. The candle cast long shadows, obscuring the streak of gold in the stone wall just beyond. But the radiant lamp washed out the shadows, and caught the glimmer of gold embedded in the rock.

People with hearts enlightened by the Holy Spirit enjoy the glorious inheritance of life with God. Your outlook determines your outcome, and your outlook depends on the spiritual enlightenment of the heart.

PHYSICAL HEART FOCUS
Alcohol has seven calories per gram.

❤ Stabilizer in Turbulence

ISAIAH 26:3

You will keep him in perfect peace,
Whose mind is stayed on You,
Because he trusts in You.

IN A SENSE, WE ALL "FLY" through turbulence. Like a thunderstorm heaving with wind shear, contemporary culture makes staying on your life–course difficult.

Airplanes are built to handle turbulence. Each one has a vertical fin to keep the plane from being whipped side to side and a horizontal stabilizer maintaining level flight.

God made provision for the spiritual and moral turbulence with which we must cope. The heart is intended by God to be an internal stabilizer, keeping us steady in the turbulent blasts of everyday living.

SPIRITUAL HEART FOCUS

Recall a time when other people were in panic but you were calm, or imagine such a situation. Write down your ideas on how God can make you calm in the storms.

People with minds "stayed" on God are those who rely on Him even while their lives plunge into turbulent storms. They have a sense of safety and welfare that steadies them in the midst of the shrieking gales. The hearts of such people are powerful stabilizers because they are fixed on God.

PHYSICAL HEART FOCUS

Schedule exercise in your daily planner just like you do appointments, because your workout is one of the most important engagements of your day.

❤ The Lukewarm Heart

REVELATION 3:15–17

"I know your works, that you are neither cold nor hot. I could wish you were cold or hot. So then, because you are lukewarm, and neither cold nor hot, I will vomit you out of My mouth. Because you say, 'I am rich, have become wealthy, and have need of nothing'—and do not know that you are wretched, miserable, poor, blind, and naked."

JIMMY FEARED DISAPPOINTMENT and failure, so he never committed to anything, including love.

He audited his university classes for fear of not qualifying for entry. He even "audited" church. He sat and soaked, but never left the pew.

Jimmy was like the man in Jesus' parable who buried his treasure for fear it would be lost (Matthew 25:24–25). There was no risk in Jimmy's life. He refused to allow his heart to be passionate about anything, but neither would he embrace the coldness of unbelief. He hovered in a stagnant pool of indifference and complacency.

Jimmy was right about a few things: It's risky to give your heart away and sacrifice it for causes that lead to crosses.

The only problem with Jimmy and all those like him is that they miss life. Don't be afraid to let your heart get ignited for Christ and His Kingdom.

SPIRITUAL HEART FOCUS
Praise God the Holy Spirit for His ministry of igniting cold hearts. Ask Him to pour fresh fuel of revival and renewal on your heart.

PHYSICAL HEART FOCUS

Inspire yourself by remembering that whatever you do to maintain your fitness now will determine your health ten years from now.

❤ Smooth Heart

ACTS 2:46–47

So continuing daily with one accord in the temple, and breaking bread from house to house, they ate their food with gladness and simplicity of heart, praising God and having favor with all the people. And the Lord added to the church daily those who were being saved.

SOME PEOPLE HAVE A "COUNTRY ROAD" heart, layered with pebbles and potholes. Then there are "honey" hearts, sweet but grainy with beeswax.

The sincere heart is a smooth heart: no pebbles, no potholes, no flecks of beeswax. In popular culture, if a person is sincere about what he or she does, morality matters little. By this standard, even Hitler would be judged right because of the "sincerity" with which he killed all those people.

True sincerity of heart is unrippled, trustworthy as a well–paved road or well–refined honey. Such a heart has "gladness." Literally, in the Greek language of Acts 2:46, it "jumps for joy."

Allow the Holy Spirit to smooth out your heart, and you will be glad He did.

SPIRITUAL HEART FOCUS

What are the "pebbles" and "potholes" that cause your heart to damage others? What is the "beeswax" that hinders the work of God's Spirit in you? Ask God to "smooth" your heart.

PHYSICAL HEART FOCUS

For snacks, try fruit, nuts, or fresh, raw vegetables.

❤ The Hung–Up Heart

PHILIPPIANS 3:13–14

Brethren, I do not count myself to have apprehended; but one thing I do, forgetting those things which are behind and reaching forward to those things which are ahead, I press toward the goal for the prize of the upward call of God in Christ Jesus.

SHAQ O'NEAL, THE BASKETBALL STAR, says his stepfather gave him the passion to succeed in the game. For one thing, Phil Harrison wouldn't let his stepson keep his trophies in the house.[10] Reportedly, Harrison feared the trophies would get Shaq more focused on past accomplishments than on future goals.

When the heart gets hung up in the past, momentum is lost. Some people set up trophy rooms in their heart. There's nothing wrong with celebrating accomplishments, but if your heart is primarily a shrine of your "good ole' days," it loses its future focus. Give a quick hoorah to what you achieved yesterday, and then focus on the future. That's the way you move forward.

SPIRITUAL
HEART FOCUS
Thank God for enabling your past achievements. Ask Him to prepare you and help you focus on what lies ahead.

PHYSICAL HEART FOCUS
Set some mileposts on your journey to total heart health that mark achievement of goals along the way, and celebrate each time you pass one. Check your weight and BMI.

March

God ultimately gives us
what our hearts really want.

❤ What Touches the Heart

JOHN 11:32–35

Then, when Mary came where Jesus was, and saw Him,
she fell down at His feet, saying to Him, "Lord, if You had been here,
my brother would not have died." Therefore, when Jesus saw her weeping,
and the Jews who came with her weeping, He groaned in the spirit
and was troubled. And He said, "Where have you laid him?"
They said to Him, Lord, come and see." Jesus wept.

NOTHING REVEALS A PERSON'S TRUE CHARACTER as much as that which touches their heart.

Basketball star David Robinson is noted for his commitment to Christ. "A couple of things have touched our hearts as we've grown as a family," Robinson says of himself, his wife, and their three children. Those concerns include parents trying to feed their children and the education of disadvantaged kids.

What touches the heart results in action, so the David Robinson Foundation channels hefty chunks of his paychecks into poverty–scarred communities.[11]

Even though Jesus knew He had power to raise Lazarus from the dead, His compassionate character is revealed in His tears over Mary's pain. Consider what really touches your heart and you will know yourself truly.

> SPIRITUAL
> HEART FOCUS
> Dare to pray as did Bob Pierce,
> founder of World Vision:
> "Let my heart be broken with
> the things that break
> God's heart."

PHYSICAL HEART FOCUS

Soups are great for the diet–conscious *connoisseur*, but watch out for high fat and salt content in some canned products.

❤ The Holdout Heart

GENESIS 6:5-6

Then the LORD saw that the wickedness of man was great in the earth, and that every intent of the thoughts of his heart was only evil continually. And the LORD was sorry that He had made man on the earth, and He was grieved in His heart.

BERTRAND RUSSELL, THOUGH A MILITANT nonbeliever, concurred with Jesus that evil lies in the heart, and "from our hearts it must be plucked out."[12]

Imagine living in a world where the singular focus of people is to do evil. This was the spiritual and moral environment in which Noah clung to God and His righteousness. Were it not for Noah, the holdout against evil, the world would have ended right there.

When the world's heart is set on evil, God has individuals whose hearts are set on Him. Then God uses people with holdout hearts to keep the world going. "Noah found grace in the eyes of the LORD," says Genesis 6:8. This is no surprise, since "the eyes of the LORD move to and fro throughout the whole earth, to show Himself strong on behalf of those whose heart is loyal to Him" (2 Chronicles 16:9).

You can make a huge difference in your world by "holding out" for God!

> **SPIRITUAL HEART FOCUS**
> There is a point when your determination to walk by God's truth overcomes your desire to follow the tempter. Stay faithful and you will reach that objective.

PHYSICAL HEART FOCUS

Develop the discipline of a polite "No" when offered supersized portions or second helpings at meals.

❤ God's Heart–Sigh

GENESIS 6:6

And the LORD was sorry that He had made man on the earth, and He was grieved in His heart.

JO BETH SIGHED SUDDENLY while she was cross–stitching. "What's the matter?" I asked.

"I have to pull all this out," she said.

"Why?"

Jo Beth replied, "I didn't count right at first, and if you don't start right, the whole pattern will be distorted."

If you don't start right, you won't end up right.

God started right with His universe.

He gave people freedom. Humanity used liberty to mess up the pattern. "Sorry" comes from a Hebrew root, "to sigh." In that Divine sigh was deep heart–pain. Sin's extent meant God would begin again with humanity.

God's heart–sigh is not judgment, but hope. God will pick up the pieces and start again when liberty is abused and leads to destruction.

If you feel God sighing over you, don't assume it's wrath. If you are His child, it is the signal He's going to wipe the slate of your heart clean and give you another opportunity.

> SPIRITUAL
> HEART FOCUS
> Thank God for loving you so much He is willing to "sigh" over you, to cleanse you, and to allow you to begin again.

PHYSICAL HEART FOCUS

When dining at a fast–food restaurant choose a salad with vinegar and oil rather than the burger and fries.

❤ Heart Assurance

1 JOHN 3:18–21

My little children, let us not love in word or in tongue, but in deed and in truth. And by this we know that we are of the truth, and shall assure our hearts before Him. For if our heart condemns us, God is greater than our heart, and knows all things. Beloved, if our heart does not condemn us, we have confidence toward God.

HEALTH INSURANCE IS IMPORTANT, but heart assurance is vital. A compassionate, loving lifestyle is assurance we're in God's family.

A wife working to put her husband through seminary became terminally ill in his senior year, but she kept going until she wore out. She was brought to the graduation ceremony on a cot. When he got his diploma, the young preacher descended the platform, went to the cot, and kissed his wife. "I wouldn't be here without your sacrificial love," he said.

No one questioned his love for her; the deed was proof enough. Not even your own conscience can accuse you of not loving God when you are stepping off the platform to demonstrate your love.

SPIRITUAL HEART FOCUS
Ask the Father for opportunities to demonstrate your love for Him through your service to others.

PHYSICAL HEART FOCUS
Choose exercise levels that challenge you without exhausting you.

❤ Speaking from the Heart

LUKE 6:45

*"A good man out of the good treasure of his heart brings forth good;
and an evil man out of the evil treasure of his heart brings forth evil.
For out of the abundance of the heart his mouth speaks."*

THE MAN SLAMS THE DOOR as he arrives home from a frustrating day. The woman shrieks with anger at her disobedient children. When you shake an apple tree, apples rain down. The real you comes out when you're shaken. The fruit of your true heart thuds into view.

"That guy made me lose my temper!" The person who says that already had the temper inside. "That woman (or man) made me lust!" Nope, the lust was there already.

Apple trees don't blame anyone for the presence of apples.

Today's victim mentality encourages us to blame others for what comes out of us. Tragically, this blinds us from the opportunity to take responsibility for what's in our hearts.

But if you evaluate what comes out when your "tree" is shaken, your heart can be healed!

SPIRITUAL HEART FOCUS
Pray for the kind of heart that brings good fruit that blesses others rather than the heart that sickens others with rotten fruit.

PHYSICAL HEART FOCUS

Excess pounds wear down your joints as the years pass, so exercise and watch your weight now for a healthy body in "old age."

❤ When God Hardens the Heart

EXODUS 4:21

And the LORD said to Moses, "When you go back to Egypt, see that you do all those wonders before Pharaoh which I have put in your hand. But I will harden his heart, so that he will not let the people go."

IT'S UNTHINKABLE FOR GOD, who is love, to make somebody's heart so hard they can't respond to Him. Then what's with Pharaoh?

The Egyptian ruler's heart melts one minute and freezes the next. Plagues come, and he softens. But before the Hebrews can pack their mules, he changes his mind. Finally, God Himself hardens Pharaoh's heart.

Think of it like this. Place a chunk of clay and an ice cube under a broiling sun. The clay hardens, but the ice melts. Nothing has changed about the sun. Its heat is constant. The difference is in how the objects respond to the same sun.

> **SPIRITUAL HEART FOCUS**
> Pray for the Lord to keep your heart soft and pliable toward Him.

God ultimately gives us what our hearts really want. For the heart that has hardened itself toward Him, God finally gives it the insensitivity to Him it has craved. But for the heart that has yearned for Him, He gives Himself. This is blessing.

It's not God who makes our hearts unresponsive, but our own choices.

PHYSICAL HEART FOCUS

Make sure there is slow, deliberate, planned advance in your exercise programs, gradually increasing the challenge without rushing or pushing yourself.

❤ Total Return

1 SAMUEL 7:3

Then Samuel spoke to all the house of Israel, saying, "If you return to the
LORD with all your hearts, then put away the foreign gods and
the Ashtoreths from among you, and prepare your hearts for the LORD, and
serve Him only; and He will deliver you from the hand of the Philistines."

WHEN YOUR REPENTANCE is as notable as your sin was infamous, the heart has made its way back to God, to paraphrase Charles Haddon Spurgeon. That means getting rid of the "foreign gods." Your heart is the Holy of Holies of the bodily temple. There is to be only one Occupant—the living God. True repentance dethrones all the idols and seats the Lord in His reserved place.

Baal and Ashtaroth worship were at the core of pagan culture. Today, when we bow to the "god of this age" (2 Corinthians 4:4), we are worshiping the deities of our pagan culture.

Until the idols are gone, there is only partial repentance, or maybe none at all.

SPIRITUAL
HEART FOCUS
Tell God that you want your
heart reserved for Him alone
and that your desire is for
all the idols there to be torn
down and dethroned.

PHYSICAL HEART FOCUS
Keep healthy foods in your pantry, and remove the ones that would tempt you.

❤ True Beauty

1 PETER 3:3–4

Do not let your adornment be merely outward—arranging the hair, wearing gold, or putting on fine apparel—rather let it be the hidden person of the heart, with the incorruptible beauty of a gentle and quiet spirit, which is very precious in the sight of God.

TWO WOMEN LOOK IN THE MIRROR. Both want a makeover. The first woman, wealthy, can pay the $75,000 tab. The other woman, poor, has to remain—to her mind, at least—ugly.

You might not be able to do anything about your physical features, but there's a beauty available for everyone.

Inner beauty radiates outward as external beauty. Inner beauty is heart–beauty, that of a "gentle and quiet spirit." "That leaves me out," you may think, because your personality is expressive, assertive, and extroverted. But the person with a gentle and quiet spirit is one who has dignity, who is not boisterous in her assertiveness or crass in her expressions.

In today's parlance, we call this "class." It's an incorruptible beauty. Age doesn't mar it. In fact, such beauty is enhanced by the years. Go for this makeover!

SPIRITUAL HEART FOCUS
Pray for the Holy Spirit to beautify your interior and radiate it to and through your exterior.

PHYSICAL HEART FOCUS
You don't have to experience "middle-age sag" nearly so much if you continue your diet and workout regimen throughout your life.

❤ The Delusional, Stubborn Heart

JEREMIAH 23:17

They continually say to those who despise Me,
'The LORD has said, "You shall have peace" ';
And to everyone who walks according to the dictates of his own heart,
they say, 'No evil shall come upon you.' "

THE EASIEST PEOPLE TO FOOL are those so stubborn they refuse to open their hearts to truth.

"Stubbornness" means "twisted" as well as "hardened." The unwillingness of the stubborn–hearted comes from a deluded view of reality.

Stubbornness of heart makes people refuse to admit bad things can really happen to them. They are above tribulation and trial, or so they think. They listen to the seers who predict happy times, but stubbornly close their hearts to the sages who warn them of consequences. Hitler was stubborn–hearted to the end. When the Allies landed at Normandy, his aides were afraid to awaken him, because he still believed in his own invincibility.

SPIRITUAL HEART FOCUS

Ask God to break stubbornness off your heart and to cause it instead to be discerning and yielded to Him.

The stubborn heart is deadly, because it embraces the lies and delusions it wants to hear. Its opposite is the heart yielded to God and His truth.

PHYSICAL HEART FOCUS

Don't measure your heart–health progress in huge leaps, but in each small step, and take satisfaction in each one.

❤ Inadequate Lift

EZEKIEL 28:5

*"(By your great wisdom in trade you have increased your riches,
And your heart is lifted up because of your riches)."*

THERE ARE TWO ROCKET ENGINES for lifting the heart—haughtiness and humility.

The haughtiness lift is like the missile that soars then sputters. The gravitational push against the pride–fired heart is heavier because "God resisteth the proud" (James 4:6 KJV).

The humility lift takes the vessel higher and higher. The humble heart knows it must keep receiving fresh fuel, that it cannot sustain itself. It does not lift itself through riches—material things—but through God's power. While He resists the proud, He gives grace to the humble (James 4:6).

Augustine, in *The City of God*, suggests we all live in two cities. Part of the heart lives in a city where the populace is prideful but believes itself humble. The other side of the heart dwells in a town where people are humble but believe they are prideful.

The only way to get the lift of humility is to admit your pride.

SPIRITUAL HEART FOCUS

Ask the Holy Spirit to help you evaluate where you are relying on your own accomplishments for your "lift," and ask Him to transform your heart into one of genuine humility.

PHYSICAL HEART FOCUS

Eating the right kinds of foods in the right amounts will maximize your opportunity to live a long and productive life.

❤ The Meditating Heart

PSALM 19:14

Let the words of my mouth and the meditation of my heart
Be acceptable in Your sight,
O LORD, my strength and my Redeemer.

WHEN YOU MEDITATE, you talk to yourself. The Hebrew word for "meditate" means to "say again."

The meditating heart reads a Bible passage, then "talks it over" internally. The rabbis sang the Psalms, mystics journaled, and prophets talked the Word of God back to themselves.

Memorizing Scripture helps meditating.

Meditating on Scripture is like the tune that lingers in your head all day. You whistle, sing, and strum because your life is consumed with the song. Meditating is to have God's Word of the day echo in every moment.

Start your day with God's Word. Find ways to keep it before you in multiple forms. Think about the meanings and implications for you.

The meditating heart is a well–nourished heart!

SPIRITUAL HEART FOCUS

Open your Bible to Psalm 103. Meditate upon and pray through the first five verses, allowing the Holy Spirit to lead you.

PHYSICAL HEART FOCUS

As good diet and exercise become your lifestyle, some health problems may diminish, but never change or discontinue prescribed medications without consulting your physician.

♥ The Wise Heart

The wise in heart will receive commands,
But a prating fool will fall.

WISDOM INVOLVES THE HEAD and the heart.

If you follow only your heart, then your uncontrolled emotions will drive you over the cliff. Use only your head and you'll miss the nuanced bends in the road and plummet over the precipice.

Once I had a monkey on my back, a big need in our ministry. A solution was recommended, and my heart liked it, but my head wasn't sure.

So I prayed, but I forgot to ask the Lord for wisdom. I went with my heart. However, one morning I awakened to the realization I had gotten a monkey off my back but had a gorilla in my arms!

My mistake was going forward before my head and heart were in agreement.

Wise–hearted individuals "receive commands" from both the head and the heart. If they're wise, they know to wait until head and heart are compatible before deciding.

Wiseheartedness will keep you from foolhardiness.

SPIRITUAL HEART FOCUS
Seek the Lord for the wisdom to wait until your head and heart are in agreement before implementing decisions.

PHYSICAL HEART FOCUS

Vary your exercise, using the three types—cardio, resistance, and stretching.

♥ 'Braveheart'

PSALM 27:14
Wait on the LORD;
Be of good courage,
And He shall strengthen your heart;
Wait, I say, on the LORD!

HOW TALL IS A GIANT?

Ten of the twelve spies Moses sent into the Promised Land assumed they knew the measure. Israelite soldiers quaking in front of Goliath thought they knew.

Actually, they all would have been wrong. A giant is tall as Joshua and Caleb, who believed in God more than the colossuses of Canaan. David was a greater giant on the battlefield that day than Goliath.

SPIRITUAL HEART FOCUS
Ask God to give you a courageous heart, the heart of a spiritual giant.

A real giant is a "braveheart," a person with courage to wait on the Lord. The invaders are whooping in, but the man or woman of courage holds the ground. "Don't run," they tell themselves. "Wait for the word of the Commander." That's the person of spiritual courage, waiting on God, confident He will lead the battle.

Ernest Hemingway said courage is grace under pressure. In truth, bravery is fear plus prayer. Giants may quake, but their stature reaches to the heavens, where their hearts are made brave.

PHYSICAL HEART FOCUS
Exercise and relieve tension at your desk by slowly rolling your head forward, then side to side several times.

❤ The Pierced Heart

ACTS 2:37–39

Now when they heard this, they were cut to the heart, and said to Peter and the rest of the apostles, "Men and brethren, what shall we do?" Then Peter said to them, "Repent, and let every one of you be baptized in the name of Jesus Christ for the remission of sins; and you shall receive the gift of the Holy Spirit. For the promise is to you and to your children, and to all who are afar off, as many as the Lord our God will call."

YOU KNOW YOU'VE BEEN HEARD when your audience asks, "Wow! What should we do about this?"

In his Pentecost sermon, Peter pierces the hearts of listeners. "God has made the man you crucified both Lord and Christ," he tells them, and they answer, "What should we do?"

Zing! Right into the heart. Now those who had mocked the dying Lord melt under the truth of His love.

Hebrews 4 says God's Word is a two-edged sword, cutting on entry and exit. The Word says, "All have sinned and fall short of the glory of God" (Romans 3:23), and "the wages of sin is death, but the gift of God is eternal life in Christ Jesus our Lord" (6:23).

Believers' hearts are pierced with the message that our sin crucified Christ. The proof that the sword of the Word has stabbed your heart is being compelled to ask, "What should I do about this?"

> **SPIRITUAL HEART FOCUS**
> What have you done about the fact that Christ died for you? If you have received His free gift of grace, worship Him for it. If not, ask Him for it and thank Him for taking the penalty of your sin.

PHYSICAL HEART FOCUS

Limit caffeinated drinks to one or two a day, and drink water the rest of the time.

♥ The Tablet

PROVERBS 3:3
Let not mercy and truth forsake you;
Bind them around your neck,
Write them on the tablet of your heart.

FRENCHMAN JEAN–JACQUE ROUSSEAU believed the inner human being was a *tabla rasa,* a "blank slate," born good but defiled by culture.

God's truth shatters this idealism: "In sin my mother conceived me" (Psalm 51:5), and "All have sinned and fall short of the glory of God" (Romans 3:23).

People are not hapless victims of society's polluting influences; instead, they willingly give their heart tablets to the powers of darkness.

But the Bible shows that when we give our hearts to Jesus, He erases the filthy scrabble and gives us each back a pure, clean heart. The devil would love to fill it up again with sordid scratching, but we are to allow only the Lord to write on the tablet of our heart through His Holy Spirit.

He pens on our inner person kindness and truth. Truth is principle and kindness is action. It is through this combination inscribed on the heart tablet that we are able to live effectively on the internal and external levels.

> **SPIRITUAL HEART FOCUS**
> Ask the Lord to write kindness and truth on the tablet of your heart with regard to specific situations you face currently.

PHYSICAL HEART FOCUS
Vary the places you walk, jog, or run to keep boredom from your routine.

❤ Plans of the Heart

PROVERBS 16:1

The preparations of the heart belong to man,
But the answer of the tongue is from the LORD.

SOMETIMES WE WRITE PLANS on our heart tablets.

Plans are the arrangements and preparations to carry out some desire. The evil heart is full of schematics on how to execute seductions.

But methods of blessing are in the plans written out on the hearts of those who love God. "A plan in the heart of a man is like deep water, but a man of understanding draws it out" (Proverbs 20:5 NASB). Others are refreshed by the plans in the heart of those who follow God.

You can make the heart encyclopedic with dreams and schemes, but God alone knows the outcome. Write your plans of goodness on your heart, but submit even those for God's editing and revision.

SPIRITUAL
HEART FOCUS
Consider the desires and plans
that fill your thoughts and
ask God to change them
to conform to His
will for you.

PHYSICAL HEART FOCUS

Set aside a planned time for exercising daily and stick with it.

❤ Tuning the Heart

PSALM 119:36
Incline my heart to Your testimonies,
And not to covetousness.

ELECTRONIC MESSAGES ARE ZIPPING all around you, available to any receiver tuned to pick them up.

"Speak to me, O God," we sometimes pray. The truth is, like the electronic messages riding their frequency bands, God never stops speaking. If you're not hearing God, it may be that your heart is not tuned to His frequency.

A radio tuner resonates at the frequency you choose and ignores all the thousands of others. If the tuner attempted to resonate at all the frequencies, the radio would go crazy trying to sort them all out. If you've heard overlapping radio signals and static, you understand how confusing it can be.

SPIRITUAL HEART FOCUS
Ask God to help you set your heart's focus on Him and His Word.

Spiritually, there are zillions of messages oscillating at a given moment. The devil never stops trying to get our attention. Spiritual static and overlapping signals cause confusion in our inner beings.

Set your heart on God's frequency and you will hear clearly.

PHYSICAL HEART FOCUS

Eat slowly, so you can begin to sense how little food it really takes to make you feel satisfied. This will help you know when to stop.

❤ The Envious Heart

PROVERBS 23:17

Do not let your heart envy sinners,
But be zealous for the fear of the LORD all the day.

A SMALL-TOWN MERCHANT WAS JEALOUS of his competitor. A genie popped up before him. "Whatever you ask I will do for you, and double for the man you envy so much."

"Then make me blind in one eye," said the envious merchant.

Envy is an energy consumer. It eats you up, devouring passion and zeal. Invest your creative juices in envy and there's less left to spark you to success. Envy also releases emotional and mental toxins into your spiritual bloodstream. Your life is polluted so much you even will accept injury to yourself if it can be multiplied against those of whom you're jealous.

The fear of the Lord is the cure of the envious heart. One of the results of reverencing the Lord is respecting His sovereignty. Freedom from envy comes from worshiping God as the Absolute One who has the right to send His refreshing rain on the unrighteous as well as the righteous (Matthew 5:45).

SPIRITUAL HEART FOCUS
Consider those you envy. Thank God for His blessing on their lives, and ask Him to bless them even more!

PHYSICAL HEART FOCUS
Don't be envious of the physical attributes and appearance of others, but be satisfied to take care of the body God gave you.

♥ The Singing Heart

EPHESIANS 5:19

Speaking to one another in psalms and hymns and spiritual songs,
singing and making melody in your heart to the Lord.

MUSIC IS A BAROMETER of our character.

Music streams through the Scriptures. In fact, when we get to Heaven, preaching will be finished, but music will be in its fullest power.

"He brought me up . . . out of the miry clay" and "put a new song in my mouth," says the Psalmist (Psalm 40:2–3). God lifts us from the mire and puts us in the choir!

Hezekiah, Josiah, and Nehemiah were all great reformers, building again the choirs of Israel and Judah. Martin Luther brought reformation and hymns such as "A Mighty Fortress Is Our God." John and Charles Wesley embraced the parish of the world with the Lord's songs.

SPIRITUAL
HEART FOCUS
Ask God to put a new song
in your heart.

If you were to write a history of the evangelical church, you would have every reason to title it *The Sound of Music.*

Unleash your heart to make melody to the Lord, and it will throb with vitality!

PHYSICAL HEART FOCUS
Before you go grocery shopping, decide the aisles you're going to skip, especially those with fat–stuffed snacks.

❤ Songs for the Heart

1 SAMUEL 16:23

And so it was, whenever the spirit from God was upon Saul, that David would take a harp and play it with his hand. Then Saul would become refreshed and well, and the distressing spirit would depart from him.

"ALL YOU LISTEN TO ARE THOSE VIOLINS," said one of our sons to me as we rode along. My car radio is almost always set on the "violin station."

A while back I was in a friend's car. The radio was on a station reporting a summary of the day's events in our city—murder, mayhem, rape, wrecks, political skullduggery, ethical breaches in business—enough trash for a landfill.

I decided to go back to my violins.

King Saul needed the violins, too. David's harp filled the function. God allowed an evil spirit to torment Saul, because that's what Saul opened himself to receive. God honors our choices. David's Spirit–inspired, harmonic songs soothed the king's troubled heart.

> SPIRITUAL HEART FOCUS
>
> Ask the Lord to fill your heart with His music and give you strength to turn off the music that troubles your heart.

Everywhere we go, the noises of earth batter us with chaos. The heart is troubled with the cacophony. But God's music stills the troubled heart. Get it in you and be refreshed.

PHYSICAL HEART FOCUS

Walking your dog regularly combines a romp for Rover and exercise for you.

❤ Don't Be a Heart Melter

DEUTERONOMY 1:28-30

*"[You said] 'Our brethren have discouraged our hearts, saying,
"The people are greater and taller than we; the cities are great and fortified
up to heaven; moreover we have seen the sons of the Anakim there.'"
Then I said to you, 'Do not be terrified, or afraid of them. The LORD your
God, who goes before you, He will fight for you,
according to all He did for you in Egypt before your eyes.'"*

A "HEART MELTER" IS A PERSON who discourages others, who liquefies their inner strength, like the ten shaky spies who checked out the Promised Land.

SPIRITUAL HEART FOCUS

Ask God to solidify, stabilize, and strengthen your own heart, and then use you to solidify the hearts of others.

Every group has its heart melters. In strategic planning for an organization, leaders sometimes do an analysis by which they survey the institution's strengths, weaknesses, opportunities, and threats (SWOT). Heart melters focus on the threats rather than the opportunities. A "heart solidifier," as Moses, Joshua, and Caleb were to the Hebrews, does not ignore reality. He or she sees the threats. But the solidifiers encourage the inner strength of the team or group by getting everyone to see the opportunities. Moses' own heart was solid and stable with his faith in God. Heart melters transmit their own shakiness to team members, but heart solidifiers share their faith and strength.

PHYSICAL HEART FOCUS

Before you dine out, plan what you will avoid and stick to it.

❤ The Proud Heart

DEUTERONOMY 8:13–14; PROVERBS 16:5

And when your herds and your flocks multiply, and your silver and your gold are multiplied, and all that you have is multiplied; when your heart is lifted up, and you forget the LORD your God who brought you out of the land of Egypt, from the house of bondage. . . .

Everyone proud in heart is an abomination to the LORD; Though they join forces, none will go unpunished.

PRIDE IS THE NUMBER ONE OBSTACLE to human growth.

Pride starts early in our lives. It's what makes us fire God as CEO of the heart and put ourselves on that throne. Pride presents the illusion of adequacy when we are empty, ability when we are hapless, and superiority when we are inferior in skill and talent.

The proud heart disgusts the Lord. Consider a father who wants to teach his son to drive. The boy has been controlling racecars on a video game, and he proudly believes his driving skills are actually better than his dad's. The pride is an abomination to the father because he knows it can lead to disaster for his child.

God opposes the proud heart because He loves us and knows how it can mislead us (James 4:6). He gives unmerited favor to the humble heart because it is teachable, correctable, and leads to effective living.

SPIRITUAL HEART FOCUS
What are some of the illusions pride has stirred in you? Ask God to make your heart humble, teachable, and correctable.

PHYSICAL HEART FOCUS

Eat several small meals during the day and you'll be less hungry in the afternoon when you're most tempted to snack.

♥ The Reflector

PROVERBS 27:19

As in water face reflects face,
So a man's heart reveals the man.

THE ELDERLY MAN IS UNUSUALLY VIBRANT and active. He helped crack the Nazi grip on Europe. Then he launched into another career, earned a doctorate and, in his eighties, became an educator. Sunday by Sunday you can see this hero at our church. You would know him by his strong countenance.

At one point, his physical heart said "Enough!" The gentleman had quadruple bypass surgery. But his face never lost the glow of a man with a strong spiritual and moral heart.

What will your demeanor reveal today about the condition of your heart? Energize with God and His Word and—even though your physical heart may be weary, as in the case of my friend—your spiritual and moral heart will reflect God's strength within you!

SPIRITUAL HEART FOCUS
Ask God to keep your spiritual and moral heart strong no matter what the condition of your physical heart.

PHYSICAL HEART FOCUS
Be realistic about the limitations of medical science to maintain your physical health.

❤ The Truth That Won't Stay Under

ROMANS 1:18–19

For the wrath of God is revealed from heaven against all ungodliness and unrighteousness of men, who suppress the truth in unrighteousness, because what may be known of God is manifest in them, for God has shown it to them.

BILLY AND ZEKE PLAY A MEAN GAME of water dodgeball.

Billy is the bully, but Zeke is the sneak. He tries to submerge the ball until he can get close and whack Billy. Zeke has a hard time keeping the buoyant ball down, though. He pushes and squeezes, but the ball keeps spurting back to the surface. You can't suppress a beach ball in the depths of a swimming pool!

God has put His truth deep inside us. He has written His Law on our hearts (Romans 2:15). The only way a human being can deny God is to try to suppress the truth tucked away in the depths of their soul.

SPIRITUAL HEART FOCUS
Ask God to bring His truth up to the surface so you can see it plainly.

But that truth is irrepressible. It insists on bobbing to the surface. Men and women weary themselves trying to hold it down, but it won't stay under. Let the truth emerge and you'll wonder why you ever wanted to keep it submerged!

PHYSICAL HEART FOCUS
Supplement your heart–healthy diet with a daily multivitamin.

♥ The Fatal Flaw of the Self-Exam

1 CORINTHIANS 4:3–5

. . . I do not even judge myself. For I know of nothing against myself, yet I am not justified by this; but He who judges me is the Lord. Therefore judge nothing before . . . the Lord comes, who will both bring to light the hidden things of darkness and reveal the counsels of the hearts. . . .

HARRY SHAVES HIS CHEST, attaches the probes of the do–it–yourself electrocardiogram machine, and pushes the button. He looks at the little peaks and valleys on the printout. "Yep, lot's of them," he says to himself. "I must have a really healthy heart!" The potentially deadly flaw of Harry's self-exam is that he has not been trained to read the health of his own heart, and this flaw can prove fatal because the printout may be full of danger signals he cannot understand.

> **SPIRITUAL HEART FOCUS**
> Submit the motives and intents of your heart to God. Ask Him to examine them and purify you at the deepest level.

Ancient philosophers like Seneca and Plato believed the individual human conscience should be the standard for measuring the ethics of behavior. Contemporary humanism has bought into that potentially fatal flaw.

Paul understood he was not qualified for a do–it–yourself spiritual heart exam. "I am not aware of anything wrong," he says, "but this doesn't make it right." Only God can do the life–saving heart exam, through His Word and Spirit.

PHYSICAL HEART FOCUS

A formula for poor diet: FF x 2 = PD. That means too much fast food equals a poor diet of high calories, high fat, and low nutrition.

❤ The Spectator Heart

MATTHEW 13:3–4, 19

Then He spoke many things to them in parables, saying: "Behold, a sower went out to sow. And as he sowed, some seed fell by the wayside; and the birds came and devoured them. . . . When anyone hears the word of the kingdom, and does not understand it, then the wicked one comes and snatches away what was sown in his heart. This is he who received seed by the wayside."

ANCIENT PALESTINE HAD UNWALLED GARDENS. Paths bordered and linked the little orchards. Over time, many people walked the paths, and the rocky soil would be hardened like concrete. At planting time, sowers scattered seed, and some fell on the path edges. There it wouldn't germinate, and birds gobbled it.

A certain woman goes to church and the seed of God's Word is scattered. But she is on the periphery. She shrinks back from a genuine commitment to the Lord. Spiritually, her heart is for the birds. It doesn't germinate God's truth because the devil is able to steal it.

> SPIRITUAL HEART FOCUS
> Declare to God your resolve for passionate commitment and ask Him to fill your heart with His truth.

When God's Word truly penetrates your heart it will "save your souls" (James 1:21). God's truth will change your thinking, your feelings, and your choices. Resolve not to be a mere spectator, but a man or woman of passionate commitment to Christ and His Kingdom, and the seed will root and transform you.

PHYSICAL HEART FOCUS

Twelve thousand steps equals six miles of walking and burns 600 calories. Check your steps with a pedometer.

❤ The Shallow Heart

MATTHEW 13:20–21

"But he who received the seed on stony places, this is he who hears the word and immediately receives it with joy; yet he has no root in himself, but endures only for a while. For when tribulation or persecution arises because of the word, immediately he stumbles."

JESUS' EARTHLY HOMELAND RESTED on a limestone shell, covered by a thin layer of rich soil. Seed sown where the limestone hadn't been broken up withered quickly because roots couldn't develop.

Shallow–hearted people take in the Gospel seed quickly, believing it will position them for rewards and prosperity. But when testing comes the shallow–hearted person will turn away from Christ every time.

SPIRITUAL HEART FOCUS
Ask God to intensify your hunger for His Word and commit yourself to systematic study and memorization of the Scripture.

Put your roots down deep in God's Word. Study it daily, meditate upon it, pray it. Do this individually and with others. Allow God to break up the rocky soil that encases your heart, even though it may be painful. Get serious about the Lord and watch Him change your heart!

PHYSICAL HEART FOCUS

When dieting, break your overall goal into small segments, and celebrate the loss of one pound because it leads ultimately to the loss of 20, if you stay with it.

❤ The Suffocated Heart

MATTHEW 13:22

"Now he who received seed among the thorns is he who hears the word, and the cares of this world and the deceitfulness of riches choke the word, and he becomes unfruitful."

IT'S HARD TO BE PROSPEROUS and grow and go with God.

Prosperity often suffocates the spiritual heart, cloaking the dynamics of life in Christ. This is why Jesus said it is easier for a camel to go through a needle's eye than for a rich man to enter the kingdom of God (Matthew 19:24).

God does not call us to poverty. True, Jesus told the rich young ruler to sell all he had and give the proceeds to the poor (Matthew 19:21). But Jesus did not give that direction to all the wealthy people He met. The problem with the rich young man was that his possessions were suffocating his spiritual heart.

SPIRITUAL HEART FOCUS
Ask the Heavenly Father to help you not to be suffocated by your possessions.

We are to learn to live with poverty and with wealth, to say with Paul, "I know how to get along with humble means, and I also know how to live in prosperity" (Philippians 4:12 NASB). Living with prosperity means not letting possessions suffocate your spiritual heart.

PHYSICAL HEART FOCUS
Good diet is a lifestyle, not a fad.

❤ The Spiritually Sensitive Heart

MATTHEW 13:8, 23

"But others fell on good ground and yielded a crop: some a hundredfold, some sixty, some thirty. . . . But he who received seed on the good ground is he who hears the word and understands it, who indeed bears fruit and produces: some a hundredfold, some sixty, some thirty."

"ENJOYED YOUR SERMON, PASTOR," the man said Sunday after Sunday. Then I happened on some information about his lifestyle. "Enjoyed your sermon," he said the next Sunday, as usual. I pulled him aside, and asked, "What are you going to do about it?"

People with spiritually sensitive hearts bear fruit because their hearts are receptive.

Good soil knows the sharpness of the hoe, the slicing of the plow, the dampness of the rain. God is your heart's gardener. He will stir your heart and open it. His Spirit will soak it with softening moisture.

SPIRITUAL HEART FOCUS

Submit your heart to God for His "gardening" work to make it spiritually sensitive and receptive to His word.

If you are in relationship with God through Jesus Christ, you can say with Paul, "And not only that, but we also glory in tribulations, knowing that tribulation produces perseverance; and perseverance, character; and character, hope. Now hope does not disappoint, because the love of God has been poured out in our hearts by the Holy Spirit who was given to us" (Romans 5:3–5).

PHYSICAL HEART FOCUS

For healthy weight loss, exercise alone is not enough, but there must be an overall program that includes dieting.

♥ Idol Factory

ROMANS 1:21–23

Although they knew God, they did not glorify Him as God, nor were thankful, but became futile in their thoughts, and their foolish hearts were darkened. Professing to be wise, they became fools, and changed the glory of the incorruptible God into an image made like corruptible man—and birds and four-footed animals and creeping things.

THE HEART THAT DOESN'T WORSHIP GOD cranks out idols. A Dostoevsky character says if there is no God all things are permissible. The heart that denies the living God deifies everything!

Fearful they would leave out a god, the Athenians finally erected a catchall statue "To An Unknown God" (Acts 17:16–34).

To understand the idols your heart is prone to produce, ask yourself some key questions. What do you fear above all else? At the end of that fear might be an idol. What do you think about when you don't have to concern yourself with anything else? The makings of an idol can lie about in those thoughts.

> SPIRITUAL HEART FOCUS
> Ask God to reveal the idolatry in your life and shut down the idol factory.

You can shut down the idol factory by confessing the sin of idolatry in your own life, identifying and unmasking your personal idols, renewing your faith in the true and living God, and giving Him the totality of your worship.

PHYSICAL HEART FOCUS

If you want to grow thinner, decrease your dinner.

❤ Give It A Rest!

PSALM 116:7
Return to your rest, O my soul,
For the LORD has dealt bountifully with you.

THE HEART'S GATEWAY PULSES two and a half billion times in an average lifetime.

Blood surges through the gate at about eight gallons a minute during intensified activity, like kissing your sweetheart or scampering up stairs.

Though it seems never to stop, the heart rests twice as long as it beats. God designed the physical heart for a balance of work–rest, work–rest, with a two–to–one edge for the rest phase!

SPIRITUAL HEART FOCUS

Ask God to give you patience in the midst of your troubles and faith to trust Him for His work of wholeness in you.

The Psalmist tells his spiritual heart to give it a rest. Crisis had caused it to pump feverishly. The reason an anxious heart can rest is because if you are in relationship with God, He will deal "bountifully" with you.

That means He is working to resolve your crisis and meet your needs.

If God is working on your behalf, why should your heart labor? Give it a rest on the big bed called faith!

PHYSICAL HEART FOCUS

Be patient with your weight loss. It took time to gain extra weight and it will require time to lose it. Check your weight and BMI.

April

The only question that counts
in the operating room and in daily living is:
"What's going on inside the heart?"

❤ Troubles, But Untroubled

JOHN 14:1

"Let not your heart be troubled; you believe in God, believe also in Me."

"WE ARE NOT GOD'S COSMIC PETS," said E. Stanley Jones.

When we receive Christ, God doesn't place us in a cushy world of health and wealth, isolated from troubles.

Jesus promises us something better. In the midst of troubles, our spiritual heart can be untroubled!

To believe in God is to believe in Christ, and to believe in Christ is to believe in God. Therefore, if you are in Christ you are in a "zone" where even the troubles become the components of His blessing in your life.

SPIRITUAL HEART FOCUS

Ninety days ago you embarked on a plan to implement a spiritual routine that includes at least a half hour a day of personal time with God and His word. Our hope is that you now feel this to be a lifestyle rather than a forced practice.

For instance, a woman weaves a magnificent quilt. At one point she uses a thread whose tint troubles the daughter for whom she is making it. The color is grim. But when the quilt is done, the unattractive color is now beautiful, seen in the context of the whole.

You can be untroubled in the midst of your troubles when you know Jesus is using hardship to make your life a lovely whole.

PHYSICAL HEART FOCUS

If you took up the 21–40–90 day challenge to exercise and eat right, perhaps you now feel this routine is so much a part of your day you can't do without it!

❤ Heart Sizes

JAMES 5:16

*Confess your trespasses to one another, and pray
for one another, that you may be healed.
The effective, fervent prayer of a righteous man avails much.*

SOME YEARS AGO A LOCAL HEART ASSOCIATION invited city leaders to a presentation by cardiologists. The physicians displayed four human hearts floating in jars of formaldehyde.

The heart of a middle–aged person killed instantly in an accident was normal size. The next was the heart of an executive who died of a heart attack during a high–powered bargaining session with a client; it was twice normal size. Third was the heart of a coronary victim who was cheating on his wife; it too was enlarged. Displayed finally was the heart of a person who had suffered a heart attack, survived, and changed his lifestyle in the years before his death. The heart was appropriately the normal size, although it had once been stricken.

> ### SPIRITUAL HEART FOCUS
> Ask God to show you sins of the past that struck your spiritual heart. Acknowledge and confess the sins and declare to God you are turning from them.

You may have suffered a spiritual heart attack in the past through a moral failing or some other sin. Repentance, which begins with acknowledgment and confession of sin, is a change in lifestyle that heals your spiritual heart. And repentance is good for your physical heart, too!

PHYSICAL HEART FOCUS
Add whole grain (not instant) oatmeal to your diet. It's a natural enemy of bad cholesterol (LDL).

❤ Rhythms of the Heart

MATTHEW 5:3–4
*"Blessed are the poor in spirit,
For theirs is the kingdom of heaven.
Blessed are those who mourn,
For they shall be comforted."*

RENUNCIATION AND PARTICIPATION are the rhythms of a healthy spiritual heart.

The poor in spirit renounce pride, acclaim, and fame, and they embrace humility. Spirit poverty recognizes that the inner temple is vacant without the Holy Spirit.

> **SPIRITUAL HEART FOCUS**
> Pray for balance in your life. If you tend to the ascetic, ask the Father to give you a heart for others. If you are most often an activist, ask the Lord to give you a hunger to be separated unto Him.

Mourners not only weep for themselves and their own tendencies to fall short of the glory of God, but their tears also fall for a fallen world. This sensitivity comes from their participation in society.

Renunciation alone is spiritual suicide. Participation alone is spiritual death by suffocation. Mystics tend to the first, while activists tend to the second. But the spiritually healthy person practices both renunciation and participation, separation and involvement.

Before sunrise, Jesus separated Himself and went to hidden places to pray. But in the searing daylight, He was out with the people. This is the rhythmic syncopation of a healthy heart.

PHYSICAL HEART FOCUS
Try jumping rope as a great aerobic exercise that also improves your balance.

❤ How Not to Fear Bad News

PSALM 112:7

He will not be afraid of evil tidings;
His heart is steadfast, trusting in the LORD.

THE PSALMIST WAS NOT AFRAID of bad news because his heart was steady.

Bad news in the electronic media age is like the sudden storms at sea. Billowy clouds dressing the morning in lacy loveliness suddenly become heavy shrouds cloaking the sky in gray death. Gentle breezes shift into howling wraiths. Seas calm as a swan's back mutate into the serrated jags of a dinosaur's spine.

If you trust in the Lord the storm won't capsize you. "Steadfast" means to be upright. God is like the great rocks off the California and Oregon coasts. The waves bash against them, but they are unmoved. When you trust in God, you are anchoring yourself to His stability.

In fact, in the Hebrew original, "trust" means to scamper to God for refuge. When the tides of bad news crash in, run to the Rock!

SPIRITUAL HEART FOCUS

Confess to your Heavenly Father the anxieties of your heart, the things you dread. Willingly turn over these things to His loving heart and capable care.

PHYSICAL HEART FOCUS

Confess to God anxieties you have about your body and exercise and dietary habits.

❤ Magnetic Pole

PSALM 112:4

Unto the upright there arises light in the darkness;
He is gracious, and full of compassion, and righteous.

ONCE, CHRIST'S FOLLOWERS WERE KNOWN as "People of the Way."
They had fixed their hearts on Jesus, who is the Way.

A friend gained new perspective on the importance of knowing the Way while he crossed the Atlantic on a freighter one December. During the day, fog cloaked the horizon. At night, it seemed the whole world disappeared.

One night in the middle of the ten–day crossing, he climbed above the ship's bridge and looked down on the place where the ship was steered. A soft green glow penetrated the glum darkness. A softly lit glass dome stood on a pedestal, and inside was the ship's compass. No matter how dark and stormy, the needle pointed to magnetic north, and the helmsman knew how to steer. The ship came to its destination even though there seemed no sense of direction.

Fix your heart on Jesus and His Way, and the directional light will glow in your darkest night.

SPIRITUAL HEART FOCUS

Thank God for His truth and commit yourself to following it no matter how deep the darkness around you. Ask God to sharpen your vision of Him and His Word.

PHYSICAL HEART FOCUS

Follow through with a weekly exercise plan that will help you reach your weight–loss and physical health goals.

❤ Hero Measure

1 SAMUEL 17:4

A champion went out from the camp of the Philistines, named Goliath, from Gath, whose height was six cubits and a span.

ONE OF THE MOST REVEALING MEASURES of your heart and mine is the quality of our heroes.

The Philistine heart was disclosed in their champion, Goliath. Arrogant, vicious, angry, unbelieving, scornful—that was the heart of Goliath and the people who hoisted him to hero status.

You can measure the heart of a nation by noting those to whom its people pay exorbitant salaries, place on popular magazine covers, and listen to endlessly on the electronic chatter circuit.

Are you a member of the cult of the famous, the religion of celebrity? Do you worship in the temple of the illustrious by seeking your identity in the heroes of the hour? Your heroes reveal your heart.

SPIRITUAL HEART FOCUS
Spend some time worshiping and adoring Christ as your Hero and the Champion of your salvation.

For Israel that day there was only one champion, David. For we who live in this celebrity–glutted hour there can be only one Hero—the Lord Jesus Christ. Enshrine Him as your Champion, and watch what happens to your heart!

PHYSICAL HEART FOCUS
Enlist a friend to exercise with you several times a week.

❤ Risking Heart

MATTHEW 14:28–29

Peter answered Him and said, "Lord, if it is You, command me to come to You on the water." So He said, "Come." And when Peter had come down out of the boat, he walked on the water to go to Jesus.

BEING A CHRISTIAN IS AN exhilarating adventure.

A believing heart gets out of a safe boat at the command of Jesus and dares to go into the turbulence of a stormy world.

You can take the risk when you know Jesus is calling you to climb out of the boat, when you know He is out there where you are headed, and when your focus is on Him above all else.

The call to risk comes when you feel dissatisfied when you compare the place where Jesus is with the place where you are. Hudson Taylor, safe in England, saw Jesus in impoverished China, and Taylor had to step out. C. T. Studd, son of wealth, beheld the Lord in Africa, and he abandoned estates to live in the jungles. Chuck Colson saw Jesus in prisons, and although he was a former inmate who cringed at confinement, he went out on the waters to Jesus.

To what "waters" is Jesus calling you?

SPIRITUAL HEART FOCUS

Ask the Lord to give you discernment to see Him on the "waters," and courage to step out into the place to which He calls you.

PHYSICAL HEART FOCUS

Get daring! If you usually use two or more spoons of sugar in your coffee or tea, change to a sugar substitute.

❤ Places in the Heart

EPHESIANS 4:26–27

"Be angry, and do not sin": do not let the sun go down on your wrath, nor give place to the devil. Let him who stole steal no longer, but rather let him labor, working with his hands what is good, that he may have something to give him who has need.

IN WAR, CONQUERING ARMIES ESTABLISH BASES in enemy territory, and there they store armaments and launch forays.

The devil seeks to build bases in our hearts. Sometimes we willingly give him the ground. Paul uses anger as one example. It is as if anger in the heart were a huge plot of land we surrender to the enemy for the establishment of his base of operations within us.

Galatians 5:19–21 identifies other places in the heart where the adversary can set up a fortress: "immorality, impurity, sensuality, idolatry, sorcery, enmities, strife, jealousy, outbursts of anger, disputes, dissensions, factions, envying, drunkenness, carousing" (NASB), and similar mindsets and behaviors.

SPIRITUAL HEART FOCUS
Ask the Holy Spirit to reveal the places in your heart where the enemy is able to operate. Confess the sin, and ask Jesus to capture your every thought.

We demolish the devil's places in our hearts by refusing to accept notions, attitudes, and lifestyles that contradict Christ's truth, and when we allow Him to take captive our every thought and conform us to Himself (2 Corinthians 10:5–6).

PHYSICAL HEART FOCUS

Keep a small notebook, record all you ate and drank today, and use the data to improve tomorrow's choices.

❤ Purposes of the Heart

1 CHRONICLES 29:17–18

I know also, my God, that You test the heart and have pleasure in uprightness. As for me, in the uprightness of my heart I have willingly offered all these things; and now with joy I have seen Your people, who are present here to offer willingly to You. O LORD God of Abraham, Isaac, and Israel, our fathers, keep this forever in the intent of the thoughts of the heart of Your people, and fix their heart toward You.

WHAT ONE THING IS WORTHY of becoming the central purpose of your heart, the objective so great you are willing to give it your total energy and treasure? For David, it was the building of God's temple. Paul said, "For to me, to live is Christ" (Philippians 1:21).

SPIRITUAL HEART FOCUS
Ask the Holy Spirit to help you sort through all the purposes of your heart, to bring them together under the one great purpose of being in His will, and to preserve that passion in you forever.

"What's your business?" you ask someone. "Insurance," is the answer. The answer reveals the purpose of the heart. So we conclude, "He is *in* insurance." So, ultimately, the highest purpose of the heart must be to be *in* Christ.

This means being in Christ's destiny, eternity in Heaven. In the present age, being *in* Christ's destiny means being in His will now. This is the ultimate "business" of every follower of Jesus Christ. This is the "magnificent obsession" that must be preserved forever in your heart.

PHYSICAL HEART FOCUS

If you stick to a new exercise and diet program for 90 days, you have a much greater chance of it becoming your heart–healthy lifestyle.

❤ Paint Job

MATTHEW 23:25–26

"Woe to you, scribes and Pharisees, hypocrites! For you cleanse the outside of the cup and dish, but inside they are full of extortion and self–indulgence. Blind Pharisee, first cleanse the inside of the cup and dish, that the outside of them may be clean also."

A HEART SURGEON OPENS A PATIENT'S CHEST and finds a heart gray with sickness. But rather than probing for the cause of the ailment, the physician takes a brush and paints the heart bright pink! That certainly would not cure the sick heart.

"Paint–job religion" is popular these days. Keep a few rules. Nod at God. Toss the church a bone. Placate the preacher.

But the only question that counts in the operating room and in daily living is this: "What's going on inside the heart?"

Jesus' treatment plan for sick hearts is always inside out. A clear glass cup or bowl may have surface dirt. You can wash it all off, but you still have dirt, because the inside gunk has not been removed. Wash the inside, and the whole thing sparkles.

The Lord doesn't paint over sickened hearts. He heals the inside, and then the color of health glistens on the outside, too!

> **SPIRITUAL HEART FOCUS**
> Ask the Great Physician to probe deep into the core of your heart and cut out all the disease spread within by sin.

PHYSICAL HEART FOCUS

To lengthen your life, maintain a normal body weight for your height.

❤ When the Heart's Not in It

ISAIAH 29:13

Therefore the LORD said:
". . . these people draw near with their mouths
And honor Me with their lips,
But have removed their hearts far from Me,
And their fear toward Me is taught by the commandment of men."

AMOS 5:21

"I hate, I despise your feast days,
And I do not savor your sacred assemblies."

SPIRITUAL HEART FOCUS
Renew your commitment to a genuine relationship with your Heavenly Father.

GOD HATES RELIGION that merely goes through the motions. Many people rationalize that if the body is in the right position and the spoken formula precise, then Heaven is happy. "Hate" is a strong word. In Old Testament Hebrew it means loathing something so much you get rid of it as fast as possible—like biting into a rotten egg. When our hearts are not involved in our relationship with God, our religious rituals are disgusting to His palate.

Some people ask, "How little can I do and still make God happy?" By the minimums of external compliance we try to short–circuit grace and keep just enough of the law to keep us on the happy–face side of God. Not only does this repulse God, but it cheats us. The heart wholly yielded to Him experiences His joy and peace. Heartless religion produces only bondage to rules and guilt.

PHYSICAL HEART FOCUS
A healthy lifestyle takes planning and discipline.

❤ Fellowship of the Burning Heart

LUKE 24:32

And they said to one another, "Did not our heart burn within us while He talked with us on the road, and while He opened the Scriptures to us?"

THE FELLOWSHIP OF THE BURNING HEART began that day when two followers of Jesus were dragging themselves back to their village of Emmaus, having watched Jesus—and their hopes—die on the cross.

The flame of passion and confidence had been snuffed. But suddenly, He is beside them, at the table with them, breaking bread with them, teaching them the whole plan of God revealed in the Scriptures, and the passion returns to their hearts!

People in the Fellowship of the Burning Heart are "enthusiastic" because they are "*en* (in) *Theos*" (God)!

If you are confident that whatever the world deals you, Christ in you can handle it, you are a member of the Fellowship of the Burning Heart. If you rest in the fact that He is the Lord of history, that whatever occurs is in His scope of vision and care, that bitter crosses are bridges to empty tombs, welcome to the Fellowship!

SPIRITUAL HEART FOCUS
What is the spiritual temperature of your heart? How high is the flame burning? Ask God to pour on more fuel.

PHYSICAL HEART FOCUS
Check out your local church or community center for low–cost exercise classes.

♥ Where You Got Your Heart

HOSEA 11:7–8

"My people are bent on backsliding from Me.
Though they call to the Most High,
None at all exalt Him.

How can I give you up, Ephraim?
How can I hand you over, Israel?
How can I make you like Admah?
How can I set you like Zeboiim?
My heart churns within Me;
My sympathy is stirred."

SPIRITUAL HEART FOCUS
Thank God for the gift of your heart, and ask Him to conform your heart to His.

GREEN SLIME CAN'T produce compassion. Where did we get "heart"? Hard question for the naturalist. Whirling atoms can't account for kindness. Primeval scum couldn't produce love. The unfeeling void can't come up with mercy.

Where did we get our emotions?

We are made in the image of God and got our heart from Him. In Genesis, He looks on what He has made and says, "That's good." Such a statement is meaningless without a heart capable of emotion. "Good" means the object brings pleasure. No heart, no feeling; no feeling, no pleasure.

God has heart, and thus we do, too.

The human heart mutates under the distortion of sin. Emotions go awry, compassion is absent or twisted. But through Jesus Christ the old twisted heart is replaced by the new heart by the same One who gave us His heart at the beginning!

PHYSICAL HEART FOCUS
Obesity and diabetes go hand–in–hand, so lose that extra weight through a healthy plan.

❤ Whose Heart Is Broken?

PSALM 51:4

Against You, You only, have I sinned,
And done this evil in Your sight—
That You may be found just when You speak,
And blameless when You judge.

2 CORINTHIANS 7:10

For godly sorrow produces repentance leading to salvation, not to be
regretted; but the sorrow of the world produces death.

THE QUESTION IS NOT, "Is my heart broken *over* sin?" but "Is my heart broken *from* sin?"

Until we understand that our sin breaks God's heart, we will have only the sorrow of the world, which is regret, and not godly sorrow, which is repentance.

Regret can be merely the decision not to experience the pain of sin again. *Repentance* is the decision to turn away from sin itself because it grieves God.

David was stung by the consequences of his adultery with Bathsheba and the instigation of her husband's murder. Those outcomes washed over his family like a scourging flood.

But David really turned around when he realized his sin, ultimately, was against God, the One he loved the most.

SPIRITUAL HEART FOCUS

Ask the Holy Spirit to lead you to true repentance, not just regret over consequences.

PHYSICAL HEART FOCUS

Don't forget the three exercise strategies comprising your total fitness plan: cardio, resistance, and stretching.

❤ When the Heart Is Taxed

LUKE 12:20–21

"But God said to him, 'Fool! This night your soul will be required of you; then whose will those things be which you have provided?' So is he who lays up treasure for himself, and is not rich toward God."

TODAY IS TAX DEADLINE DAY for America. People with stressed–out hearts are trying to figure out how to settle with Uncle Sam.

Some aren't worried. They paid throughout the year through withholding or quarterly payments. They are square with the tax man, or he might even owe them money.

In Jesus' parable, the rich man hadn't made any "payments" at all. He had clung to his wealth, sating his soul and body. But on deadline day, he paid with his very soul.

> SPIRITUAL
> HEART FOCUS
> Ask the Father to help you make sure your heart is ready for its day of judgment.

Judgment is coming when our sin–debt will be levied. "Jesus paid it all," declares the old hymn, but His sacrifice does us no good if we don't receive His gift of salvation before the taxing day of the heart.

The Bible says "now is 'the acceptable time' . . . now is 'the day of salvation'" (2 Corinthians 6:2 NASB). Settle the issue with God today and you will have nothing to fear when the ultimate tax man comes!

PHYSICAL HEART FOCUS

Losing 15–20 pounds and keeping it off is manageable for most people.

❤ The Oven

HOSEA 7:6

"They prepare their heart like an oven,
While they lie in wait;
Their baker sleeps all night;
In the morning it burns like a flaming fire."

"WHAT'S COOKING?" Many a chef has been asked that question. I saw a sign in a restaurant: "Stamp out home cooking—eat out!" Another said, "Take your wife out to eat; the wife you save may be your own."

Some find cooking an art or fascinating hobby. For the person who has to prepare daily for a large family, meal preparation can become drudgery.

One oven is definitely overworked. The spiritual heart whose thermostat is not controlled by God is overheated with the cooking of plots and subterfuges. The schemes of rebellion bake deep inside the human heart.

> **SPIRITUAL HEART FOCUS**
> Ask the Father to grant that your heart will "cook" plans that lead to good and not evil plots and strategies.

Hardly anything is as fragrant as dinner cooking in the oven; few things smell worse than the smoke of a ruined supper. Good and bad things get prepared in the heart.

What's cooking in yours?

PHYSICAL HEART FOCUS
Exercise burns calories and relieves stress.

❤ Looking Inside the 'Oven'

MATTHEW 9:4

But Jesus, knowing their thoughts, said,
"Why do you think evil in your hearts?"

OLD–FASHIONED OVENS had hefty metal doors, but today's ranges come with glass viewing panels. The cook can peer inside and know exactly what's happening in the baking process.

The heart is an oven, and Jesus is the expert chef who can look inside and see exactly what's going on. Although most people rejoiced when He healed a paralytic, one group of people scowled at Him. Their mental ovens were baking reasons that Jesus' act of mercy broke the ritual law. But the Lord could see what was going on in their hearts.

> SPIRITUAL
> HEART FOCUS
> Ask God to look into your heart through His Holy Spirit, and then to show you what He sees inside.

We may feel the door of our heart is shut tight, that the things simmering inside are hidden from view. But there is One who knows where the viewing panel is. He looks inside, and His expert eyes know if the bread baking there is poisonous or wholesome.

He is the One who is "able to judge the thoughts and intentions of the heart" (Hebrews 4:12 NASB), our very motives!

PHYSICAL HEART FOCUS

Fresher is always better, so keep foods as close to their natural state as possible.

♥ The Self–Bloated Heart

ISAIAH 9:9–10

All the people will know—
Ephraim and the inhabitant of Samaria—
Who say in pride and arrogance of heart:
"The bricks have fallen down,
But we will rebuild with hewn stones;
The sycamores are cut down,
But we will replace them with cedars."

THE HEART THAT REBELS AGAINST GOD must place faith in itself. Pride enlarges the spiritual heart, as life–threatening as a swollen physical heart. The self–bloated heart leads to the idolatry of self, always a fatal disease.

The prophet Isaiah spoke out when Israel turned away from God and fell into the sins of arrogance and pride. People reasoned that if their world crumbled, they themselves could rebuild it.

The self–bloated heart wheezes with the idolatry of self. And because God's job description is ultimately too big for a human being, the heart of a man or woman trying to play God finally gives out in exhaustion.

What a huge relief to the heart that gets it right: God is God, we aren't, and therein is our ultimate peace.

SPIRITUAL HEART FOCUS
If crisis is churning in your heart, give the concern to God, and rest in His ability to meet your need.

PHYSICAL HEART FOCUS
Stretching is great for the muscles and the mind. Do some stretching exercises.

❤ The Swindling Heart

PROVERBS 12:20
Deceit is in the heart of those who devise evil,
But counselors of peace have joy.

A WHILE BACK, JO BETH AND I BOUGHT some furniture. Less than twenty–four hours later, the delivery man said I owed more money. Certain services had been tucked away in fine print. I paid, vowing never to do business with that company again.

A heart that will skew the scales in business will be deceptive in every other relationship. "It's just business," goes the mantra. But it's not, because deception becomes so routine that the deceiver unconsciously cheats spouse, children, and friends.

SPIRITUAL HEART FOCUS
Allow the Holy Spirit to weigh your heart in His balances. Are you out to get or out to give? Ask the Lord for a heart of honesty and joy.

On the other hand, other individuals focus on serving others fairly. Cheaters have the short–term pleasure of monetary profit, but the men and women who aim at others' satisfaction have enduring joy.

PHYSICAL HEART FOCUS
Set a reasonable weight–loss goal and write it down.

❤ The Support System

PSALM 104:14–15

He causes the grass to grow for the cattle,
And vegetation for the service of man,
That he may bring forth food from the earth,
And wine that makes glad the heart of man,
Oil to make his face shine,
And bread which strengthens man's heart.

GOD HAS PUT EVERYTHING ON THE EARTH essential for total heart health, and it's tragic when we use His good gifts to weaken the heart.

A man in our church got a new heart. His old one was barely fluttering because of disease. The man was pale, bent with weakness, and struggled to breathe. Then he got his new heart, and his whole body showed the benefit. Vitality returned, along with joy and confidence.

Suppose the man with the new heart began eating and drinking in excess and refused exercise. It would be as if he had spurned the opportunity for a new life. Alcohol and drug abuse, improper diet, and a lazy lifestyle constitute a perversion of God's good gifts and misappropriation of His love, which gave us the gifts in the first place.

For the sake of good health, see the earth's bounty as God's grace for wholesome living.

> SPIRITUAL HEART FOCUS
> Thank God for His good gifts, and ask Him for the wisdom to use them wisely to build and support health, not destroy it.

PHYSICAL HEART FOCUS
Even if the label says "low fat" you still can gain weight from the product.

❤ 'Big Ears'

DANIEL 1:8

But Daniel purposed in his heart that he would not defile himself with the portion of the king's delicacies, nor with the wine which he drank; therefore he requested of the chief of the eunuchs that he might not defile himself.

MICKEY MANTLE AND WHITEY FORD used to laugh at Bobby Richardson.

As his pastor, Richardson once invited me to sit in on a reminiscing session with his old baseball colleagues. Mantle and Ford recalled how, although the players could do anything they liked between games, Bobby Richardson would find a church with a Bible study or prayer meeting in session.

SPIRITUAL HEART FOCUS
Declare to the Lord your determination not to be gobbled up by fallen culture, but to stand as a godly person in the midst of it. Ask for His strength.

"Something's wrong with you," they kidded Bobby.

Later in life, Mantle decided there was something wrong with himself, with his own heart. Mickey fought alcohol abuse, and toward his life's end he declared no one should look at him as a role model.

I couldn't help but reflect on the conversation years before, and the sparkling example of Bobby Richardson. As a godly man, like young Daniel, he had set his heart in the concrete of a commitment not to be defiled by the culture.

Fame gobbled up Mickey Mantle, but Bobby Richardson was unfazed because he had set his heart on the Lord.

PHYSICAL HEART FOCUS
Sometimes the low–fat items have more sugar calories. Read the labels.

❤ The Grateful Heart

LUKE 7:37–38

And behold, a woman in the city who was a sinner, when she knew that Jesus sat at the table in the Pharisee's house, brought an alabaster flask of fragrant oil, and stood at His feet behind Him weeping; and she began to wash His feet with her tears, and wiped them with the hair of her head; and she kissed His feet and anointed them with the fragrant oil.

GOD HAS JOY IN OUR GRATITUDE, not because He needs us to thank Him, but because He knows the grateful heart is healthy.

People who knew her would have said the woman who washed Jesus' feet was morally sick. But they couldn't know that Jesus and His grace had brought her hope and reason to live. Her gratitude gushes out with her tears, or her "heart water," as Martin Luther calls them.

The alabaster vial full of perfume shows the extravagance of her gratitude. Her humility in letting down her hair and bathing the feet of the Carpenter shows the depth of her gratitude. But the woman doesn't care about any embarrassment. Her heart so overflows with thankfulness that nothing else matters.

Consider the things you get depressed over not having. Let them bring to mind what you do have, and give God the sweet fragrance of your "thank You."

SPIRITUAL HEART FOCUS
Thank God as His child for lavishing your life with blessings. Thank Him for specific things.

PHYSICAL HEART FOCUS

In addition to your spiritual journal, keep a diet and exercise journal where you record goals, experiences, and results.

❤ The Growing Heart

2 CORINTHIANS 3:18

But we all, with unveiled face, beholding as in a mirror the glory of the Lord, are being transformed into the same image from glory to glory, just as by the Spirit of the Lord.

IN CHRIST, WE START at the finish line.

Justification is an event happening the moment we receive Christ. At that instant, we are forgiven, the accusation against us is torn up, and we can stand forever without condemnation (Colossians 2:14; Romans 8:1–2).

The event of justification launches us into the process of sanctification. This is growth toward what we already have.

> SPIRITUAL HEART FOCUS
>
> Ask God to increase your hunger and thirst for His Word, leading to accelerated spiritual growth in your life.

Sanctification, to paraphrase Paul, helps us attain that for which we've been "apprehended" (Philippians 3:12–13).

Jo Beth prayed that she would hunger and thirst for God's Word. God answered her prayer by starting to awaken her every morning by 5 a.m. The first activity of her day is to study the Scripture and pray.

The goal of spiritual growth is a heart fully developed with the "glory," the character of Christ. Spiritual growth is not becoming more religious, but more Christlike.

PHYSICAL HEART FOCUS

As often as possible, eat your last meal of the day no later than 7 p.m.

❤ The Giving Heart

2 CORINTHIANS 8:1–3

Moreover, brethren, we make known to you the grace of God bestowed on the churches of Macedonia: that in a great trial of affliction the abundance of their joy and their deep poverty abounded in the riches of their liberality. For I bear witness that according to their ability, yes, and beyond their ability, they were freely willing.

THE DEEPER THEIR OWN NEED, the more the Macedonian Christians gave, revealing their true heart.

The Jerusalem Church was caught in an economic crunch brought on by drought. Meanwhile, over in Macedonia, the ruling Romans levied oppressive taxes, shut down the region's gold and silver mines, and prohibited the Macedonians from cutting down trees to build houses and ships. The situation was dire, but the Christians of Macedonia gave generously to Jerusalem.

> **SPIRITUAL HEART FOCUS**
> Thank God for your blessings, and ask Him to show you how to give in proportion to your need as well as your abundance.

They focused away from their own need to the needs of others. The world has a lot of formulas for licking poverty, but none are better than that. There is no record that the Macedonians got rich, but you can be certain God supplied the followers of Christ amid their poverty so they could continue giving.

The *getting* heart may be at the core of national economies, but the *giving* heart is the engine that drives the economy of God's Kingdom.

PHYSICAL HEART FOCUS

Be enthusiastic, but not obsessive. Obsessiveness in dieting is unhealthy, leading to anorexia and bulimia, but healthy dieting means eating on a well-balanced plan.

❤ The Grounded Heart

EPHESIANS 3:14, 16–17

For this reason I bow my knees to the Father of our Lord Jesus Christ . . . that He would grant you, according to the riches of His glory, to be strengthened with might through His Spirit in the inner man, that Christ may dwell in your hearts through faith . . .

THE GROUNDED HEART IS SO DEEPLY ROOTED it can't be pulled out of its relationship to Christ.

Someone gave Jo Beth a great big plant. She placed the huge plastic container bearing the flower on an even larger pot in our backyard. There it sat for two years, then was knocked over. Jo Beth tried to put the flower back in place, and found that it had sunk its roots through the large pot and deep into the ground. It seemed immoveable.

Our fallen culture tugs hard on our hearts. As we root ourselves in His Word, we are so deeply embedded that the strongest pull cannot uproot us.

"For I am persuaded that neither death nor life, nor angels nor principalities nor powers, nor things present nor things to come, nor height nor depth, nor any other created thing, shall be able to separate us from the love of God which is in Christ Jesus our Lord" (Romans 8:38–39).

SPIRITUAL HEART FOCUS

What is tugging on you right now, trying to pull you away from Christ? Ask God for fresh strength to resist, and to take the roots of your heart deeper into Him.

PHYSICAL HEART FOCUS

It's okay to break your diet on special celebratory occasions as long as you get back on track the next day.

❤ The Calm in the Deep

JAMES 5:8

You also be patient. Establish your hearts,
for the coming of the Lord is at hand.

FOLLOWERS OF CHRIST ARE PERPETUAL tip–toe standers!

We peer over the threshold of time, knowing the Lord can appear at any moment. He will show up in various ways in daily routine. Someday He will ride into history in His Second Coming.

When history howls with crisis and your daily responsibilities scream with problems, the way to strengthen your heart is to fix your gaze up high. Watch for what the Lord does and how He manifests Himself in the midst of the fracas.

Such an outlook leads to well–established calmness in the crisis.

A friend told me of going scuba diving in rough seas. "How were you able to dive?" I asked. "It was hard to get to the diving spot, but under the surface it was calm and serene," he said.

> **SPIRITUAL HEART FOCUS**
> Use your prayer time today to set your focus away from current events and demands of daily routine, and turn instead to the Lord. Ask Him to reveal Himself to you in all you encounter today.

The strengthened heart is full of peace when the world on the surface tosses in torment.

PHYSICAL HEART FOCUS

Stand and sit taller—it will make you look trimmer and stretch your body properly at the same time.

❤ Heart Food

HEBREWS 13:9

Do not be carried about with various and strange doctrines. For it is good that the heart be established by grace, not with foods which have not profited those who have been occupied with them.

GRACE NOURISHES THE SPIRITUAL HEART.

Diets abound these days. Books and tapes confuse us with weight–loss plans.

There is, however, no misunderstanding about the best diet for strengthening the spiritual heart. The Jews constantly were being lured back into energy–draining ritualism and legalism. No nourishment there, suggests the Holy Spirit in Hebrews.

SPIRITUAL HEART FOCUS
Have a praise party. Celebrate by reading, meditating on, and praying Psalm 103:12 and Romans 8:1–2.

Today we are lured into dead–works religion—spurred to burn candles, kiss the ground five times, give money to the right need, show up at the right church events—to make us strong spiritually.

Not so. It's all empty calories spiritually.

Grace, God's unmerited favor, is nourishing heart food. When you understand how spiritually gaunt your deeds are and how great His grace is, your heart is encouraged, strengthened, and motivated by love, not by rules.

PHYSICAL HEART FOCUS
Stressed spelled backward is *desserts!*

❤ Closed for Business

1 JOHN 3:17

*But whoever has this world's goods, and sees his brother in need,
and shuts up his heart from him, how does the love of God abide in him?*

A WHILE BACK I WATCHED A TV INTERVIEW with a popular media leftist. He rambled on about America's insensitivity to poverty and the homeless, and how the government should do more to help the poor. Then the TV host turned the tables.

"Where do you live?"

"Hollywood."

The interviewer stared at his guest. "Can you name one person who is poor?"

The man's shock and inability to name one person revealed that his passion was a sham. Some people bedeck their lives with a big neon sign flashing, "I'm for the poor!" But when the needy knock on their heart–door they find it is closed for business.

SPIRITUAL
HEART FOCUS
Ask God to purge you of false compassion and open your heart to those in genuine need.

The way we treat genuinely needy people, especially those in our spiritual family, reveals the true nature of the heart.

PHYSICAL HEART FOCUS
The journey to total heart health is a lifelong endeavor, not a day trip.

❤ Freighting the Heart

PHILEMON 10–12

I appeal to you for my son Onesimus, whom I have begotten while in my chains, who once was unprofitable to you, but now is profitable to you and to me. I am sending him back. You therefore receive him, that is, my own heart.

PLANT YOUR HEART IN SOMEBODY, and wherever they go, they carry your passion.

Onesimus was a slave who escaped from his master, Philemon. He fled to Rome, where he knew one person, Paul, who happened to be sitting in a jail cell. Onesimus was so desperate, he found Paul, who then introduced him to Christ.

Paul bottle–fed this spiritual babe with the milk of the Word. Paul gave his spiritual and emotional heart, his devotion and vision, to Onesimus.

Then Paul wrapped him up and freighted him back to Philemon, who probably was really surprised when this runaway package showed up at his front door! Somewhere there's a person in whom God wants you to plant your heart. It may be a youngster who will outlive you and will take your heart across time as well as space. Look for that special person, and be ready to "freight your heart" through him or her.

> **SPIRITUAL HEART FOCUS**
>
> Ask God to show you the person you should be discipling, the person in whom you should be planting your devotion and commitment to Christ. Also, ask God to show you how to implant your heart in that person.

PHYSICAL HEART FOCUS

Recruit a cheerleader, an encourager, who knows your goals and will cheer you forward.

❤ Straying Hearts

PROVERBS 7:25

Do not let your heart turn aside to her ways,
Do not stray into her paths.

YOU'D HAVE TO BE CRAZY OR ASLEEP at the wheel to let yourself stray into the path of an 18–wheeler.

Imagine you work in a hospital emergency room where you treat patients banged up from wrecks on the most dangerous highway in the region, the truck route where all the herds of mega–vehicles thunder along.

When your shift is done, you steer your car toward home. Five routes lead to your driveway, but you decide to take the road where all your patients that day got hit by the freight trucks.

SPIRITUAL HEART FOCUS
Ask the Holy Spirit to keep your heart awake and alert spiritually.

Not a good decision.

The proverb above symbolizes sin by the seductress. But understand that the sin could be embodied in a male as well as a female. The Bible is clear about what happens when our hearts stray into the path of sin: Sin's house is the way to Sheol, descending to the chambers of death (Proverbs 7:27).

Don't go to sleep at the wheel of your heart!

PHYSICAL HEART FOCUS
At the restaurant, avoid foods described as fried, breaded, or *au gratin*.
Check your weight and BMI.

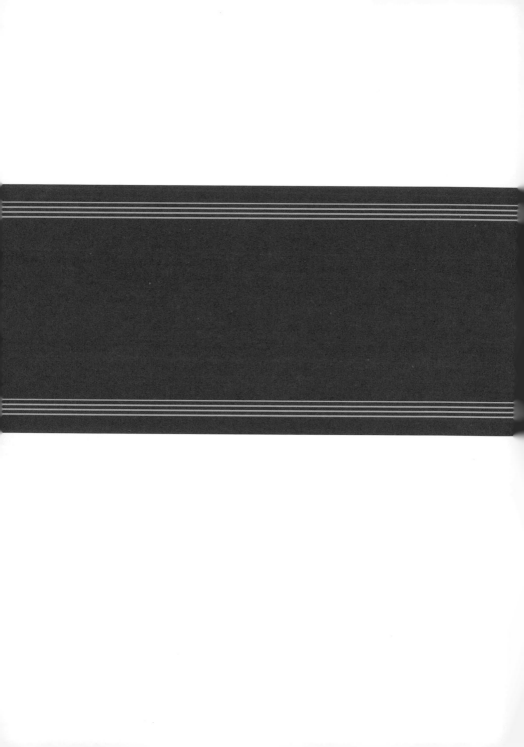

May

No one will question the
authenticity of your heart–faith when
they see your hand–faith.

♥ Dominating Fear

1 SAMUEL 21:10–12

Then David arose and fled that day from before Saul, and went to Achish the king of Gath. And the servants of Achish said to him, "Is this not David the king of the land? Did they not sing of him to one another in dances, saying:
'Saul has slain his thousands,
And David his ten thousands'?"
Now David took these words to heart, and was very much afraid of Achish the king of Gath.

FEAR DOMINATES WHEN IT BUILDS a fortress in the heart.

Achish sent out troops of taunts, and David allowed them to build their base in his heart. The result was that David had his knees knocking over—compared to Goliath—a runt of a king.

SPIRITUAL HEART FOCUS
What fears are encamped in your heart? Confess them to God and ask Him to uproot them and tear down fortresses of anxiety they have created in you.

Three elderly southern ladies braved up for a vacation in New York City. Their minds were full of nightmares of being assaulted. One evening they hurried off the street before the muggers prowled, and into their hotel elevator. A large man slipped in, leading a huge Doberman. "Sit!" said the big man. Slowly, the three women, backs to the elevator wall, slid to the floor. The man looked at them quizzically, then smiled, and finally guffawed. "Ladies, not you!" he said. "I was talking to my dog!"

When we take fear into our hearts and allow it to dominate, we will react to any perceived threat, and sometimes make idiots of ourselves.

PHYSICAL HEART FOCUS

The only time "success" comes before "work" is in the dictionary.

♥ The Brake

JOB 31:7-8

If my step has turned from the way,
Or my heart walked after my eyes,
Or if any spot adheres to my hands,
Then let me sow, and another eat;
Yes, let my harvest be rooted out.

THE EYES RACE TOWARD DISASTER if the heart does not put on the brakes.

As a senior in seminary I drove the same 75–mile route daily. My car could almost make the trip automatically. The problem was that my eyes always zoomed ahead, knowing every bend.

The reckoning day came, and a patrolman ticketed me. Unbelievably, a few weeks later, I looked down while on the same stretch, and I was speeding at the same rate as the day I got the ticket. Needless to say, my foot raced to the brake, and I slowed down the vehicle before the officer had to stop me again.

> **SPIRITUAL HEART FOCUS**
> Pray that God will give you a heart that will put on the brakes when your eyes are zipping toward disaster.

When the heart speeds along with the eyes, there is brake failure. The mission of the spiritual heart is to slow us down with caution and reason.

To put it another way, when your emotions put the pedal to the metal, give heed to the cautions of the heart!

PHYSICAL HEART FOCUS

When you have the urge to snack, wait 10 minutes. If you're still hungry, either eat fruit or drink a large glass of water with a lemon slice.

❤ Default

MALACHI 2:2

"If you will not hear,
And if you will not take it to heart,
To give glory to My name,"
Says the LORD of hosts,
"I will send a curse upon you,
And I will curse your blessings.
Yes, I have cursed them already,
Because you do not take it to heart."

IN A FALLEN WORLD, THE "CURSE" is the default position.

Jesus showed us there are only two kingdoms—that of God, the Kingdom of Light, and the kingdom of the devil, the domain of darkness. There is no third kingdom, no "kingdom of neutrality." By default, the spiritually "neutral" have registered themselves in the kingdom of darkness, the curse zone.

SPIRITUAL HEART FOCUS

Where is the spiritual neutrality in your life? Where is it you struggle to believe? Decide to choose what the Bible teaches clearly, whether you can understand it or not, and declare your decision to God.

A curse, among other things, is a ban. An individual chooses neutrality, and doesn't understand why darkness keeps choking out the light. It's because he or she is isolated from blessing—the favor, prosperity, peace, and joy of the Lord—by their own choice.

In a world gone wrong, unless the heart makes the right choice, the wrong choice will win.

PHYSICAL HEART FOCUS

Never let what you cannot do interfere with what you can do.

❤ Rocky and the Cripple

1 PETER 3:3-4

Do not let your adornment be merely outward—arranging the hair, wearing gold, or putting on fine apparel—rather let it be the hidden person of the heart, with the incorruptible beauty of a gentle and quiet spirit, which is very precious in the sight of God.

"ROCKY'S DOWN AT THE BEACH!" our boys shouted one day during vacation. I walked to the water's edge, and there was Sylvester Stallone, "Rocky."

He was the focus of everyone.

After awhile my eye caught sight of a man about Stallone's age, but a victim of stroke or some other debilitating ailment. He labored to make his way into the water. I watched as he thrashed his twisted limbs in an attempt to enjoy swimming.

Suddenly I heard a female, whose eyes were welded to "Rocky," shout, "He's my hero!" But my hero that day was the man no one saw, the guy determined to swim in the ocean despite a bent body.

God's eyes are always on "the hidden person of the heart." We can preen spiritually by trying to be hyper-religious, but that doesn't impress God. Precious in His sight is the inner character, even if it's housed in an unattractive body!

> **SPIRITUAL HEART FOCUS**
> Pray for the ability to see the beauty in the "hidden person" of others, especially those otherwise unattractive. Ask the Lord to continue to transform your character into beauty in which He delights.

PHYSICAL HEART FOCUS

God designed your body to move, so move it daily and systematically.

♥ Settling Questions

ROMANS 10:9–10

If you confess with your mouth the Lord Jesus and believe in your heart that God has raised Him from the dead, you will be saved. For with the heart one believes unto righteousness, and with the mouth confession is made unto salvation.

SIMPLE QUESTIONS CAN SETTLE THE ISSUE of whether or not you are Heaven–bound.

First, do you profess to be a Christian, a follower of Jesus Christ? The willingness to confess Him openly, not just privately, indicates saving faith.

SPIRITUAL HEART FOCUS
Review your personal answers to the questions. If they unsettle your confidence that you are Heaven–bound, make a fresh commitment to Christ. As the questions settle your faith, give God thanks.

Next, does the Holy Spirit bear witness to His presence in your lifestyle? "The Spirit Himself testifies with our spirit that we are children of God" (Romans 8:16 NKJV). When you receive Christ, the Holy Spirit brings to your heart an increasing awareness that you are a member of God's family.

Finally, do you find yourself becoming more Christlike in your lifestyle? The question is not whether you have more money, better health, or fewer problems, but whether you are being conformed more and more to Christ's image.

If the questions unsettle you, then turn them around and let them settle you. Invite Christ to be Lord and Master of your life, and the questions will affirm you are on the right path.

PHYSICAL HEART FOCUS

Make your favorite egg dishes with egg whites rather than whole eggs.

❤ Lifting Hearts

EXODUS 36:2

Then Moses called Bezalel and Aholiab, and every gifted artisan in whose heart the LORD had put wisdom, everyone whose heart was stirred, to come and do the work.

EARLY IN THE TWENTIETH CENTURY, people were excited about the prospects of dirigibles, huge balloons that would carry passengers across oceans and continents. But it was difficult to find an energy source for lift.

Hydrogen was used at first. Then on May 6, 1937, the massive *Hindenburg* crashed in Lakehurst, New Jersey. Helium, which is called a "noble" gas because it stays pure and doesn't mix with other elements like very combustible oxygen, later became the preferred means of lifting giant balloons into the air.

SPIRITUAL HEART FOCUS
Ask God to fill your heart with love for Him that will motivate you to glorify God in all you do.

Moses sought "lift" when he launched the building of the Tabernacle. He wanted people who needed no external motivation but whose hearts were full with the desire to raise the Lord's tent.

Love is the helium of that lifting heart. Moses sought people motivated by love for God. It's the same today. Your motivation to do God's noble work in the world is an indication of your love for Christ and His Kingdom.

PHYSICAL HEART FOCUS

Find someone else to encourage today on his or her program of diet and exercise.

♥ The Hands Reveal the Heart

JAMES 2:17–18

Faith by itself, if it does not have works, is dead. But someone will say, "You have faith, and I have works." Show me your faith without your works, and I will show you my faith by my works.

BELIEF IS HOUSED IN THE HEART and revealed in the hands.

I knew of a family with five children. The father died and the mother became critically ill. "Sally," age 16, became both father and mother to her siblings. She washed, cooked, got them off to school, and tucked them in at night, all the while caring for her bedridden mother. This was the teen's life, seven days a week.

SPIRITUAL HEART FOCUS
For real balance in your spiritual life, review how much of your time is spent in receiving from others versus how much time you spend in giving and ministering to other people.

"Sally, I don't see you at church much with all the other youth," said a busybody one day.

"I don't get to be there like I would love to," Sally replied.

"Then what are you going to tell God when you get to Heaven as to why you didn't go to church?"

"I guess I'll just show Him my hands," the young woman answered.

No one will question the authenticity of your heart–faith when they see your hand–faith.

PHYSICAL HEART FOCUS

Don't skip meals. That's like not fueling your car when it runs low.

♥ VE Day

1 JOHN 5:4–5

For whatever is born of God overcomes the world. And this is the victory that has overcome the world—our faith. Who is he who overcomes the world, but he who believes that Jesus is the Son of God?

THE ACCUSER ALWAYS WANTS TO REMIND you of sins committed, but your Advocate focuses you on sins remitted!

On May 8, 1945, the Nazis surrendered and "Victory in Europe" (VE) was declared. With their leader dead and the liberating forces advancing, the war was over for Hitler's evil disciples.

The moment Jesus Christ came to earth two thousand years ago, the Kingdom of Heaven invaded the sin–occupied world. At the cross, Jesus blitzed the devil's bunker. There are still holdouts, but the question of who will win is settled forever!

> SPIRITUAL HEART FOCUS
> Ask the Holy Spirit to help you focus today on victories you have experienced over the world, the flesh, and the devil. Praise God for giving you Christ's strength to overcome!

In Christ we already have the victory because our sins are forgiven. We may not have been literally in the victorious Allied armies in 1945, but we were "there" in the sense of benefiting from their victory right now. Similarly, Christ came, defeated the devil, placed us in Himself, and therefore made us victors in His victory!

Because you believe on Him in your heart, you can make today your personal "V Day."

PHYSICAL HEART FOCUS

Write down your victories on your diet and exercise goals, celebrate, and post the record where you can see it.

❤ Wooden Statue

ROMANS 6:10–14

For the death that He died, He died to sin once for all; but the life that He lives, He lives to God. Likewise you also, reckon yourselves to be dead indeed to sin, but alive to God in Christ Jesus our Lord. Therefore do not let sin reign in your mortal body, that you should obey it in its lusts. And do not present your members as instruments of unrighteousness to sin, but present yourselves to God as being alive from the dead, and your members as instruments of righteousness to God. For sin shall not have dominion over you, for you are not under law but under grace.

IT'S IMPOSSIBLE TO TEMPT a wooden statue.

Years ago, when I was a pastor in North Carolina, I sometimes traveled through a small community that had a giant wooden statue in the middle of town. What if someone tried to tempt that wooden statue to do something illegal or immoral? The wooden statue would be unfazed by the temptations because it is dead, merely wood chopped off a tree. It's impossible to tempt something that's dead.

When we receive Christ, our born–again spirit, the spiritual heart, becomes dead to sin. The mind, will, and emotions are still vulnerable, but as we learn to respond to temptation through the spirit, the temptation just can't get through.

SPIRITUAL HEART FOCUS

Ask the Holy Spirit to teach you how to respond in the spirit, not in the flesh, to temptation.

PHYSICAL HEART FOCUS

Remove your most tempting food from the house.

❤ The Cynical Heart

PROVERBS 13:12
*Hope deferred makes the heart sick,
But when the desire comes, it is a tree of life.*

CYNICISM IS IDEALISM SOURED through frustration.

Once I saw a football player with a neck injury. Frustration was on the young man's brow. A steel brace allowed him to only look right and left, but not up.

Because of the deep cultural divide in America now, people tend to look only right or left politically and philosophically. But people whose minds are biblically formed—and who consider themselves disciples of Jesus Christ—know how to look upward.

That's always the direction of hope. If you look to politicians or philosophers for idealistic dreams and plans, your heart will be sickened with frustration, cynicism, and despair.

Look beyond the right and left of the cultural wars by yanking off the steel bindings and gazing upward at God and His Kingdom, revealed in Scripture!

SPIRITUAL HEART FOCUS
Ask God to help you look above and beyond human beings and their movements as the sources of your hope, and instead see it all in Him.

PHYSICAL HEART FOCUS
Switch to skim milk, especially when you're dieting.

❤ The Saving Implant

JAMES 1:21

Therefore lay aside all filthiness and overflow of wickedness, and receive with meekness the implanted word, which is able to save your souls.

A TEEN WAS ASKED WHAT HE THOUGHT of when he considered his parents. "Big mouths," he replied. "What would you like to see?" the youngster was asked. "Big ears," he answered.

Our hearts need "big ears," because the heart is where God's Word needs to be heard so thoroughly it echoes in every facet of our being. The soul is the core of our self–awareness, our thinking, feeling, and deciding. It is the arena of spiritual growth, which begins in the regenerated spirit. Paul prayed that God's people would be "filled to all the fullness of God" (Ephesians 3:19). Sanctification, growth, leads toward this fullness and happens in the soul, the inner heart.

The human spirit receives the initial seed of God's Word, but the roots must extend into the soul, and the fruit will be manifest through the body.

SPIRITUAL HEART FOCUS

Pray for the Lord to give your heart "big ears," a deep hunger for His Word, and clarity of hearing it in the core of your being.

PHYSICAL HEART FOCUS

Check out your neighborhood or community swimming pool for water aerobics classes.

❤ Spring Fever

LUKE 24:25

Then He said to them, "O foolish ones, and slow of heart
to believe in all that the prophets have spoken!

SPIRITUAL SPRING FEVER RENDERS US as useless as the physical variety does, and the heart slow to believe is afflicted with spiritual spring fever perpetually.

The followers of Jesus walking home to Emmaus after observing the crucifixion were surrounded by prophetic truth. They had heard and read the prophecies that the Messiah would be betrayed by a friend for thirty pieces of silver, accused by false witnesses, spat upon and smitten, crucified with transgressors, His hands and side pierced, buried with the dead, and rise again, but their hearts were too woozy to see it.

The sluggish heart afflicts us, too. We study the Bible and know it in our heads, but our hearts are slow to believe and understand when things happen around us that demonstrate God's work in our day.

Shake your heart out of its spiritual spring fever!

SPIRITUAL HEART FOCUS

Ask the Holy Spirit for a heart fully awake to all God is doing in your life and in the world right now.

PHYSICAL HEART FOCUS

Plan a vacation for this summer that will include a lot of walking and biking.

❤ Jumping Heart

1 SAMUEL 2:1
And Hannah prayed and said:
"My heart rejoices in the LORD;
My horn is exalted in the LORD.
I smile at my enemies,
Because I rejoice in Your salvation."

GOD SOMETIMES ANSWERS OUR PRAYERS later to answer them better.

Immediate gratification is the demand of today's "grab it and gobble it" culture. So if God doesn't come through when we direct, many of us proceed to a self–devised solution.

In their desire for a son, Hannah and her husband prayed, spoke the right "faith formulas," and had hands laid upon them to get God's answer. Nothing happened.

SPIRITUAL HEART FOCUS
Is there a matter you've been praying about a long time on which you are tempted to give up? If the concern won't let go, keep praying, and submit to God's timing.

The problem was not the request, but their timing. Had Samuel been born fifteen years earlier, he would have been just another kid. But God knew the precise moment when the child should appear to fulfill the ministry for which God brought him into the world.

When Hannah dedicated the long–awaited child, she cried, "My heart rejoices!" Literally, she was saying, "My heart is jumping inside me!"

When your heart meets God's heart in God's timing for God's purposes, it will dance inside you.

PHYSICAL HEART FOCUS
It's okay for adults to jump rope—and it's great cardio exercise—but build gradually.

❤ Heart Certification

1 JOHN 3:21

Beloved, if our heart does not condemn us,
we have confidence toward God.

ONLY CITIZENS COMPETED IN RACES in ancient Greece. To compete in the big runs, you had to be certified by participating in shorter races.

If your heart wouldn't hold out in a shorter race, you couldn't participate in the longer ones. The runner's heart certified whether or not he could run.

Life in Christ is a great dash toward Heaven. To be in this race, you must be a citizen of God's Kingdom. Paul also writes of the heart certification when he says that to have Christ and heavenly citizenship is to have a heart indwelt with the Holy Spirit. Then, says the Scripture, "The Spirit Himself bears witness with our spirit that we are children of God . . ." (Romans 8:16).

> **SPIRITUAL HEART FOCUS**
> What does the spiritual center of your personality tell you about your relationship to God? Do you feel confident in calling Him "Abba" (Daddy)? If not, give your life to Christ and receive His indwelling Spirit. If so, give God thanks for making you His child.

This is the "certification" in which the heart doesn't condemn, but confirms that we belong to God in the deepest sense. Do you have such certification?

PHYSICAL HEART FOCUS
When golfing, walk rather than ride a cart.

❤ The Regretful Heart

2 SAMUEL 24:10

And David's heart condemned him after he had numbered the people.
So David said to the LORD, "I have sinned greatly in what I have done;
but now, I pray, O LORD, take away the iniquity of Your servant,
for I have done very foolishly."

DAVID'S HEART, IN MY BOYHOOD MISSISSIPPI–SPEAK, "beat up on him" after he took a census of Israel. He was supposed to put his confidence in God, not in the size of his populace and number of potential warriors.

Regret is not repentance, but a "self" word—half self–reproach and half self–pity. For instance, Esau wept over his losses, but not the lifestyle that caused them (Genesis 27:34).

Years ago an airplane was in trouble. A popular comedian aboard tried to calm the passengers with humor. When the plane landed safely after a harrowing few minutes, the comic said, "Now, ladies and gentlemen, you may return to the sins you gave up twenty minutes ago."

Regret gets you nowhere, but repentance puts you on the road to newness of life.

SPIRITUAL HEART FOCUS

Ask the Holy Spirit to help you discern whether you have regret or repentance in your heart.

PHYSICAL HEART FOCUS

Exercise helps you sleep better.

❤ Improper Training

2 PETER 2:10, 14

And especially those who walk according to the flesh in the lust of uncleanness and despise authority. They are presumptuous, self-willed. They are not afraid to speak evil of dignitaries . . . having eyes full of adultery and that cannot cease from sin, enticing unstable souls. They have a heart trained in covetous practices, and are accursed children.

MIKE LOOKED FORWARD TO RUNNING the marathon and leading the thousands of runners across the finish line. He exercised daily by playing tiddlywinks, confident he was building up his thumb muscles. That, Mike assured himself, would lead him to victory. Sounds silly, but many of us train ourselves inappropriately.

SPIRITUAL HEART FOCUS
Pray for wisdom to sharpen your skills for good, not for useless or even destructive goals.

If you and I hone our skills in satisfying our greed and lust, we're exercising the wrong thing. Here's a businessman who sharpens his skills at closing a deal through a slight deceit. There's a politician, developing the ability to shade meanings. Over here is a womanizer, practicing his seductive "pick-up line." When we exercise our ability to do wrong, it's as spiritually useless— and defeating—as a runner, who should be developing his legs, focusing on thumb-power instead!

PHYSICAL HEART FOCUS

Exercise is especially important as we grow older, and we should emphasize workouts that are low-impact and rhythmic, like walking, swimming, and water aerobics.

❤ Starving at the Banquet

NEHEMIAH 9:25–26

"They took strong cities and a rich land,
And possessed houses full of all goods,
Cisterns already dug, vineyards, olive groves,
And fruit trees in abundance.
So they ate and were filled and grew fat,
And delighted themselves in Your great goodness.
Nevertheless they were disobedient
And rebelled against You,
Cast Your law behind their backs
And killed Your prophets, who testified
against them
To turn them to Yourself;
And they worked great provocations."

SPIRITUAL HEART FOCUS
Pray that your banquet of material blessings will not rob you of a hunger for God and His Word.

A WIDOW BOUGHT A TALKING PARROT to ease her loneliness.

A week passed, but the parrot said nothing. The pet–shop merchant suggested buying a mirror for the cage. Still the parrot didn't talk. An exercise ladder didn't help. A little swing for the birdcage brought not a syllable.

After another ten days, the parrot finally spoke. As it died, it gasped, "Didn't they have any food to buy down at that store?"

After they conquered the Promised Land, the Israelites lived amid a banquet of plenty, yet spiritually they starved. Today we have feasts of material bounty, yet there is moral and spiritual starvation.

Amid all the things in your life, don't forget to nourish your heart on God's strengthening Word.

PHYSICAL HEART FOCUS

Walking one mile burns 100 calories. One pound of fat contains 3,500 calories.

❤ Under the Banyan Tree

ISAIAH 10:12–13, 16

Therefore it shall come to pass, when the LORD has performed all His work on Mount Zion and on Jerusalem, that He will say, "I will punish the fruit of the arrogant heart of the king of Assyria, and the glory of his haughty looks."

*For he says: "By the strength of my hand I have done it,
And by my wisdom, for I am prudent;
Also I have removed the boundaries of the people,
And have robbed their treasuries;
So I have put down the inhabitants like a valiant man.
. . . Therefore the Lord, the Lord of hosts,
Will send leanness among his fat ones;
And under his glory
He will kindle a burning
Like the burning of a fire."*

SPIRITUAL HEART FOCUS
Allow the Holy Spirit to bring to your mind those nestled under your heart. Ask the Father to grant that all those you lead—whether spouse, kids, or work associates—will grow under your heart.

SOME PEOPLE HAVE SUCH ARROGANT, dominant hearts that everything beneath them is wasted away.

In the lovely town of Lahaina, on the Hawaiian island of Maui, there is a banyan tree that covers a city block. Nothing grows under a big banyan tree. It shuts out all the light and consumes all the nutrition.

Haughty and arrogant hearts stifle the growth of others. The king of Assyria arrogantly believed he could dominate and control everyone else. His haughtiness made him believe he was in charge of everything. A person with such a heart cannot allow others to succeed or have the spotlight.

Do other people grow under your spiritual heart, or do they shrivel?

PHYSICAL HEART FOCUS

Be a food label inspector, checking for calories, fat, and sugar content.

♥ The Heart That Misses It

JOHN 14:13

"And whatever you ask in My name, that I will do, that the Father may be glorified in the Son."

JAMES 4:2–3

You lust and do not have. You murder and covet and cannot obtain. You fight and war. Yet you do not have because you do not ask. You ask and do not receive, because you ask amiss, that you may spend it on your pleasures.

SOMETIMES WE DON'T BELIEVE OUR PRAYERS are answered when actually we have rejected God's true answer.

A man was in the desert, desperately thirsty. Hope stirred as he spotted a traveler walking toward him. "Water!" the thirsty man pled.

SPIRITUAL HEART FOCUS
Seek God for the heart to receive what He wills to give you, even if it's not what you asked for.

"I have no water," replied the traveler, "but I will give you my necktie."

"I don't want your necktie; I want water!" With that, the thirsty man crawled away.

Just around a sand dune, he spotted a restaurant, and dragged himself in, knowing at last he would get water. "Sorry," said the maître d', "but we can't let you in without a necktie."

God loves us so much, He gives us precisely what our heart *needs*, not what the heart may *want* at that moment.

God knows when we really need the necktie in the desert!

PHYSICAL HEART FOCUS
Pray during your daily walk.

♥ Bull's-eye!

ACTS 2:37

Now when they heard this, they were cut to the heart, and said to Peter and the rest of the apostles, "Men and brethren, what shall we do?"

MY COLLEGE ROOMMATE, WHO PROFESSED to be an atheist, asked one afternoon, "Edwin, do you believe in God?"

"Of course I believe in God," I answered. "I'm a Christian!"

"Well, you certainly don't live like it," he replied.

His words zapped my heart.

I left the dorm room and began to pray like the people in Jerusalem who heard Peter preach at Pentecost. I rededicated my life to Christ. Not long after that, in a solitary place, God called me to full-time ministry. On Mother's Day, I walked the aisle of my home church. Someone gave me a decision card, and I wrote, "Lord, I give you all that I am, and all that I will ever be."

That self-proclaimed atheist was used by God to fire a spiritual arrow that struck at the core of my being. It changed the direction of my life. It was a bull's-eye.

> **SPIRITUAL HEART FOCUS**
>
> What words and events did God use to set the course of your life? Thank Him for the people and circumstances. Evaluate where you are in comparison to what you intended, and ask God to put you on course and/or hold you there.

PHYSICAL HEART FOCUS

To relieve tension, roll your shoulders forward three to four times, then backward three to four times, repeating the whole sequence three to four times.

♥ Burning Bucket

ROMANS 5:1–5

Therefore, having been justified by faith, we have peace with God through our Lord Jesus Christ, through whom also we have access by faith into this grace in which we stand, and rejoice in hope of the glory of God. And not only that, but we also glory in tribulations, knowing that tribulation produces perseverance; and perseverance, character; and character, hope. Now hope does not disappoint, because the love of God has been poured out in our hearts by the Holy Spirit who was given to us.

TOUGH TIMES LEAD to steel–like character.

Steel mills have hot metal ladles, huge containers filled with the seething ingredients of steel. They resemble burning buckets.

SPIRITUAL HEART FOCUS
Are you presently passing through trials? Ask God to use the testing to produce steel–like character in you. Open your heart to receive His love.

Our hearts are designed to be burning buckets into which God's passionate love has been poured!

What makes tribulation lead to the perseverance that produces stainless steel character? It's the Holy Spirit pouring the love of God into the heat and fury of suffering. It takes a blistering environment to make steel, and that's what it takes to produce unbreakable character.

PHYSICAL HEART FOCUS

Count fat grams to help make a wise choice in what you eat. For example, a small slice of cheesecake has nine grams, while a large peach has none.

❤ When the Bucket Pours

JOSHUA 14:7

*"I was forty years old when Moses the servant of the LORD sent me
from Kadesh Barnea to spy out the land,
and I brought back word to him as it was in my heart."*

WHATEVER FILLS YOUR BUCKET is what will slosh out on others.

The bucket of your heart will get bumped and stressed. Its contents will pour out. Fear filled the hearts of ten of the spies Moses sent to check out the Promised Land, and fear came out. Joshua brought back to Moses what was in his heart, which was faith in God and confidence that Israel could overcome whatever obstacles it faced.

I remember seeing a fired–up football player run to an opponent and jerk off the guy's helmet and throw it at him. Anger and bravado filled the heart of the man who threw the helmet, leading to a thoughtless action that got him and his team penalized. Is your bucket stressed? Fill it with Jesus and His Word, and the fruit and works of the Spirit will gush forth!

SPIRITUAL HEART FOCUS

Pray that blessings will pour out of your life onto others, even those who irritate and anger you.

PHYSICAL HEART FOCUS

Help relieve minor backache by stretching a few minutes daily.

♥ When God Cheers

PSALM 149:4

For the LORD takes pleasure in His people;
He will beautify the humble with salvation.

IF YOU KNOW GOD AS FATHER, you have the capacity to bring Him delight! I remember shots my sons made when they were playing basketball. I also recall A's they made on report cards. I am emotionally involved with my boys, and I delight in cheering them on.

SPIRITUAL HEART FOCUS

Consider where you are in life right now and the situations you face. Meditate on the fact that God is cheering you on if you are His child and seeking to live for Him.

When the Psalmist writes that God will "beautify the humble," it means literally He will "polish" them. Imagine a loving parent getting a child ready for the big game. Then, in the stands, the parent beams over the gleaming child and hoots and hollers for every score he makes.

Parents will cheer for other kids on their child's team, but not the way they will for their own children. In the same way, God delights in the "kids" who love Him as Father, and He cheers us on to victory.

PHYSICAL HEART FOCUS

Your fitness team may include a physician, nutritionist, and trainer, but when it comes to making the right choices, the key player is *you.*

♥ Grace Elixir

HEBREWS 13:9

Do not be carried about with various and strange doctrines.
For it is good that the heart be established by grace, not with foods which
have not profited those who have been occupied with them.

RELIGIONS ARE ABOUT LAW, what humans can do to win God's favor. Only one spiritual truth is about grace—what God has done to make us right.

This is why only Jesus' message can be called "gospel," "good news."

Law is a depressant. Human beings struggle to be good enough for God. That was the problem addressed in Hebrews 13:9. The message was that law–bound Hebrews shouldn't think a good relationship with God meant a return to the kosher table.

Grace is the elixir for the heart. It focuses on *being* right rather than *doing* right. We are made right with God in Jesus Christ. When we *are* right, *doing* right flows. This encourages the heart just like a good medicine!

> SPIRITUAL
> HEART FOCUS
> Have you slipped into the religion of *doing* rather than the relationship of *being*? Reaffirm your devotion to Jesus Christ and His grace alone as the hope of your salvation.

PHYSICAL HEART FOCUS
Add nuts and fresh fruit to your salads for a tasty, healthy change.

❤ Light the Fire Within

JUDGES 13:20

It happened as the flame went up toward heaven from the altar—the Angel of the LORD ascended in the flame of the altar! When Manoah and his wife saw this, they fell on their faces to the ground.

I ONCE HAD THE HONOR OF CARRYING the Olympic Torch. It was a double honor, because that Torch was designed by a dear friend whose wife had been my wife's college roommate. Its inscription read, "Light the Fire Within."

The experience of Manoah, father of Samson, shows us the power of the fire within us. An angel appeared to Manoah, telling him about the son he would have, and Manoah then built an altar to commemorate the angelic visitation. Sacrifices were burned on the stone platform, and the angel himself rocketed upward on the flame.

SPIRITUAL HEART FOCUS
Begin your prayer today with the question of the disciples: "Lord, teach me to pray" (Luke 11:1). Ask the Lord, to sharpen your desire to "pray without ceasing" (1 Thessalonians 5:17).

This is a picture of the prayer of a heart aflame for Christ. An angel is a messenger of God. Prayer is like a flame arising from the altar of our heart, carrying the message to God Himself!

Light the fire within through a lifestyle of dynamic prayer arising from your heart.

PHYSICAL HEART FOCUS

Overexercising is not healthy, so know your limits and build your program reasonably.

❤ Heart Sights

JOB 42:5–6

"I have heard of You by the hearing of the ear,
But now my eye sees You.
Therefore I abhor myself,
And repent in dust and ashes."

INVITE A CERTAIN FRIEND I KNOW to a symphony, and he will ask, "Who is Phil Harmonic?" Before working on a church staff, my friend was a football coach. He might not know anything about quarter notes in music, but he can tell you every nuance of every play in any quarter of any football game he watches. His eye is trained for the game.

Because of his tribulations, Job had to retrain his heart–eyes. He had focused so long on his problems that he had lost the capacity to see God clearly. His friends attempted to refocus his heart–vision to conform to their own blurry views.

SPIRITUAL HEART FOCUS
Ask God to train your heart–eyes to see Him in life transforming clarity.

Then Job saw God at a new level. Rather than fuzziness, Job's searing heartbreak burned away the film over his heart–eyes. The sight in his heart overwhelmed the mere hearing of ideas, notions, and concepts.

Objective truths and principles may reassure and guide us, but a heart trained to see God will transform us!

PHYSICAL HEART FOCUS
Quick meals often stimulate you to overeat, so eat slowly.

❤ Hearts Melted Together

GENESIS 2:22–24

Then the rib which the LORD God had taken from man He made into a
woman, and He brought her to the man. And Adam said:
"This is now bone of my bones
And flesh of my flesh;
She shall be called Woman,
Because she was taken out of Man."
Therefore a man shall leave his father and mother and be joined to his wife,
and they shall become one flesh.

WHEN A MAN AND WOMAN CLEAVE to one another, their hearts are melted together. Jo Beth and I have been married a long time, so my original wedding ring became dull and worn. One Christmas she gave me a new ring. A jeweler took the old wedding ring, melted it down, added some gold, and made me a new ring.

I have some "old gold" and a bit of "new gold." That's what it means for two hearts to cleave to one another: they are melted together.

In a sense, then, the bedroom is a fusion chamber. Sexual intimacy between husband and wife is the prime expression of the oneness of the hearts melted together. If you are already married, celebrate the oneness. If you are contemplating marriage, choose carefully the heart you want fused to yours.

SPIRITUAL HEART FOCUS

If you are married, ask the Father to intensify the heart–bond between you and your spouse and protect it from any division. If you are unmarried, seek God for the person with the right kind of heart.

PHYSICAL HEART FOCUS

Never go below 1,000 calories a day on a diet plan.

❤ Bruised Heart

EPHESIANS 4:26–27

"Be angry, and do not sin": do not let the sun go down on your wrath, nor give place to the devil.

IF YOU SLEEP ON A BRUISED HEART you wake up with a cold heart.

A husband and wife have a war. Hearts are bruised. Then comes dusk, an urgent hour. Matters must be settled before the sun disappears, and opponents skulk off to nurse wounds and strategize for another day's battle.

The bruised heart gives the devil a place to operate in a person's life. Bitterness becomes anger that becomes explosive behaviors. More bruising, more fragility. The bar of reconciliation is raised higher.

The prime responsibility for healing the bruised heart is the husband's. It is he who must reach across the bed and caress the hand of his wife. Her role is to respond. Being a spiritual leader means initiating confession and taking the first steps toward reconciliation.

When that happens, the bruised heart becomes a blessed heart. Its warmth is recovered.

SPIRITUAL HEART FOCUS
When there's war in your house or in your circle of friends, pray that God will always use you as an instrument for healing bruised hearts.

PHYSICAL HEART FOCUS

With your doctor's approval, take a quality vitamin and mineral supplement daily.

❤ Heart Creep

GENESIS 3:1

Now the serpent was more cunning than any beast of the field which the LORD God had made. And he said to the woman, "Has God indeed said, 'You shall not eat of every tree of the garden'?"

COSMIC COLLAPSE BEGINS with a simple question.

The destruction of a heart starts with a small matter. Physically, cholesterol builds up slowly, a creeping adversary. Spiritually, little sins coalesce into a heart–stopper.

"Bill" visited our church awhile back. He seemed to have the world tied in a knot and hoisted over his shoulder. No one knew that years earlier Bill would place an occasional bet on a ball game. Eventually, "occasional" became "constant." Finally, Bill was covered with gambling debts.

One day he awoke to the reality of the deceit that had crept into his heart. He realized he had become insensitive to twisting the truth. "I could lie, and it didn't bother me at all," he said later.

> **SPIRITUAL HEART FOCUS**
> Ask the Holy Spirit to expose the things creeping into your heart that could destroy you. Renounce them and turn away from them by receiving Christ's liberating truth.

What creeps up on your heart today becomes its essence tomorrow. Stop the creep before it becomes a crushing mountain of death.

PHYSICAL HEART FOCUS

For an easy "as–you–go" exercise, tighten your abdominal muscles ("abs") 10 to 15 times every time you think about it.

❤ Blaming Heart

GENESIS 3:11–12

And He said, "Who told you that you were naked? Have you eaten from the tree of which I commanded you that you should not eat?"
Then the man said, "The woman whom You gave to be with me, she gave me of the tree, and I ate."

ONCE, WHILE RUSHING TO CATCH an airplane, I ran over my own suitcase and tried to blame it on Jo Beth. In the garage, I had remembered that I needed my suit, so I left the suitcase at the car, zoomed back to get my suit, and put it in a hanging bag. Then I hopped in the car, threw it in reverse, and smashed my suitcase! I growled at Jo Beth, "This is all your fault! You should have had my suit packed!"

People who are voted "Most Likely to Succeed" sometimes don't. Often, it's because they passed on blame for a personal failure. I was late for the airplane because I had overscheduled, not because of Jo Beth.

We develop blaming hearts because we deceive ourselves into thinking our mistakes are never our own. In the end, it's our own heart we run over and crush.

SPIRITUAL HEART FOCUS
Ask God for the ability to see your own mistakes and the courage to take responsibility for them.

PHYSICAL HEART FOCUS
Parents should begin early teaching their children good dietary and exercise habits.

♥ 'Ouch Place'

HOSEA 6:1
Come, and let us return to the LORD;
For He has torn, but He will heal us;
He has stricken, but He will bind us up.

GOD SOMETIMES WOUNDS US in order to heal us.

Dr. Gatlin, our doctor when I was a kid, made house calls. He probed and asked, "Does that hurt?" He kept punching until he found the "ouch place." When he heard the wince, he pushed harder, knowing he had located the problem.

He wounded us to heal us.

The Holy Spirit searches our hearts, probing for the "ouch place." When He touches it, we may weep, or feel angry, or even experience heartache. We think He's wounding us, when in reality He's healing us.

When you feel the "ouch" in your heart, welcome the work of the Holy Spirit convicting you of the sin that can destroy you. Allow Him to apply the healing medicine of Christ's salvation to the "ouch place."

SPIRITUAL HEART FOCUS
Think about where you feel the spiritual "ouches," and meditate on what God may be saying to you through the sensitive spots in your spiritual heart.

PHYSICAL HEART FOCUS

Soreness is part of regular exercise, but if pain develops and persists, stop the activity and consult a physician. Weigh today and check your BMI.

June

Begin with an obedient heart
and you will get
an understanding heart.

❤ Heart Business

LUKE 2:49–50

And He said to them, "Why did you seek Me? Did you not know that I must be about My Father's business?" But they did not understand the statement which He spoke to them.

SOMETIMES THE APPARENT BUSINESS is not the real business.

I read about MBAs who are trained to identify the actual enterprise of a corporation. For example, when the automobile appeared, buggy–makers folded. However, say the experts, had the buggy companies understood they were not really in the buggy–making business, but the transportation business, they would have survived.

Jesus had a clear understanding of the business of His heart. When He spoke the words recorded in Luke 2:49, Jesus was an apprentice carpenter. His business was to make things, one might conclude. But Jesus knew the enterprise of His heart was the carpentry of human lives. His business was to craft human beings!

> **SPIRITUAL HEART FOCUS**
> Commit yourself to be about the Father's business, and express your willingness to set aside personal agendas for the sake of His work in and through you.

Using your immediate ambition, trade, and skill is not the core business of your heart. Loving God and others is. When you discover that, you won't lose your heart when your earthly enterprises fade and fail.

PHYSICAL HEART FOCUS

When you eat out, save calories by drinking club soda or water.

♥ T–Shirt Love

JOHN 21:15–17

Jesus said to Simon Peter, "Simon, son of Jonah, do you love Me . . . ?"
He said to Him, "Yes, Lord; You know that I love You."
He said to him, "Feed My lambs."
He said to him again a second time, "Simon, son of Jonah, do you love Me?"
He said to Him, "Yes, Lord; You know that I love You."
He said to him, "Tend My sheep."
He said to him the third time, "Simon, son of Jonah, do you love Me?" Peter was grieved because He said to him the third time, "Do you love Me?"
And he said to Him, "Lord, You know all things; You know that I love You."
Jesus said to him, "Feed My sheep."

SPIRITUAL HEART FOCUS
Submit your understanding of love for the Holy Spirit's evaluation, and ask Him to help you love as God loves.

LOVE IS MORE THAN an inscription on a T–shirt.

Peter missed the point and was wounded that Jesus kept asking him if he loved Him. Jesus was asking, "Do you love me unconditionally with your whole heart?" and Peter answered every time, "Yes, I'm Your friend."

Jesus was dealing diamonds and Peter offered marbles.

The business of the heart is loving God and others with heavenly love, devoid of self–interest. This can be incredibly difficult. But don't lose heart in trying to do the business of the heart, because it is possible for the Holy Spirit to spread heavenly love through you. Make your heart available for Him to do business there. Don't stop with the T–shirt.

PHYSICAL HEART FOCUS

When fat is required in cooking, use olive oil or polyunsaturated vegetable oils when possible.

♥ Optimistic Heart

ROMANS 15:13

Now may the God of hope fill you with all joy and peace in believing, that you may abound in hope by the power of the Holy Spirit.

BILLY BOB WAS A PERPETUAL CANDIDATE for sheriff in a certain Texas town. He would only get a handful of votes, but he campaigned seriously in every election.

He knocked on a door to solicit support. "I'm Billy Bob, and I want your vote for sheriff." The lady threw a fit. "You're the sorriest excuse for a man I've ever known. You're a kook, and nobody in their right mind would vote for you!"

Back at his car, Billy Bob, ever the optimist, wrote by her name, "Maybe."

The hope that God implants in the heart of His people isn't based on fudging the facts or wishing flimsily. The New Testament Greek word for "hope" means *expectation* that the desire will come true. This is not a 50–50 proposition; it's 100 percent on target.

In Christ, the hopeful, optimistic heart is an expectant heart.

SPIRITUAL HEART FOCUS
Ask the Father to align your wishes and desires with His, and you will have ground for expectant hope.

PHYSICAL HEART FOCUS

Today's steps toward total heart health may seem small, but you can't get there without them.

♥ Is There A Heart in There?

PROVERBS 17:16

Why is there in the hand of a fool the purchase price of wisdom,
Since he has no heart for it?

HARRY HAD BEEN ON A LONG TRIP and collapsed on his sofa. When his children returned from elementary school, Harry pretended to be asleep.

"Do you think he's dead?" his daughter asked her brother. "I'll see." She pried open Harry's eye and peered inside. "No, he's still in there," she reported.

C.S. Lewis wrote of "men without chests," describing people who live heartless, thoughtless lives. Similarly, the Book of Proverbs speaks of people with no heart capable of receiving wisdom. Imagine a homeless person buying a piano. There is no place to house the instrument. So it is with those who have no heart. They seek treasures for which they have no capacity.

SPIRITUAL HEART FOCUS
Consider the capacity and readiness of your heart to receive God's deepest truth. Ask the Father to give you a heart capable of seeing and embracing God's profound revelation.

God's revelation is available to all, but people who have no heart for it will not receive it. Only the Lord can give you a heart for His truth.

PHYSICAL HEART FOCUS
Slice and freeze fresh fruit in individual portions for quick, healthy snacks.

❤ Eloquence of the Whole Heart

1 CHRONICLES 29:9

Then the people rejoiced, for they had offered willingly,
because with a loyal heart they had offered willingly to the LORD;
and King David also rejoiced greatly.

A WEALTHY FAMILY THREW A BANQUET. A famous actor was asked to quote lines, and he spoke the twenty–third Psalm magnificently, to great applause. The host spotted a godly man and requested him to repeat the same passage. The man stumbled through the verses. When he finished, a holy hush settled over the room.

Everyone wondered: Why was there applause for the actor and deep reverence as the old man quoted the same Bible verses?

The actor himself understood. "The difference between him and me is that I know the Psalm, but he knows the Shepherd."

One can know the Bible with mental sharpness and even display emotions like the finest actor. But there is an eloquence that comes from knowing God with one's whole heart that goes beyond human abilities. The voice may be halting, the grammar fractured, but the eloquence of whole–heart devotion is what God uses to transform lives!

SPIRITUAL HEART FOCUS
Ask the Holy Spirit to form the eloquence of your heart. Give the Lord the totality of your mind, will, and emotions.

PHYSICAL HEART FOCUS
All foods affect heart health, so make wise choices.

❤ Impossible Health

MATTHEW 19:24–26

"And again I say to you, it is easier for a camel to go through the eye of a needle than for a rich man to enter the kingdom of God." When His disciples heard it, they were greatly astonished, saying, "Who then can be saved?" But Jesus looked at them and said to them, "With men this is impossible, but with God all things are possible."

THE DISCIPLES HAD JUST WATCHED a fabulously wealthy young man reject Christ because he was unwilling to pay the price of following the Lord. Jesus tells His disciples that the bar is impossibly high to qualify to be God's child. "Then who can make it?" they fret.

This is why the Gospel is Good News. To make a desperately wicked heart acceptable to God— to form a new person qualified for the Kingdom— is impossible for man, even at his most religious. But God specializes in the impossible.

You and I are not good enough for Heaven, but that's no problem for God, who infuses us with the innocence of the only begotten Son!

SPIRITUAL HEART FOCUS
Recognize it is impossible for you to save yourself, and rest in Christ by throwing your eternal destiny on Him.

PHYSICAL HEART FOCUS
Know your family history of cardiovascular disease.

♥ The Religious Heart

1 SAMUEL 16:7–8

*But the L*ORD *said to Samuel, "Do not look at his appearance
or at his physical stature, because I have refused him.
For the L*ORD *does not see as man sees; for man looks at the
outward appearance, but the L*ORD *looks at the heart."*

*So Jesse called Abinadab, and made him pass before Samuel. And he said,
"Neither has the L*ORD *chosen this one."*

"HERE COMES THE JUDGE!"

Samuel arrives to fanfare. "Why have you come to our fair city?"
The prophet replies, "I have come to sacrifice." A sweeping sigh of relief
rises. "Whew! He's come for religious reasons, not to
meddle with our personal lives and secret dealings."

Samuel actually has come to Bethlehem to
seek the Lord's man to replace failed King
Saul. People may think a little religion is
good, as long as it doesn't stick its nose into
their business. But God goes deeper than that:
He looks into the very heart.

When God searches young David's heart, it's
not for the purpose of exposing his weaknesses, but
his promise and potential. If the religious types at
Bethlehem had understood that, they all would have presented themselves
to the judge!

> SPIRITUAL
> HEART FOCUS
> Ask the Holy Spirit to sharpen
> your discernment in recognizing
> the potential in people,
> especially in your spouse,
> children, or others whom you
> can encourage.

PHYSICAL HEART FOCUS

Accept your doctor's advice about your weight loss and exercise program.

❤ Power of a Positive Testimony

1 JOHN 1:1-4

That which was from the beginning, which we have heard, which we have seen with our eyes, which we have looked upon, and our hands have handled, concerning the Word of life—the life was manifested, and we have seen, and bear witness, and declare to you that eternal life which was with the Father and was manifested to us—that which we have seen and heard we declare to you, that you also may have fellowship with us; and truly our fellowship is with the Father and with His Son Jesus Christ. And these things we write to you that your joy may be full.

TESTIMONIES ARE REPORTS OF THE WORK God is doing in people's hearts.

Often, testimonies focus on the negative. Folks center their stories on how sordid their lifestyles were. Sometimes testimonies are more about the old way of living than about the new.

SPIRITUAL HEART FOCUS
Give God thanks for all the victories you have won through Him.

It's refreshing to hear the testimonies of our young people. All could report their flaws and falls. But I love to hear them talk about situations where they experienced the power of Christ in their transformed hearts.

Jesus, not us sinful human beings, is the star of such positive testimonies. When He touches and transforms you, you want to testify and declare what He's done. Center your testimony on Him, not yourself, and everyone who hears will know your heart has been truly transformed!

PHYSICAL HEART FOCUS

Record your progress and experiences along the way—including times you "fell off the wagon" of your diet and fitness plans—and encourage others with your report.

❤ Heart in the Studebaker

LUKE 23:45–46

Then the sun was darkened, and the veil of the temple was torn in two. And when Jesus had cried out with a loud voice, He said, "Father, 'into Your hands I commit My spirit.'" Having said this, He breathed His last.

JOHN 10:29–30

"My Father, who has given them to Me, is greater than all; and no one is able to snatch them out of My Father's hand. I and My Father are one."

I HOPPED IN MY COLLEGE ROOMMATE'S Studebaker, and the medical student shouted, "Don't sit on that!" The paper–wrapped object was a human heart, cut from a lab cadaver. I held it, but soon knew I had neither the qualifications nor the authority to hold a heart in my hand.

The devil tried with all his might to pull Jesus away from His Father and divide the Godhead. At the beginning of Jesus' ministry, in the wilderness, and on the cross, the adversary yanked but could not pull Jesus' heart from the Father's hand.

Our hearts are in Jesus' hand, He's in the Father's hand, and we are inseparable from our God from here to eternity!

SPIRITUAL HEART FOCUS

Celebrate your safety and security in God's hands. Recommit your heart to His care.

PHYSICAL HEART FOCUS

For a quick, high–fiber breakfast, try whole–grain cereal sweetened with a small amount of honey.

❤ World Peace and the Heart

MATTHEW 15:19–20

"For out of the heart proceed evil thoughts, murders, adulteries, fornications, thefts, false witness, blasphemies. These are the things which defile a man, but to eat with unwashed hands does not defile a man."

WHEN THE UNITED NATIONS WAS TAKING SHAPE, there was a public forum open to anyone. The elites were there, and so were people off the street. The auditorium vibrated with the hope of deliberation replacing destruction in the ever–changing relations among countries.

"Are there any questions?" the moderator asked after discussions. A housewife waved her hand. "Yes, Madam?"

The woman asked, "What do you propose to do about human nature?"

This is the fundamental question not only regarding global peace, but personal peace. The story of the woman at the United Nations forum may be an urban legend, but it's no legend that Jesus Christ has the power to do something about human nature by giving each individual a new heart!

SPIRITUAL HEART FOCUS
Pray for peace in the world. Pray for global evangelism and missions and that individuals everywhere will be transformed by Jesus Christ into people of peace.

PHYSICAL HEART FOCUS

If you're tempted to eat late snacks, set an early cut–off time for eating, and don't go beyond it.

♥ Heart Golf

PHILIPPIANS 3:8–11

Yet indeed I also count all things loss for the excellence of the knowledge of Christ Jesus my Lord, for whom I have suffered the loss of all things, and count them as rubbish, that I may gain Christ and be found in Him, not having my own righteousness, which is from the law, but that which is through faith in Christ, the righteousness which is from God by faith; that I may know Him and the power of His resurrection, and the fellowship of His sufferings, being conformed to His death, if, by any means, I may attain to the resurrection from the dead.

I ENJOY GOLF AND ALWAYS LOOK for ways to improve. One day I learned a simple secret that can help even a runt drive a ball a long way. That afternoon I felt the power was in me to hit the ball well, but it wasn't happening. A friend offered a tip. I tried his idea and slammed the ball. His approach added power to my swing.

Golfing instructors sometimes say, "Let the club do the work." Many golfers try to use their own muscle power to make the difference, but body position and club choice are vital.

Trying to make a fleshly heart do spiritual work and bear spiritual fruit is like attempting to golf under your own power. Salvation in Jesus Christ means the heart now has resurrection power. In our own strength, we are limited, but, as Paul put it, "I can do all things through Christ who strengthens me" (Philippians 4:13).

SPIRITUAL HEART FOCUS
Confess to God the sin of attempting to produce spiritual fruit through the power of your own flesh. Ask Him to use you as an instrument empowered by Christ's resurrection life.

PHYSICAL HEART FOCUS
Eat intelligently. Know what foods are good for you, and build your diet around them.

❤ Biopsy

JEREMIAH 12:3

But You, O LORD, know me;
You have seen me,
And You have tested my heart toward You.
Pull them out like sheep for the slaughter,
And prepare them for the day of slaughter.

HEART DOCTORS LIKE MY FRIENDS Mike Duncan and Rick Leachman use complex instruments to examine the deepest regions of the human heart. A surface exam is inadequate to diagnose and treat life–threatening disease.

The Old Testament laws were great for understanding surface problems, but Jesus came to probe deeper—right down to the level of attitude.

Attitude is crucial. Jeremiah says God tests our heart's attitude toward Him.

In a biopsy, a physician cuts out a piece of tissue and removes it from the body. Then the material is examined for evidences of disease.

SPIRITUAL HEART FOCUS
Is your attitude toward God shaped by a view of Him as Giver of law or grace? Ask the Lord for a fresh vision of His grace.

God biopsies our heart's attitude toward Him, because the way we regard Him determines how we regard all else. Allow grace to shape your attitude toward God, and you will fulfill the Law.

PHYSICAL HEART FOCUS

Substitute an after–dinner walk in place of dessert.

❤ Three Types of Anger

ECCLESIASTES 7:9

Do not hasten in your spirit to be angry,
For anger rests in the bosom of fools.

WE'VE ALL SEEN FOLKS EAGER to pick a fight. Their hearts fume with eagerness to be angry.

Among the main excuses people give for being angry are:

Rodney Dangerfield anger—Some people always feel demeaned. In their eyes, they "get no respect."

Smothers Brothers anger—Tom's famous punchline to his brother, Dick, was, "Mom always liked you best." This is the anger of neglect, perceived or real.

Joe McCarthy anger—The 1950s–era senator understood the dangers of communism, but his heart seethed with anger so broad it targeted even many innocent people. This is generalized anger, lumping whole classes of people into one despised group.

The heart constantly boiling with anger resides in a fool's chest, says the Scripture. If you have an angry spirit, treat it as you would any other sin and receive God's grace and forgiveness.

> **SPIRITUAL HEART FOCUS**
> Ask God to go to the root of your anger and tear it out. Confess your anger as sin. Ask the Lord's forgiveness and trust His grace.

PHYSICAL HEART FOCUS

Take time to enjoy your food. Sit down to eat. Be aware of when you're full.

❤ The 'Unwrapper'

No one has seen God at any time. The only begotten Son, who is in the bosom of the Father, He has declared Him.

JESUS CHRIST IS THE HEART of the Father.

Just as your heart is "you," so "the only begotten Son," Jesus, is God. To explain or declare means to unfold the meaning of something. Jesus Christ "unwraps" God so that all people can know Him.

Jesus shows us the All Powerful One who leans toward the lowly. Through Christ we see the Holy One who loves sinners. When God the Father's heart beats, it is the compassion and mercy of God the Son pulsing within.

Your heart "unwraps" you, too. If your physical heart is strong, people will comprehend you as hardy and healthy. If your moral heart is strong, people will see you as a positive, principled person. If your spiritual heart is powerful for Christ, people will know you as a godly person.

Your heart will "unwrap" the real you!

> **SPIRITUAL HEART FOCUS**
> Pray that the Holy Spirit will create in you a heart that reveals you to others as a godly man or woman

PHYSICAL HEART FOCUS

When you take in more calories than you burn off, you gain weight—every time. Increase your caloric expenditure by walking 20 minutes a day.

❤ When the Heart Cries 'Father!'

MATTHEW 6:9

"In this manner, therefore, pray:
Our Father in heaven,
Hallowed be Your name."

"OUR FATHER" IS THE MOST COMPACT SUMMARY of biblical faith, a title for God that opens the door to all life's relationships.

"Our Father" opens the door to the unseen world, telling us that behind the veil is a personal, loving, powerful Almighty Father.

"Our Father" opens the door to the seen world, giving meaning in the midst of suffering.

"Our Father" opens the door to our relationships with others. Jesus doesn't tell us to pray "*my* Father," but "*our* Father."

"Our Father" opens the door to healthy self–relationship. "Father" reminds us that if we matter to no one else, we matter to Him.

"Our Father": two words that embrace the heart of our relationship to God. Embrace them as yours.

> SPIRITUAL
> HEART FOCUS
> Pray the Lord's Prayer, found
> in Matthew 6:9–13.
> Use the prayer as an
> outline to express your
> personal prayer.

PHYSICAL HEART FOCUS

Be on the lookout for noticeable health changes or prolonged fatigue, and consult your physician.

❤ When the Heart Cries 'Daddy!'

GALATIANS 4:6

And because you are sons, God has sent forth the Spirit of His Son into your hearts, crying out, "Abba, Father!"

THE ONLY WAY WE CAN KNOW GOD as "Abba" or "Daddy" is with our heart.

As we read in yesterday's devotion, referring to God as "Father" is wonderful. Yet the word can be too broad and nebulous.

The New Testament records 275 times when Jesus called God "Father" in a manner so personal it offended the religious establishment. They knew God as Father with their heads, but He knew God as Father with His heart!

"Abba" was the way a small child addressed her father. Today, important prayers at institutional settings, like dedications and inaugurations, often begin with a pretentious–sounding *"Faw–ther Gawd."* But people who know by the witness of the Spirit that they are His kids can call Him "Abba," "Daddy."

George Washington is the "father" of my country, but I'm not authorized to call him "Daddy." Does your heart feel free to call God "Abba"?

SPIRITUAL HEART FOCUS

If you can't call God "Abba," you need to receive His only begotten Son.

PHYSICAL HEART FOCUS

Bless your family by making total heart health diet and exercise your lifelong practice.

♥ Hearing the Whole Band

PSALM 19:8
The statutes of the LORD are right, rejoicing the heart;
The commandment of the LORD is pure, enlightening the eyes.

WHEN I WAS IN SEMINARY, Jo Beth and I lived in a small campus apartment near a high school. If the wind was blowing our way, we could hear all the instruments of the practicing band. But if the wind was blowing the wrong way, only the percussion thumped through.

Some of us were brought up to hear only the drumbeat of *judgment, judgment, judgment*. Others, with hearts tuned to the theology of contemporary culture, hear only the flighty piccolo of *mercy, mercy, mercy*.

SPIRITUAL HEART FOCUS
Ask the Holy Spirit to tune your heart to hear the totality of God's music.

The heart must hear the whole band. When it does, it rejoices like a music lover hearing all the harmonies, played by all the instruments. When your heart hears the full music of God, it listens to the percussion of justice and the piccolo of mercy in beautiful conjunction.

Separate, they are incomplete, like an unresolved chord. Together, they compose the music of joy.

PHYSICAL HEART FOCUS
Enlist a friend to walk with you two or three times a week at the local mall.

❤ The Size of the Cross

EPHESIANS 3:14-19

For this reason I bow my knees to the Father of our Lord Jesus Christ, from whom the whole family in heaven and earth is named, that He would grant you, according to the riches of His glory, to be strengthened with might through His Spirit in the inner man, that Christ may dwell in your hearts through faith; that you, being rooted and grounded in love, may be able to comprehend with all the saints what is the width and length and depth and height—to know the love of Christ which passes knowledge; that you may be filled with all the fullness of God.

JAYNIE WAS TOURING A GREAT CATHEDRAL with her grandfather. Never before had she seen a full–size cross, and suddenly she stood before a huge crucifix bearing the sculpted form of Jesus.

"Pa–Pa, who's that on that cross?" she asked. The little girl's granddaddy gently explained about Christ's atonement, and the child then invited Christ to set up residence there. Jaynie grasped not only the physical size of the cross, but also its spiritual immensity.

The cross is tall enough to span the distance from this fallen world to the Throne of God, and its beams are wide enough to cover sinners like us.

It's big enough to fill the heart with all the fullness of God.

> **SPIRITUAL HEART FOCUS**
> Have you trivialized the cross to a mere piece of jewelry? Ask God for fresh insight into the size and scope of the cross of Jesus Christ, and repent if necessary for the sin of minimizing or underestimating it.

PHYSICAL HEART FOCUS

Calories are your allies for supplying energy—they only become your enemies when you let them run wild in your daily diet.

♥ Twice His

ISAIAH 43:1

But now, thus says the LORD, who created you, O Jacob,
And He who formed you, O Israel:
"Fear not, for I have redeemed you;
I have called you by your name;
You are Mine."

I LIKE TO VISIT A CERTAIN SHOP with model sailboats, and while there I recall the story of a Dutch boy who spent months crafting a functional toy sailboat. He would take the little vessel to the canals and launch it, then fish it out with a stick.

One day a wind carried the model out to sea. The boy was brokenhearted. Months later, he spotted his lost boat in a shop window, and he bought it back.

The young lad clutched the little boat and said, "I made you and I bought you. You are twice mine!"

God created you, but when an ill wind arose, you set the sail of your heart to run before it into a sea of sin. You were lost from your Maker. But with the immense price of Jesus' blood, God bought you back.

You are twice His!

SPIRITUAL HEART FOCUS

Consider the imagery of your heart as a sail. What winds drive it? Yield your heart to the wind of the Holy Spirit. Praise God for recovering you when you were lost.

PHYSICAL HEART FOCUS

A wise choice today would be to eat 3 ounces of salmon (1 fat gram) rather than 3.5 ounces of hamburger (8 fat grams).

❤ The Enchanted Heart

REVELATION 9:21

*And they did not repent of their murders or their sorceries
or their sexual immorality or their thefts.*

"I ALMOST GOT CHOPPED UP!" reported my friend, an avid amateur
astronomer. Long before dawn he lay in the middle of a golf course to
look at the brilliant stars, and he was so enchanted by
the glimmering galaxies that he didn't hear the
lawnmower coming over the hill.

"Follow your heart," says the world. But
the enchantments of the heart can surprise us
with sudden death.

"Sorceries" are any techniques by which the
fallen culture tries to enchant our hearts. The
Greek term is *pharmakeus*, from which we get
"pharmacy," and it means "a spell–giving potion."

When the heart gets hypnotized by the enchantments of
the world, it becomes distracted from the very things that can tear it apart.

> **SPIRITUAL
> HEART FOCUS**
> What enchants your heart to the
> extent it distracts you from all
> else, including dangers?
> Ask the Lord to so control your
> heart that nothing can allure
> it away from Him.

PHYSICAL HEART FOCUS

Avoid alcohol while dieting, and when you hear of health benefits of wine, beer, and
other beverages, balance that information with facts about the negatives of drinking.

JUNE 21

♥ Primacy of the Obedient Heart

1 SAMUEL 15:22
So Samuel said:
"Has the LORD as great delight in burnt offerings and sacrifices,
As in obeying the voice of the LORD?
Behold, to obey is better than sacrifice,
And to heed than the fat of rams."

BEGIN WITH AN OBEDIENT HEART and you will get an understanding heart. A man studied a complex blueprint. It was too much for him to understand, so he zeroed in on the smallest component. Then he moved on to another tiny portion of the job, following the design meticulously. At last he stood back. Now he could see the whole and understand the blueprint.

> **SPIRITUAL HEART FOCUS**
> Rather than fretting about what you do not understand, ask God to help you carry out what is clear to you, as revealed through His Word.

Often when people listen to a sermon, hear teaching, or read the Bible, they fret because the principles don't seem clear to them. But the spirit understands what the mind cannot grasp. As you walk in the spirit obediently, your mind slowly awakens to knowledge. Obedience precedes understanding.

PHYSICAL HEART FOCUS

Resistance exercise helps fight osteoporosis in women, and stretching contributes to flexibility and joint health in both men and women.

❤ Smiling Heart

JONAH 4:6-8

And the LORD God prepared a plant and made it come up over Jonah, that it might be shade for his head to deliver him from his misery. So Jonah was very grateful for the plant. But as morning dawned the next day God prepared a worm, and it so damaged the plant that it withered. . . . Then he wished death for himself, and said, "It is better for me to die than to live."

WHAT PUTS A SMILE IN YOUR HEART that erupts onto your face?

Someone showed me a picture and said of the person in the photo, "I hardly recognized him because he's smiling." I studied the portrait. "In fact," said my friend, "he's a handsome guy, but I never thought of him that way before."

A smile makes a big difference in your appearance. The problem is, like Jonah, many times we have only a facial smile and not a heart smile. Jonah's heart was rebellious. He smiled because in his attempt to run from God he wound up under a scorching sun, and then found some momentary shelter.

> **SPIRITUAL HEART FOCUS**
> What puts a smile on your face? Seek God for the deep joy that causes your heart to smile and your face to express it.

When the tree died, so did the smile.

If your heart smiles from its love for God, obedience to Him, and joy in His service, the smile won't fade!

PHYSICAL HEART FOCUS
Use olive oil and vinegar for salad dressing.

❤ The Anchoring of the Anchor

JAMES 1:17

Every good gift and every perfect gift is from above, and comes down from the Father of lights, with whom there is no variation or shadow of turning.

MANY A PERSON'S HOPE IS ANCHORED to the heart, but where is the heart anchored?

A city of oil rigs lies in the Gulf of Mexico. When a hurricane rages through the petroleum metropolis, all the focus turns to anchoring the rigs. People with anchored hearts trust their emotions, their instincts, and their dreams. But if a heart is unanchored, the personality gets wrecked when the storms sweep through.

The only place to anchor the human heart is in the immutable heart of God. He tells Moses His name is "I AM WHO I AM" (Exodus 3:14). Not "I Was," or "I Will Be," but "I AM"—constant, changeless, and faithful.

You can anchor your heart to God's heart!

SPIRITUAL HEART FOCUS
Ask God to help you link your hopes, dreams, ambitions, plans, and sources of happiness and strength to the one great anchor—Him!

PHYSICAL HEART FOCUS

Whole–grain bread, oatmeal, and brown rice are good complex carbs to add in moderation to your diet.

❤ The Eclipsed Heart

2 CORINTHIANS 4:3–4

But even if our gospel is veiled, it is veiled to those who are perishing,
whose minds the god of this age has blinded, who do not believe,
lest the light of the gospel of the glory of Christ,
who is the image of God, should shine on them.

THE MOON HAS NO GLORY OF ITS OWN; it shines only with the sun's radiance. When the moon falls behind earth's shadow, sunlight is blocked and reflected loveliness is darkened.

Human beings once shone with God's glory, but it was lost through sin. Now our hope is to reflect the glory of Christ.

However, the prince of darkness desires to impose his shadow over our hearts so that we do not sparkle with God's "Sonlight." Through its own motion the moon slips into the massive shadow of earth, an eclipse. Likewise, our own actions bring us into the state of the eclipsed, darkened heart, but we can avoid this by deciding to walk in the light.

> SPIRITUAL
> HEART FOCUS
> Ask Jesus Christ to remove
> the veil of unbelief from your
> mind, and take the shadow of
> doubt off your heart.

The more darkness one chooses, the more darkness one has. Those who choose not to see will not see. The heart that selects the veil gets the veil.

Move out of the shadows of unbelief and into God's glorious light revealed in Jesus Christ!

PHYSICAL HEART FOCUS
"Crunches" will help trim your waistline.

❤ Getting Your Heart's Delight

PSALM 37:4
Delight yourself also in the LORD,
And He shall give you the desires of your heart.

I REALLY WANTED THAT JOB. I prayed, confessed, stood on the Word, but I didn't get the position.

I prayed to marry a certain girl, but it didn't happen. I planned to build bridges as a career, but I didn't become an engineer. I ran for president of the student council, prayed to be elected, but got clobbered.

The desires of my heart on all those issues were not aligned with delighting in the Lord.

God's desires for me were better than my own dreams. The job I did get was much more fulfilling. I married the ideal girl and have been blessed beyond my expectations. I didn't become a bridge builder, but God has allowed me to be part of building churches. And had I been elected president of the student council I would have missed the church job that changed my life!

We get confused when our desire becomes our delight, but we get it right when our delight in the Lord determines our desire.

> **SPIRITUAL HEART FOCUS**
> Set aside your fondest desires. Tell the Lord you're nailing them to the cross. Ask Him to cause your heart to delight in Him above all else and to desire what He desires.

PHYSICAL HEART FOCUS

If you don't enjoy eating fish, add a fish oil supplement to your vitamin list as an alternative source of "fishy" nutrients.

♥ When God's Heart Is Turned Over

HOSEA 11:8

"How can I give you up, Ephraim?
How can I hand you over, Israel?
How can I make you like Admah?
How can I set you like Zeboiim?
My heart churns within Me;
My sympathy is stirred."

WITH THREE SONS, JO BETH AND I KNOW what it's like to be concerned intensely for our children. We feel their pain, wounds, rejections, and victories.

Now those heart-stirrings are extended to our grandchildren. It goes on and on, part of the heart and its love and relationships.

The reason we're bound up in the lives of our kids is because we are made in the image of God. Through Hosea, God tells His rebellious covenant children that His heart churns with compassion for them.

If you're God's child, His heart is turned over because of your disobedience, yet it also burns with compassion for you. Let this knowledge motivate you, as it does me, to not want to grieve the heart of our loving Father.

His heart goes out to you!

SPIRITUAL HEART FOCUS

A covenant is an agreement between two partners. God promises to save you if you trust Him. Renew your side of the covenant with God by affirming your faith in Christ as Savior and Lord of your life.

PHYSICAL HEART FOCUS

If you're a "meat and potatoes" person, substitute a green vegetable for the potatoes, and eat smaller portions of meat.

♥ 'That's My Boy'

MATTHEW 3:16–17

When He had been baptized, Jesus came up immediately from the water; and behold, the heavens were opened to Him, and He saw the Spirit of God descending like a dove and alighting upon Him. And suddenly a voice came from heaven, saying, "This is My beloved Son, in whom I am well pleased."

MY HEART TAKES GREAT PLEASURE in our three sons. I thrill at Cliff's music, Ben's intellectual insights, and Ed's creative zest.

I have many sons and daughters spiritually, and although I delight in them all, others don't hold my heart quite like my biological sons. Our natural children have a special place in our hearts no one else can occupy.

When we receive Christ, we become "joint heirs" with Him, and we are merged into His relationship with the Father! (Romans 8:17)

SPIRITUAL HEART FOCUS

Meditate on the fact that when God sees you, if you are one with Christ, He takes the same pleasure in you as He does in Jesus. Let this thought lead you to worship God for receiving you this way.

When Jesus allowed John to baptize Him, Jesus was signaling His willingness to be identified with sinners and to take on the mission of atoning for the world's sins. At that point, the Father expressed His immense pleasure in His Son.

If you are one with Jesus Christ, God the Father takes the same pleasure with you that He does with His only begotten Son!

PHYSICAL HEART FOCUS

When using weights, note that sometimes weighted full range of motion can damage joints.

❤ The Calloused Heart

PSALM 17:10
They have closed up their fat hearts;
With their mouths they speak proudly.

A BUSINESSMAN TOLD ME, "Every transaction I get involved in makes me realize more calluses are being built on my heart."

Literally, an unfeeling heart is one enclosed in its own fat. A thick layer of flesh keeps the heart from being sensitive. A callus is a thickening of the skin from rubbing and pressure, and is relatively insensitive.

So it is with the heart. In an effort to protect ourselves, we try to turn off our feelings. Yet not only do we shield ourselves from those who irritate and stress us, but we're isolated from those we care about the most.

> SPIRITUAL
> HEART FOCUS
> Ask the Holy Spirit to do surgery on your heart, remove the calluses, and restore the sensitivity of your spiritual and emotional heart.

Most often, calluses have to be cut off or shaved down by a physician. Is your heart becoming calloused? Allow the Holy Spirit to cut off the layers making you insensitive!

PHYSICAL HEART FOCUS
Make sure your lower back is fully supported when doing sit–ups or crunches.

♥ Giving from the Heart

2 CORINTHIANS 9:7

*So let each one give as he purposes in his heart, not grudgingly
or of necessity; for God loves a cheerful giver.*

"I NEED SOME EXTRA MONEY to run the household while you're away on business," she whispered as they entered church.

"Sure," he replied.

At the pew, he pulled out a wad of cash for the house. The wife thought it was for the collection, and plopped it in the plate.

SPIRITUAL HEART FOCUS
Consider your giving habits. Do you plan and give purposefully to the church? Repent for happenstance, accidental giving. Ask the Lord for a heart that gives with cheer.

"I know God keeps records, and He's credited me with the big bucks we gave the church," the man joked later.

"How much would you have given?" the friend asked. The man answered with a much lesser amount than his wife had given accidentally. "Then that's the amount God credited to your account," replied the friend.

The cheerful giver contributes in a planned, purposeful way, not accidentally. God looks on the heart, not the offering plate.

PHYSICAL HEART FOCUS

Draw a "line" in the plate—no sweets today.

❤ Heart Without Walls

ECCLESIASTES 2:10–11

Whatever my eyes desired I did not keep from them.
I did not withhold my heart from any pleasure,
For my heart rejoiced in all my labor;
And this was my reward from all my labor.
Then I looked on all the works that my hands had done
And on the labor in which I had toiled;
And indeed all was vanity and grasping for the wind.
There was no profit under the sun.

ORIGINALLY, A GARDEN WAS A WALLED–IN PLACE, a sanctuary with boundaries guarding it from the untamed jungle.

Today many people believe that the way to a happy heart is to tear down the walls around the garden of their heart. They give their heart whatever pleasure it craves. But in the end, as with Solomon, they become cynical and wonder, "Is this all there is?"

Boundaries are essential for peace and joy. Israel's sin tears down its protective wall, and it becomes "trampled down" (Isaiah 5:5).

> **SPIRITUAL HEART FOCUS**
> Do you have solid boundaries defining your spiritual and moral limits, or do you live by the "anything goes" philosophy? Ask the Lord to help you establish good boundaries in your heart.

A well–hedged garden is a paradise, but a garden without walls becomes a jungle. Your heart was made to be a garden, fragrant with the joy and peace of God. Without the walls—the healthy boundaries of positive values—your heart becomes a tangled mess.

PHYSICAL HEART FOCUS

When hunger pangs start, eat an apple. Check your weight and BMI.

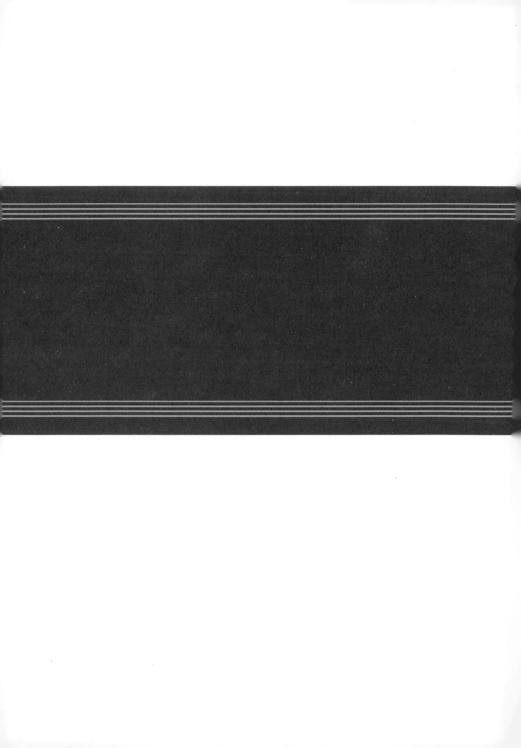

July

The lips pray deceitfully
when their words contradict the heart.

♥ Forgiving from the Heart

MATTHEW 18:34–35

"And his master was angry, and delivered him to the torturers until he should pay all that was due to him. So My heavenly Father also will do to you if each of you, from his heart, does not forgive his brother his trespasses."

HEART FORGIVENESS involves four stages.

First comes acknowledgement of the hurt. In Jesus' parable, denial of the existence of the debt would have made forgiveness meaningless.

Next is the acknowledgement of hatred. A grudge develops, and forgiveness won't come unless we confront the hatred growing in us. We will hide behind the little verbal shield that says, "I love that person who hurt me; I'm not angry!"

Healing comes through truthfulness, not a whitewash. "You hurt me and I hated you," is the way the pendulum swings. It's based on the recognition that the wound inflicted on you was no worse than the grudge or the hate with which you thrust back.

But if it's forgiveness from the heart, there will be a fourth element—an invitation to the restoration of relationship and restitution where necessary. This engages the heart and completes the stages of forgiveness.

Are there situations in which you need to go all the way to heart forgiveness?

SPIRITUAL HEART FOCUS
Ask God for the wisdom and strength to walk through all the stages of forgiveness.

PHYSICAL HEART FOCUS

Flatten your stomach with a combination of strength training, short intense cardiovascular workouts, and good nutrition.

♥ Inventory of the Heart

PSALM 44:21
Would not God search this out?
For He knows the secrets of the heart.

MY DAD HAD A COUNTRY STORE. Periodically, he closed it down, and we'd count every item on hand. The inventory was tedious, tiresome work, but essential for keeping the enterprise profitable.

Invariably, on some hidden shelf, we found a useless product collecting dust. We knew not to spend precious money on restocking that item.

It's important to do an inventory of the spiritual and moral heart. What's in there causing pain, motivating actions, influencing the self and others? The hidden things—such as unresolved resentments, empty beliefs, doubts, and lustful imaginations—crowd out the good and pure.

The only way you find the hidden items is to conduct an inventory. The Holy Spirit knows the back shelves of your heart, and He knows what's there. Allow Him to conduct the inventory.

It's the way to keep your heart profitable.

> **SPIRITUAL HEART FOCUS**
> Ask the Holy Spirit to inventory your heart of the items there that are useless and unprofitable. Make a list in a journal, and repent for each thing.

PHYSICAL HEART FOCUS

If you're a runner, run indoors on a treadmill to avoid extreme weather and air pollution.

❤ The Sluggard's Heart

PROVERBS 13:4
The soul of a lazy man desires, and has nothing;
But the soul of the diligent shall be made rich.

LAZINESS IS NOT JUST ABOUT how hard you work, but what you're willing to work at.

Ironically, a sluggard wholeheartedly craves something good, but the heart is too lazy to do anything about obtaining it!

For example, a man sought counsel about how to attract women. The adviser told him to lose 40 pounds and improve his hygiene. The man kept eating and neglecting his appearance. He enjoyed his self–pity and was too lazy to discipline himself.

Many people work hard at making a living but not on how to live. A sluggard will work feverishly at getting married but not on making a marriage. He or she will do all that's necessary to have children but won't work hard on parenting. The lazy person will strive to be popular but won't work on healthy relationships.

The diligent heart, however, is willing to work for the things it earnestly desires. Rather than merely wishing, such a person takes action. While the sluggard bemoans unfulfilled wishes and poverty, the diligent celebrates success and prosperity.

SPIRITUAL HEART FOCUS

Ask the Lord to raise in your heart the passion for His good things and the determination to "apprehend that for which you have been apprehended" (Philippians 3:12 KJV).

PHYSICAL HEART FOCUS
Take a Vitamin D supplement, especially in winter months.

❤ A Nation's Heart

ISAIAH 51:7

"Listen to Me, you who know righteousness,
You people in whose heart is My law:
Do not fear the reproach of men,
Nor be afraid of their insults."

"BLESSED IS THE NATION whose God is the LORD," says Psalm 33:12. Countries rooted in God's word don't have to fear the scorns, snarls, and derisions of opponents.

The era of terrorism is ablaze with threatenings and revilings. The terrorist age is a test of the hearts of nations. If a people honor God as revealed in the Bible and through their Hero Jesus Christ, they need not succumb to fear.

Not every citizen of a country will honor God. The way a nation makes Him its Hero is by rooting His principles in its heart. Alexis de Tocqueville came to America in the early 1800s to study its successful revolution after living through disastrous upheaval in his native France. In America he discovered a "new state of things" created by the "religious aspect of the country."[13]

SPIRITUAL HEART FOCUS
Pray that America's heart will be centered on God and His word.

As long as the national heart enshrined God's principles, she was safe, even under threat and attack.

PHYSICAL HEART FOCUS

Tell close friends or family about your heart-healthy diet and exercise goals, and report your successes so they can cheer you on.

❤ Snake–Proofing the Heart

ROMANS 16:17–18

Now I urge you, brethren, note those who cause divisions and offenses, contrary to the doctrine which you learned, and avoid them. For those who are such do not serve our Lord Jesus Christ, but their own belly, and by smooth words and flattering speech deceive the hearts of the simple.

SHOCK COLLARS SAVE QUAIL DOGS. A defanged snake is hidden under a bush, and an electric collar is placed on the dog. When the dog catches the snake's scent and pokes under the bush, a slight surge of electricity shocks the dog. After two or three jolts, the dog stays away from snakes.

Unsuspecting people are like the naïve hounds. They are lured easily by the slithering smoothness and glib flattery of people wanting to sink their fangs into their hearts.

Rather than being jolted, it's better to recognize the lairs where the snakes may hide. Such places are marked. Wherever traps are sprung to snare the weak and lead people away from sound biblical truth, a serpent is hiding.

Don't be naïve, but have an alert heart.

SPIRITUAL HEART FOCUS

Ask the Lord to increase your desire for sound doctrine and your alertness to those who would try to draw you into conflicts and traps.

PHYSICAL HEART FOCUS

When walking, jogging, or running at night, wear light–colored clothes with reflectors.

❤ Bamboozled

2 SAMUEL 15:5–6

And so it was, whenever anyone came near to bow down to him, that he would put out his hand and take him and kiss him. In this manner Absalom acted toward all Israel who came to the king for judgment. So Absalom stole the hearts of the men of Israel.

HOW DOES THE HEART get bamboozled?

David's son Absalom, a prince, enslaved people's hearts. Individuals bowed respectfully, and Absalom would say something like, "No, don't bow in front of me; you're my dear friend, not a mere subject!"

To "steal" in the Hebrew means getting something by stealth. People whose hearts throb for the approval of their heroes can get bamboozled.

Jesus Christ is more powerful than the deceiver, so your heart can't be stolen through brute force unless you allow it. You were born into the captivity of sin, but in Christ your sin debt is cancelled, unlocking your chains of servitude.

The only way your heart can be stolen is through bamboozlement. But if you know you are accepted and approved by God through Christ's grace, no trickster will be able to enslave your heart!

> **SPIRITUAL HEART FOCUS**
>
> Are you a master at stealth? Are you easily taken in by the bamboozlers? Ask the Holy Spirit to reveal your points of vulnerability. Confess the sin of using flattery to get people to yield to your wishes.

PHYSICAL HEART FOCUS

When dining out, order an appetizer for the main course.

❤ The Pain of Loss

JOB 2:13

So they sat down with him on the ground seven days and seven nights, and no one spoke a word to him, for they saw that his grief was very great.

HEARTACHE COMES BY DEGREES. Job's friends saw his grief–swathed figure, and they were speechless. His heart was experiencing the deepest degree of pain.

The heartache of human loss is the most intense pain any creature can experience. Job's misery reaches this deepest degree because he has lost his family.

Christ comes to remove the pain of eternal loss. In Revelation 21:1, John reports that ultimately, in Heaven, "there was no more sea." To a man imprisoned on the island of Patmos, the ocean symbolized separation and loss.

> **SPIRITUAL HEART FOCUS**
> In loss, allow the Holy Spirit to comfort your heart with the knowledge that someday you will be in the presence of all you care about the most.

In Heaven, we will have the wonderful peace of the removal of the fear of loss. Because of Christ, we will never again experience that deepest degree of heart pain that comes with separation from those for whom we care the most!

PHYSICAL HEART FOCUS

Regular exercise improves balance in older adults.

❤ When the Heart 'Loses' God

PSALM 139:7
Where can I go from Your Spirit?
Or where can I flee from Your presence?

"Pastor, I've lost God!" the young man cried.

"What happened?" I asked.

"I rededicated my life to Christ," he replied. "I've started reading my Bible and praying more, but God doesn't seem to be there anymore."

Then he told me he had taken a girl to a motel and spent the night with her. "I thought it would be a night of bliss, but it was horrible. And since then I can't find God."

I opened the Bible to Psalm 139. When I read the words, "when I make my bed in hell, behold, thou art there," he began to weep. The student realized that God was there that night, watching and grieving.

We would all overcome temptation much easier if we understood that we meet God in those places where we think we can hide in the darkness.

> SPIRITUAL HEART FOCUS
> Are you experiencing the sense of "losing" God from your heart? The question is not "Where is God?" but "Where are you?" Reach out to Him in confession and repentance. Your heart will find that He never left.

PHYSICAL HEART FOCUS
Dip your bread in olive oil and herbs rather than butter.

❤ Smoking Gun

ROMANS 2:14–15

When Gentiles, who do not have the law, by nature do the things in the law, these, although not having the law, are a law to themselves, who show the work of the law written in their hearts, their conscience also bearing witness, and between themselves their thoughts accusing or else excusing them).

I ACCEPTED CHRIST AS MY SAVIOR at age 11, and have never doubted my salvation.

At college I drifted spiritually, but deep in my heart I knew I still belonged to God. The witness of the Spirit within me was the "smoking gun," the clear proof.

The evidence both defended and accused me. I was assured of my salvation, but I also knew I was guilty of sin. Ultimately, that led me to repentance, and my lifestyle and worldview changed.

God holds us accountable because the "smoking gun" is in every person, even those who reject Him. A person is guilty because the eternal law of God is objective, not subjective. Like the law of gravity, God's law is based not on our feelings, but on the reality of its existence.

The fact that every human being has a sense of right and wrong is the "smoking gun." The evidence can lead us to innocence or guilt. The choice is ours.

> SPIRITUAL HEART FOCUS
> What is the witness of your conscience? Is it your accuser or defender? Receive the grace of Jesus Christ and the witness of the conscience in the cosmic courtroom will defend you!

PHYSICAL HEART FOCUS

Choose a trainer carefully. A good trainer will ask about your medical history.

♥ Great Makeover

2 CORINTHIANS 4:16

Therefore we do not lose heart. Even though our outward man is perishing, yet the inward man is being renewed day by day.

THE LOSS OF HEART IS DISCOURAGEMENT, no hope of improvement.

When I received Christ at age 11, I was not an instant spiritual giant. I could have looked at the godly people I respected and lost heart because of the spiritual growth gap.

But accepting Christ launches the Great Daily Makeover. Gradually, we are transformed into Christ's image (Romans 8:29). This occurs in tiny increments as we fellowship consistently with Him through prayer, His word, and worship.

SPIRITUAL HEART FOCUS
Pray for accelerated spiritual growth and for the encouragement to know that as you commune daily with Christ His makeover is advancing in you.

A wealthy, cultured gentleman adopts a street waif. The day the adoption papers are signed, the boy is in the family. But daily he has to learn how to live as a member of the family. It takes years to transform a kid off the streets into a polished person.

I had eleven years to learn how to be a sinner. I still have a long way to go to measure "to the stature of the fullness of Christ" (Ephesians 4:13), but my heart is encouraged with the fact that daily His makeover of me is progressing!

PHYSICAL HEART FOCUS

Exercise contributes to increased muscle mass and strong flexible bodies.

❤ Intentional Breaking

2 CORINTHIANS 4:7–10

But we have this treasure in earthen vessels, that the excellence of the power may be of God and not of us. We are hard-pressed on every side, yet not crushed; we are perplexed, but not in despair; persecuted, but not forsaken; struck down, but not destroyed—always carrying about in the body the dying of the Lord Jesus, that the life of Jesus also may be manifested in our body.

A TREE IS CUT DOWN, stripped of its bark, and sawn into pieces before it forms the elegant structure of a sailing ship. Granite is blasted, pounded, and cut before it becomes the base of a mighty bridge. A field is slashed and turned over, reborn as the cradle of nourishing grain.

SPIRITUAL HEART FOCUS
Ask God to use all your heartbreaks to heal your heart.

Had trees, stone, and sod the ability to speak, they would report that tribulation is the instrument of transformation.

When the Holy Spirit inspired Romans 5 in his heart, Paul could remember the pride of his lineage, his academic background, and his titles (Philippians 3:4–7). When Jesus appeared to him on the Damascus road, Saul of Tarsus lay in the dust, a blinded, broken man. But the man with a broken heart arose with a healed heart.

The heartbreak you experience can be God's means of deeper healing if you will receive it that way.

PHYSICAL HEART FOCUS

"Good fat" food sources include olive oil, canola oil, and avocados. Add a "good fat" item to your menu today.

❤ About Face

PSALM 51:17

The sacrifices of God are a broken spirit,
A broken and a contrite heart—
These, O God, You will not despise.

IN MILITARY TERMS, there's a big difference between "as you were" and "about face."

A general walks into the room and soldiers snap to attention. But when his presence is informal and he wants the troops to relax, he says, "As you were."

Soldiers also know "about face!" means to turn and go in the opposite direction.

Sometimes people do an "as you were" and call it repentance. They stop committing the sin for the moment. But a contrite heart is one crushed because of its sin to the point the individual eagerly turns and goes in the opposite direction.

"As you were" is the position of the sorry heart, but "about face" is the direction of the contrite heart.

> **SPIRITUAL HEART FOCUS**
> When you ask God for forgiveness, don't pray out of mere regret, but allow the Holy Spirit to break your heart over sin.

PHYSICAL HEART FOCUS

People who eat fish at least once a week have 30 percent lower risk of heart disease.

♥ Hearts on Tiptoe

ROMANS 8:23

Not only that, but we also who have the firstfruits of the Spirit,
even we ourselves groan within ourselves, eagerly waiting for the adoption,
the redemption of our body.

WHAT CAUSES YOU TO stand on tiptoe?

I was late to a basketball game with standing room only. A player on my favorite team was making a crucial shot. At the back of the crowd, I craned to watch, standing on tiptoe, holding my breath.

To "groan," according to New Testament Greek, is breathless expectancy, the eager anticipation that raises you on tiptoe to eyeball what you yearn to see.

Creation is on tiptoe waiting for the manifestation of God's children (Romans 8:19), because when our salvation is consummated at the coming of Christ, the grip of the fall will be broken off from nature.

And even while nature is on tiptoe watching for its redemption, our spiritual hearts catch their breath and look with expectancy for the coming of the Lord.

People with tiptoe hearts have a future they're excited about!

SPIRITUAL HEART FOCUS
Ask the Lord to break through the dullness of your daily routine with the awareness that every tick of the clock brings history closer to the end of the age and the coming of Christ.

PHYSICAL HEART FOCUS
Folic acid supplement is essential to women of childbearing age.

❤ Holy Place or Trash Bin?

MATTHEW 23:27–28

"Woe to you, scribes and Pharisees, hypocrites!
For you are like whitewashed tombs which indeed appear
beautiful outwardly, but inside are full of dead men's bones and
all uncleanness. Even so you also outwardly appear righteous to men,
but inside you are full of hypocrisy and lawlessness."

SCIENTISTS ON A SUBMARINE PLUNGED into one of the deepest parts of the ocean. A searchlight caught a glimmer far away. Eagerly, they steered the craft toward the shining objects, only to discover beer cans!

God didn't intend the magnificent oceans to be a trash receptacle, yet that's how they are used constantly.

The human being is the temple of God, says Paul (1 Corinthians 6:19). The body is the outer court, the soul the inner court. The spirit, symbolized by the heart, is the Holy of Holies, where God is to be enthroned.

SPIRITUAL HEART FOCUS
Use Philippians 4:8 as a prayer guide, devoting your heart to be focused on that which is honorable, right, pure, lovely, and of good reputation.

When you and I take in moral garbage and spiritual perversions, these things litter our hearts like beer cans trashing the sea floor, or, worse, the Holy of Holies being used as a garbage bin!

Watch what you take into your heart, because you may be trashing the holy place.

PHYSICAL HEART FOCUS
When eating at a fast-food restaurant, order a salad or grilled chicken.

❤ Devolution of the Heart

ROMANS 1:21–23

Although they knew God, they did not glorify Him as God, nor were thankful, but became futile in their thoughts, and their foolish hearts were darkened. Professing to be wise, they became fools, and changed the glory of the incorruptible God into an image made like corruptible man— and birds and four-footed animals and creeping things.

EVOLUTION IS THE RELIGION of the secularized world. Utopians believe the path of the race has been ever upward physically, culturally, and spiritually.

Actually, in a fallen world, devolution is the trend. Since the fall, things have been sinking lower and lower.

Spiritual evolutionists used to teach that primitive people were animists who evolved to a higher state, monotheism, the worship of one God.

SPIRITUAL HEART FOCUS

Ask the Father to deal with the idolatry of your heart. Allow the Holy Spirit to reveal your multiple "ultimate" allegiances, and Christ to set you free from them.

Research, however, shows humanity began with the high worship of one God, and since then has devolved into idolatry. Hinduism has thousands of deities. Sophisticated western spirituality also has plummeted into polytheism, the worship of many gods, especially in occultism and New Age religion.

When a fallen human being returns to the worship of the true and living God, the devolution of the heart halts, and Christ lifts it upward!

PHYSICAL HEART FOCUS

Pushups and situps can be done easily at home to work the chest, triceps, and abdominal muscles.

❤ The Heart Harp

PSALM 9:1

I will praise You, O LORD, with my whole heart;
I will tell of all Your marvelous works.

PSALM 138:1

I will praise You with my whole heart;
Before the gods I will sing praises to You.

WE ARE HERE TO BE WORSHIPERS first and workers second.

God put the universe together with purpose, and there's not one useless thing anywhere. God created humans to be worshipers.

If we don't accept our high mission the very stones will cry out! (Luke 19:40) God created us in His image for fellowship, and the zenith of fellowship is worship.

This is why God gave us a heart. The human heart is a many-stringed instrument, covering the widest range of chords. When we sin, we take this glorious harp and hurl it into the mud, where it lies rusted, broken, unstrung.

Jesus Christ comes and picks up the heart-harp, cleanses it from the mire and restrings it. Through His Spirit, the music returns to the heart.

The worship comes first because the work done by a worshiper will have eternity in it.

> SPIRITUAL
> HEART FOCUS
> Choose psalms that express worship to God, and word them into your own expressions of worship, praise, and gratitude.

PHYSICAL HEART FOCUS

Buy some fresh fruit, place it in an attractive bowl or plate, and have it readily available when the craving for a snack hits.

♥ Dressing Down

EZEKIEL 16:10, 14–16

*"I clothed you in embroidered cloth and gave you sandals of badger skin;
I clothed you with fine linen and covered you with silk. . . . Your fame went
out among the nations because of your beauty, for it was perfect through
My splendor which I had bestowed on you," says the Lord GOD. . . .
"But you trusted in your own beauty, played the harlot because of your
fame, and poured out your harlotry on everyone passing by who would
have it. You took some of your garments and adorned multicolored high
places for yourself, and played the harlot on them. Such
things should not happen, nor be."*

SPIRITUAL HEART FOCUS
Does darkness shroud your heart? Are you trying to substitute religious behavior, legalism, ritual, and reputation for the garments of light? Ask God to strip off the darkness and robe your heart in His light.

IN THE BEGINNING, God clothed our hearts in the light of His holiness and wisdom.

When we rebelled against God, we ripped off the garments of glory and dressed down, exchanging robes of light for rags of darkness.

We have a yearning for the bright garments, but we want to design them ourselves.

Herod Agrippa dressed appropriately for his worst and last day. He swathed himself in a royal robe, a cheap imitation of the garment of light, and accepted the flattery that hailed him as a god. At that moment, the worms in his body penetrated vital organs, and Herod collapsed into a putrid death (Act 12:21–23).

When we receive Christ Jesus, we are clothed in Him (Galatians 3:27). To be arrayed with Christ means the heart is dressed again with the garment of light!

PHYSICAL HEART FOCUS

Increase the servings of fruits or vegetables in your diet daily.

❤ Belief's Big Test

ROMANS 10:10

For with the heart one believes unto righteousness,
and with the mouth confession is made unto salvation.

"YOU DON'T KNOW WHAT you really believe in until you're confined to a bed in a hospital," said the seriously ill woman.

"What do you mean?" the pastor asked.

"You get your meaning in life from being excessively attractive or by working. I don't look good anymore, and I can't get up and work."

When you're flat on your back, your true belief emerges. If your gods go on vacation when you have a crisis, they are false.

The heart is the core of belief. Real life springs up from the believing heart— life that doesn't fade under fire or lose its faith in a hospital room.

Hope and faith that stand up when you are flat on your back prove the validity of the belief in your heart!

SPIRITUAL
HEART FOCUS
Ask God to enlarge
your heart's capacity for trust
in Him, and then to pour
in more faith.

PHYSICAL HEART FOCUS
A strong, flat stomach can mean a strong lower back.

❤ Tune Out the 'Anxiety Frequency'

ISAIAH 35:4
Say to those who are fearful–hearted,
"Be strong, do not fear!
Behold, your God will come with vengeance,
With the recompense of God;
He will come and save you."

ANXIETY IS LISTENING to the static in your heart. The cure for the anxious heart is getting its dial set precisely on God's frequency.

Stress generates static. The heart–dial set on God floods the psyche with the awareness that God is in charge, and what we can't handle, He can.

> **SPIRITUAL HEART FOCUS**
> Think about each concern for anxiety in your life. What does God's Word say about them? Pray Scriptures that express God's truth relating to your specific anxieties.

Physically, anxiety causes high blood pressure, crazy fluctuations in the heartbeat, and cardiac arrest. Anxiety takes aim at the spiritual heart, too, causing it to feel rising pressures of doubt and even a shut–down of faith.

To squelch the static, first take courage, "be strong." That means grabbing hold of God's promises and refusing to turn loose. Second, "do not fear!" Don't let fear drown out faith. Finally, recognize that God will fight for you. Even if you are in the middle of tribulation, He will rescue you.

Get the heart on God's frequency, and the static of anxiety fades.

PHYSICAL HEART FOCUS
Begin your day with a cup of high–fiber cereal low in sugar.

❤ Not Built to Collapse

1 CORINTHIANS 15:21–22

For since by man came death, by Man also came the resurrection of the dead. For as in Adam all die, even so in Christ all shall be made alive.

DEATH WAS MAN'S "GIFT" to himself. God didn't design the heart to get sick and die. Human beings introduced decay and death into the world through their rebellion.

Albert Speer, Hitler's architect, said Hitler ordered him to design massive structures according to the theory of "ruin value"—what a building or monument might look like after centuries.

Human beings can try to disguise death and decay, but the reality is that "in Adam all die."

But Christ brings a new quality of life to the human heart. This life spans the material world and the spiritual world. A person who has Christ continues to have His life even when he's lying in an intensive care unit with a flat line on a brain scan.

> SPIRITUAL HEART FOCUS
> Celebrate today the fact that although Adam brought you death, you are reborn in Christ, who brings you life!

The new heart Jesus brings us is not designed according to the theory of ruin value, because it experiences no ruin, no decay, just the constancy of His vibrant life surging within.

PHYSICAL HEART FOCUS

Cardio workouts done properly will increase your metabolism, contributing to weight loss.

♥ Overcoming Vertigo

ISAIAH 5:20

Woe to those who call evil good, and good evil;
Who put darkness for light, and light for darkness;
Who put bitter for sweet, and sweet for bitter!

PILOTS ARE SUBJECT TO VERTIGO, a confusion of the horizon. Up is perceived as down and down as up.

Disaster results from vertigo.

Sometimes the moral and spiritual heart experiences vertigo.

The cultural horizon seems to change. What was once good is deemed evil and vice versa.

SPIRITUAL HEART FOCUS
Pray for the nation, that she will find her way back to God's truth to overcome cultural vertigo.

Pilots must make a crucial choice to trust either their instruments or their senses. The dials show objectively that the plane is flying upside down. Yet the pilot feels he's right–side up. His subjective experience tells him one thing and the objective instruments another.

God's Word is the instrument that will keep us on the right course, in the right position, and at right altitude, and the Word will save us from death itself!

Trust the truth, not your confused heart.

PHYSICAL HEART FOCUS

Vegetarian dieters can get protein from nuts and beans and cheese.

❤ Where the Heart Can Stand

PHILIPPIANS 4:1

Therefore, my beloved and longed–for brethren,
my joy and crown, so stand fast in the Lord, beloved.

To STAND FIRM WE MUST use big truth in everyday places and apply cosmic principles in contemporary situations.

That means we must train our hearts to sense the whole sweep of eternity in the mundane events of the routine world.

Towers can be toppled, but the cross still stands. Candidates and movements come and go, but the age–old Gospel rises over people and nations, invulnerable to the assaults of intellectual, cultural, and physical persecution.

Today's shallow society doesn't want to look at the big questions. The preference is for the bottom line of the ten easy steps to a "new you." But the ten easy steps are carved out of mud. When the rains come, they wash away.

For stability, the heart must stand on the ten truths carved into stone.

SPIRITUAL HEART FOCUS
Allow the Holy Spirit to reveal the shaky places where you may be trying to stand. Establish your stand in each of these areas on His revealed truth.

PHYSICAL HEART FOCUS

If you have previous knee injuries, check with your physician before beginning weightlifting exercises.

❤ Hearts Full of Questions

PROVERBS 15:28
The heart of the righteous studies how to answer,
But the mouth of the wicked pours forth evil.

SOME QUESTIONS ARE INNOCENT, seeking information. Others are rhetorical, designed to make a point. Then there are questions intended to snare and trap.

Good people ask good questions for good reasons. Evil people use questions to cast doubt and undermine.

Philosophers, from good and bad hearts, ask big questions such as, "If God is good, how can there be pain?" This is like a four–year–old asking why Mommy and Daddy just stand by while a doctor gives her a painful shot. The parent has the big picture the child's heart cannot yet grasp. The child may be confused momentarily, but knows deep inside her mommy still loves her.

SPIRITUAL HEART FOCUS
It's time to turn over your unanswered questions to God. Don't let them be a barrier to trusting Him. Rest in the promise that you will know even as you are known (1 Corinthians 13:12).

Unanswered questions do not negate God or His love. They simply mean the heart does not yet have the capacity to understand the answers. One should never abandon faith simply because all the heart's questions cannot be answered.

PHYSICAL HEART FOCUS
Decrease or eliminate trans fats from your diet.

❤ Note to the Heart

NEHEMIAH 7:5

Then my God put it into my heart to gather the nobles, the rulers, and the people, that they might be registered by genealogy. And I found a register of the genealogy of those who had come up in the first return.

WHEN I DATED JO BETH, I wrote her little notes, signed "Luv ya!"

They were aimed at her heart, because if the heart's not in it, there is no romance.

God aimed at Nehemiah's heart, assigning him a job requiring much passion. If Nehemiah's heart wasn't in such a huge task, he wouldn't succeed.

Literally, God fastened His direction to Nehemiah's heart. I wrote Jo Beth notes because I wanted her to think constantly of my love. She could fasten the scraps of paper to her diary, or paste them on her mirror.

> **SPIRITUAL HEART FOCUS**
> What has God put into your heart to do that is yet undone? Ask for strength and opportunity to accomplish God's will.

When God puts a note in your heart's mailbox, it's fastened there. The motivation to do His will is persistent. When you do wrong, the note is there in the form of your conscience. When you do right, God's note is there, confirming your actions.

Heed the note God fastens to your heart!

PHYSICAL HEART FOCUS

When you are in a rush, carry fruit or a healthy protein bar for a snack.

❤ Tangled Passions

1 JOHN 2:15–16

Do not love the world or the things in the world. If anyone loves the world, the love of the Father is not in him. For all that is in the world—the lust of the flesh, the lust of the eyes, and the pride of life—is not of the Father but is of the world.

SOMETIMES THE HEART'S PASSIONS get as tangled as a jungle.

A man married a widow with an adult daughter. Then the man's father wed the widow's daughter, which made the first man's stepdaughter his stepmother and his wife the mother–in–law of her father–in–law. Then the first man's stepdaughter, who was also his stepmother, had a son. That meant the child was his wife's grandson, which made the man grandfather of his half–brother!

SPIRITUAL HEART FOCUS
Recommit yourself in prayer to the priority of God and His Kingdom in your life.

Such confusion characterizes people who want to love God but at the same time give their hearts to the world. They attempt to set their hearts on loving God, who is Spirit, while also being passionate about the flesh.

The way to untangle your passions is to center your heart on God. As Jesus said, "Seek first the kingdom of God and His righteousness" (Matthew 6:33).

PHYSICAL HEART FOCUS
An exercise secret: Do a little and do it often.

❤ The Loving Cup

EPHESIANS 3:17–19

That Christ may dwell in your hearts through faith; that you, being rooted and grounded in love, may be able to comprehend with all the saints what is the width and length and depth and height—to know the love of Christ which passes knowledge; that you may be filled with all the fullness of God.

"MY HEART'S A LOVING CUP," a friend tells his kids.

"Daddy, how's your loving cup?" his little daughter asks. "Almost empty," he replies. She begins hugging him, and he says, "It's getting fuller and fuller!" Finally he shouts, "My loving cup is full again!"

Some people drain our cups. Thank God for the "filling people." Family members should be fillers of one another, not drainers. Relationships in the church ought to fill us, not empty us.

Ultimately, it is Jesus Christ Himself who fills us to the top. Once, while healing a woman, the Bible says Jesus felt the power flowing out of Him (Mark 5:30). But Jesus knew how to keep His loving cup full. Daily, He communed with the Father, getting energized for the works of compassion ahead.

Your loving cup gets drained every day, too, so go daily to the Lord and ask Him to fill you up.

SPIRITUAL HEART FOCUS
Are you a "drainer" or a "filler"? Ask God to help you be the kind of person who pours love and encouragement into others.

PHYSICAL HEART FOCUS
To help you feel full, eat more vegetables.

❤ Two Hearts, One Benefit

ECCLESIASTES 4:9–10
Two are better than one,
Because they have a good reward for their labor.
For if they fall, one will lift up his companion.
But woe to him who is alone when he falls,
For he has no one to help him up.

JO BETII AND I HAVE TWIN GRANDDAUGHTERS who are alike in many ways but with markedly different hearts. One has a heart for fun and the other for perfectionism. Miss Perfection puts away her pencils, arranges the food on her plate by careful categories, and makes her bed neatly. Miss Fun is the opposite. She goes through life merrily, leaving scattered papers, a jumbled closet, and wrinkled sheets in her wake. Two different hearts, sharing the same bedroom.

Some parents might conclude one type is right, the other wrong, and attempt to remold one child's heart into the type of the other.

Actually, two hearts in one relationship should benefit one another. Our cut–up can learn seriousness from our perfectionist, and our perfectionist can be taught by our cut–up how to lighten up.

If you are in a relationship with someone whose heart beats to a different drum than yours, try to learn from him or her rather than allowing the varying hearts to spark conflict.

> **SPIRITUAL HEART FOCUS**
> Ask God to help you learn from people in your life whose personalities, interests, and expressions differ from yours.

PHYSICAL HEART FOCUS
Do your ab workout at the end of your exercise routine, right before you stretch.

❤ The Tongue Reveals the Heart

JAMES 1:26

If anyone among you thinks he is religious, and does not bridle his tongue but deceives his own heart, this one's religion is useless.

"STICK OUT YOUR TONGUE!" Dr. Gatlin commanded when I was a child, because it told him about my health. Spiritually, that's also true. The tongue, the way we speak, reveals the condition of the heart.

To be "religious" means to be ceremonious and pious. So here comes Mr. Sanctimonious or Ms. Pious, smug in the confidence that they are the community's nearest thing to God. Everyone in their path who knows them scampers out of the way, lest they get blistered by flamethrower tongues!

Their gullible hearts swell with devout confidence of their superior spirituality when, in fact, their religion is meaningless to them and unprofitable to everyone else.

They stick out their tongue and it tells all.

> **SPIRITUAL HEART FOCUS**
> Who have you wounded with your sarcasm, criticism, or angry words? Seek God's forgiveness, ask Him for the way and opportunity to express your sorrow, and ask people's forgiveness.

PHYSICAL HEART FOCUS
Substitute artificial sweeteners for sugar.

♥ Going Through the Motions

MATTHEW 13:15

"'For the hearts of this people have grown dull.
Their ears are hard of hearing,
And their eyes they have closed,
Lest they should see with their eyes and hear with their ears,
Lest they should understand with their hearts and turn,
So that I should heal them.'"

THE DULL HEART MERELY GOES through the motions.

I heard a preacher say he could stand in the pulpit and preach in his sleep. Thank God that's not true for most preachers I know.

Unfortunately, it's not only a few preachers who lose their fire; some people who sit in the pews do too. They hear sermons and religious platitudes for so long their hearts become dull and coated with layers of sluggishness. They go through the motions of religion.

SPIRITUAL HEART FOCUS
Pray for spiritual breakthrough in your life, your church, and your world.

But when the heart gets sharp, it understands. People with sharp hearts put together all they've heard and read, and they see what was once invisible to them. The Gospel makes sense. They get the meaning of speech that was once a foreign language.

When the heart understands, we no longer merely go through the motions. Instead, there is spiritual breakthrough and revival!

PHYSICAL HEART FOCUS

When beginning as a runner, ease in with a half–mile or mile walk and some stretching prior to the run.

❤ Heart Prayers

PSALM 17:1–3

Hear a just cause, O LORD,
Attend to my cry;
Give ear to my prayer which is not from deceitful lips.
Let my vindication come from Your presence;
Let Your eyes look on the things that are upright.
You have tested my heart;
You have visited me in the night;
You have tried me and have found nothing;
I have purposed that my mouth shall not transgress.

A FAMILY SAT DOWN for Sunday dinner. "O God," prayed the daddy, "thank you for our church and pastor and all our blessings, amen." During the meal the children listened as the man criticized everything for which he had just thanked God.

"Daddy," his small daughter interrupted, "did God hear you when you prayed a few minutes ago?" The dad replied, "Yes, of course."

The little girl showed confusion. "Did He also hear what you were just praying when you were talking to Mommy?" Now the daddy was confused. "Uh, I guess so."

"Then which prayer did God believe?"

The lips pray deceitfully when their words contradict the heart.

> **SPIRITUAL HEART FOCUS**
> Consider that your speech may contradict your prayers. Repent and ask God to help you always be consistent in speaking to others what you speak to Him.

PHYSICAL HEART FOCUS
Choose a certified, experienced trainer.

❤ Building on a Lie

PSALM 78:38
But He, being full of compassion, forgave their iniquity,
And did not destroy them.
Yes, many a time He turned His anger away,
And did not stir up all His wrath.

FUDGE THE SPECS IN CONSTRUCTING a building and the whole thing may tumble down.

After the 1906 San Francisco earthquake, a commission was appointed to study why the city was so devastated. It was discovered that more damage was done because buildings were not constructed according to code specifications than by the earthquake directly! Lies were hidden in the footings, foundations, and frames, and the buildings couldn't stand the shaking.

> **SPIRITUAL HEART FOCUS**
> Are you "on again, off again" in your commitment? Do you fudge God's principles in your daily lifestyle? Are you full of anxiety? Ask God to help you be steadfast in faith.

The Psalmist says the Hebrews in the wilderness had lies in their hearts. They murmured against God, refusing to trust Him. God had promised to care for the Hebrews if they would entrust themselves to Him. But again and again, they broke their side of the covenant.

The way to have a stable life amid tremors of crisis is to have a consistent commitment that trusts in God no matter what. Such devotion honors His Word and builds according to His "specs."

PHYSICAL HEART FOCUS

Experiment with different healthy food combinations to discover the diet plan that works for you. Check your weight and BMI.

August

Jesus Christ is the
Liberator of the heart.

❤ The Mute Heart

JEREMIAH 4:19

O my soul, my soul!
I am pained in my very heart!
My heart makes a noise in me;
I cannot hold my peace,
Because you have heard, O my soul,
The sound of the trumpet,
The alarm of war.

A WORKER FELL PARTIALLY INTO a vat of hot lead. "Get a doctor . . . call an ambulance!" his workmates screamed.

"It's too late for a doctor. Can anyone tell me about God?" the injured man begged.

Three hundred people were ready to save the man's life physically, but no one could tell him how to meet God, said a man who saw the accident. "Then why didn't you tell him?" his friend asked. "I couldn't," the man replied. "Those men have heard me cuss and lose my temper. . . . My life closed my lips."

> SPIRITUAL
> HEART FOCUS
> If you encountered a situation today in which you had mere moments to prepare a person to meet God, could you do it? Ask God to strengthen the witness of your heart, behavior, and voice.

Jeremiah was the opposite. His heart could not be mute. It pounded with the passion to tell people the truth, to warn them of judgment, to point them to salvation.

When you know God's good news your heart can't remain mute. That's why it's important to have a life that won't close your lips!

PHYSICAL HEART FOCUS
The best remedy for muscle soreness is rest.

❤ Profaning Heart

LEVITICUS 22:32

"You shall not profane My holy name, but I will be hallowed among the children of Israel. I am the LORD who sanctifies you."

"GOD" AND "JESUS" ARE PROFANED constantly on television and in movies, thereby proving, in an indirect way, the truth of the Gospel.

No one ever shouts "O Buddha!" or "Holy Mohammed!" Cursing is driven by the powers of darkness that loathe hearing people speak reverently of Jesus and God. So the devil and his demons love to hear people speak these names irreverently.

When a person uses God's name—including "Jesus"—profanely, he or she is saying, "I'm not even afraid of God." It was He who commanded that His name not be used in vain, and people who do so openly show that their hearts have no reverence for God and His Law.

SPIRITUAL
HEART FOCUS
Spend time today blessing
God's Name in all its forms
identified in the Bible.

PHYSICAL HEART FOCUS
A reasonable weight-loss goal is two pounds per week.

❤ Drunk Heart?

1 SAMUEL 1:13

Now Hannah spoke in her heart; only her lips moved,
but her voice was not heard. Therefore Eli thought she was drunk.

"HANNAH" HAS GOTTEN A BAD WRAP in contemporary lingo, associated with being hardhearted. Even back in biblical times she was wrongly labeled!

SPIRITUAL HEART FOCUS
Seek God for the resolute strength to live for Him, even when others criticize and misjudge you.

The mother of Samuel was a pure woman. One day she was praying in the depths of her heart, and her mouth moved with the silent expressions within. Eli, the priest, concluded she was drunk.

Eli added two and two and got five, and in doing so he revealed two things: his own lack of discernment and the low state of worship in that period, when drunks might indeed have been at the altar.

If your heart is passionate for God, people will misjudge and mislabel you. Immature people delight in being "misunderstood." Don't try to be controversial and mislabeled. But neither let people's opinions quench the passion of your heart for God.

PHYSICAL HEART FOCUS
For snacks, eat fruit and fresh–cut veggies.

♥ Opening the Heart

ACTS 13:48–49; 16:14

Now when the Gentiles heard this, they were glad and glorified the word of the Lord. And as many as had been appointed to eternal life believed. And the word of the Lord was being spread throughout all the region. . . . Now a certain woman named Lydia heard us. She was a seller of purple from the city of Thyatira, who worshiped God. The Lord opened her heart to heed the things spoken by Paul.

ON ONE SIDE OF HEAVEN'S GATES is a sign, reading, "Whosoever will may come." The other side bears the words, "Chosen from the foundation of the world."

Paul preached the Gospel at Antioch, and the Bible reports that people rejoiced, and those who had been appointed believed (Acts 13:48). "Appointed" means assigned to a particular place. God enrolled those who believed in His Book of Life (Revelation 21:27).

People can't believe in something unless they've heard about it. Those we "nominate" through our witness, God "elects."

God Himself opens hearts to belief. Our mission is not to batter down the doors of people's hearts, but to announce Christ's salvation to them. That's the meaning of "preach" or "proclaim."

Don't hold back your witness because you don't know the elect. Your mission is to share; God's work is to open the heart.

SPIRITUAL HEART FOCUS

Ask God to lay on your heart specific people with whom you need to share the Gospel, and to give you the opportunity and strength to do so.

PHYSICAL HEART FOCUS

Plan a reward for yourself for reaching your weight-loss and exercise milestones.

❤ Liberator of the Heart

LUKE 4:18–19

"The Spirit of the LORD is upon Me,
Because He has anointed Me
To preach the gospel to the poor;
He has sent Me to heal the brokenhearted,
To proclaim liberty to the captives
And recovery of sight to the blind,
To set at liberty those who are oppressed;
To proclaim the acceptable year of the LORD."

JESUS CHRIST IS THE LIBERATOR of the heart!

In the inaugural speech beginning His earthly ministry, Jesus quoted the prophetic words given through Isaiah to lay out His platform.

Jesus' plan is based on what God has done in history, the forgiveness now available for us, and the liberation that comes when we accept God's work of breaking our shackles.

SPIRITUAL HEART FOCUS
Consider the bondage of your heart without Christ and praise Him for setting you free.

When through faith we claim Christ's righteousness, we are assured of His love and are freed to love God, ourselves, and others. When we know God is pleased with us out of sheer grace, we're on top of life.

As the French and Italians poured into the streets to welcome their liberators after World War II, let's cheer joyfully and receive with open arms our great Liberator, Jesus Christ!

PHYSICAL HEART FOCUS

Decreased caloric consumption plus exercise is essential for weight loss.

♥ Mysteries of the Heart

1 CORINTHIANS 4:1

*Let a man so consider us, as servants of Christ
and stewards of the mysteries of God.*

MYSTERY LIES AT THE CORE of my heart.

I can't explain why God would love and use an average, small–town guy, sitting on a stump at the University of Alabama, struggling with his personal identity and destiny. Many people had more ability and talent or were more "churchy" in their lifestyles. Yet God was kind and gracious, and He chose me for both eternal life in Christ and service as a pastor.

That reinforces to me that I am here only by His grace and kindness.

The greatest mystery was not penned by Sir Arthur Conan Doyle or Agatha Christie, but by the Holy Spirit. We're inspired to wonder why God would love the world, and why, specifically, He would love you and me!

> **SPIRITUAL HEART FOCUS**
> Ponder the way you are managing the mystery of salvation granted to you, and ask God to help you be an effective steward of His mysteries.

Whether or not we understand it, we are stewards—earthly keepers—of that mystery, and we are responsible for sharing it with others. Don't wait for your heart to understand. Share the mystery of God's love with someone today!

PHYSICAL HEART FOCUS

Enjoy nonfat frozen yogurt topped with fresh fruit as a sundae alternative.

♥ When the Heart Yearns to Tell

ACTS 18:24–26

Now a certain Jew named Apollos, born at Alexandria, an eloquent man and mighty in the Scriptures, came to Ephesus. This man had been instructed in the way of the Lord; and being fervent in spirit, he spoke and taught accurately the things of the Lord, though he knew only the baptism of John. So he began to speak boldly in the synagogue. When Aquila and Priscilla heard him, they took him aside and explained to him the way of God more accurately.

WHEN YOUR HEART AWAKENS to God's love and grace, it becomes fervent in spirit, and it yearns to tell others the good news.

I read a letter to a popular newspaper advice columnist in which the writer was complaining about a pushy friend. This friend apparently was a new believer who was trying to "convert everybody she knows." The columnist advised the letter writer to tell the zealot to shut up or leave.

SPIRITUAL
HEART FOCUS
Ask the Lord to help you
witness with effectiveness,
not with a style that drives
people away.

Sometimes our passion to tell can prevent us from being heard, but there are important principles for sharing the Gospel that should govern us all. First, be sensitive to timing. Know when to share and when to be silent. Second, listen. Be patient with people's questions and concerns. Third, watch for the strategic moment the Holy Spirit will bring about.

When the heart yearns to tell, the greatest priority should be to be heard.

PHYSICAL HEART FOCUS

Munch a celery stick with a tablespoon of reduced–fat natural peanut butter.

♥ Really Important Stuff

ACTS 16:9–10

*And a vision appeared to Paul in the night. A man of Macedonia stood
and pleaded with him, saying, "Come over to Macedonia and help us."
Now after he had seen the vision, immediately we sought to go to Macedonia,
concluding that the Lord had called us to preach the gospel to them.*

GOD'S WAY IS ALWAYS INSIDE OUT, bottom–up.

Emperor Claudius was sleeping as the most important thing to
happen in his reign occurred. Miles away, a sleeping Paul saw the form of
a man bidding him to come to Macedonia—Greece—with the Gospel.

From the heart of the Father to the yearning Macedonian to
the heart of the willing Jew went the call. It led to the
moment when the good news of Christ moved from
the Middle East westward.

The biblical view that would produce the
great democracies began its journey that night.

That's the way the really important stuff
happens in the world—from God's heart to a
yearning human heart to the willing heart of
another person.

Nero fiddled while Rome burned, and Claudius
slept while the Gospel blazed in human hearts. Don't let your heart be
caught sleeping when God calls.

SPIRITUAL HEART FOCUS

What yearning has God placed
in your heart? What work
has God given you passion to
do? Yield to God's call
in your heart.

PHYSICAL HEART FOCUS

Squeezing a tennis ball will increase strength in your forearm and grip.

❤ When the Heart Fasts

MATTHEW 6:16–18

"Moreover, when you fast, do not be like the hypocrites, with a sad countenance. For they disfigure their faces that they may appear to men to be fasting. Assuredly, I say to you, they have their reward. But you, when you fast, anoint your head and wash your face, so that you do not appear to men to be fasting, but to your Father who is in the secret place; and your Father who sees in secret will reward you openly."

PHARISEE HEARTS LOVED FANFARE. They whitened their faces to make themselves look gaunt so everyone would admire their "spirituality."

Flaunted "religion" flourishes today. You see it in religious types who contrive sacred–sounding speech, activists sacrificing for the rainforest, politicians advertising their concern for the little guy, and celebrities rationalizing support of indecency as free speech.

SPIRITUAL HEART FOCUS
Consider a fast from electronic media. Ask the Lord for guidance in carrying it out and for clarity in hearing Him.

It might be appropriate to fast physically now and then, but there ought to be a more frequent fast of the heart. One way is through an electronic media fast. Our church was challenged years ago to lay off media for a certain period. That meant the glut of mindless programming was laid aside. Hearing God rather than talking heads became the priority. Heart–fasting is truly secret, but it becomes evident in your enhanced countenance and witness.

PHYSICAL HEART FOCUS

Chew sugarless gum while preparing meals to help you resist temptation to sample.

❤ Religious Spirit

ACTS 16:16–18

Now it happened, as we went to prayer, that a certain slave girl possessed with a spirit of divination met us, who brought her masters much profit by fortune-telling. This girl followed Paul and us, and cried out, saying, "These men are the servants of the Most High God, who proclaim to us the way of salvation." And this she did for many days. But Paul, greatly annoyed, turned and said to the spirit, "I command you in the name of Jesus Christ to come out of her." And he came out that very hour.

THE HEART CHARACTERIZED BY a religious spirit is vulnerable to toxic faith.

That was the sad case of the young woman Paul encountered at Philippi. Paul was annoyed by her because he could see her heart and that the devil was working a subtle plot through her.

Satan loves to hide in religion, one of his most insidious inventions. He disguises himself as an angel of light so he can worm his way into a person's confidence (2 Corinthians 11:14). Ultimately, the devil wants to take over, and uses religion to gain a foothold in people's hearts.

> **SPIRITUAL HEART FOCUS**
> Ask for discernment to see when your own heart is manifesting a religious spirit rather than the Holy Spirit, as well as the ability to recognize it in others.

The religious spirit robs true faith of its credibility and misrepresents Christ and His Gospel of grace. If you're "religious," get over it and become a true disciple in relationship with Jesus Christ.

PHYSICAL HEART FOCUS

To save money and calories when you eat out, get one entrée and share it with your dining partner.

❤ Setting the Heart's Course

PROVERBS 23:12

Apply your heart to instruction,
And your ears to words of knowledge.

THERE COMES A POINT when each of us must choose the heart's direction. To not choose is itself a choice to drift meaninglessly through life.

Applying our hearts to discipline means we set our course on a straight line toward a specific goal.

As a college freshman, my heart drifted spiritually. But a voice whispered inside, "There's something I want you to do." At two o'clock one morning the quiet voice became a roar. I fell on my knees and prayed, "Lord, I give you all that I am and all that I'll ever be."

SPIRITUAL HEART FOCUS
Is it time to set or redirect the course of your heart to conform to God's will? Even if you don't understand the specifics of His will, commit your ways to Him and He will establish your paths.

Ultimately, that would mean changing my school, major, and career. The new course of my heart sent me out under new disciplines, new instructions.

I've doubted a lot of things, but I have never been uncertain of that defining moment in my life when the course of my heart was set.

Say "yes" to God's call on your life, and the course of your heart will be established.

PHYSICAL HEART FOCUS

Check into resistance–band training as a good low–impact exercise plan. Consult with a gym or your trainer.

❤ Heart Shapers

But now, O LORD,
You are our Father;
We are the clay, and You our potter;
And all we are the work of Your hand.

SIGNIFICANT PEOPLE IN OUR LIVES are the hands
God uses to give shape to our hearts.

Many of my teachers had little confidence I
could accomplish anything, but Miss Edwards
looked at me and believed in me. She saw
something in my heart not even I knew was
there. John Christmas, a coach in junior high
school, also was one of the instruments God
used to sculpt my heart.

The enemy of our souls has his tools and shapers,
too. Their aim is to mar the beauty of God's image in us.

But the special people who believe in us and encourage us to our best
are led by the Holy Spirit as they chisel away and shape our hearts.
Sculpting is always a violent business. We might think of these people
with twinges of pain because they disciplined us. But without them you
would be missing some of your best qualities.

SPIRITUAL HEART FOCUS
Thank God for the people He has used to shape your heart. Ask Him to use you effectively to shape the hearts of others in your care.

PHYSICAL HEART FOCUS
When dining at a restaurant, avoid creamy dressings. Instead, order a light dressing
on the side.

♥ Dead Flies

ECCLESIASTES 10:1

Dead flies putrefy the perfumer's ointment,
And cause it to give off a foul odor;
So does a little folly to one respected for wisdom and honor.

FOOLISHNESS IN THE HEART is like dead flies in perfume.

You order a glass of iced tea and lemon in a restaurant. You add sweetener and stir. Suddenly, you spy an object in the little tempest. On close examination, you see it's not a lemon seed, but a fly! You give the waiter the tea glass, pointing out the fly. The waiter takes a spoon, flips out the fly carcass, and gives you back the glass. But you demand a fresh glass of tea. The presence of the fly corrupted the whole thing.

In Ecclesiastes, Solomon tells us that a silly indiscretion spoils a life's reputation. A teenager goes on a joyride in a stolen car, and the mistake tracks him for life. A shopper bags a twenty-dollar T–shirt, and she is labeled a thief the rest of her days.

Make wise choices now. Don't let a single fly land in your heart. It will pollute your entire life.

SPIRITUAL
HEART FOCUS
Ask the Lord to help you
make wise choices.

PHYSICAL HEART FOCUS
You commit to a total heart healthy lifestyle, but you must renew the choice daily.

♥ Get Your Heart Right

ECCLESIASTES 10:2

A wise man's heart is at his right hand,
But a fool's heart at his left.

IN EIGHTEENTH–CENTURY FRANCE, representatives in the National Assembly loyal to the king and status quo sat on the right, and those advocating change sat on the left.

The idea sticks today in the designation of the two wings of political thought.

But political divisions are not the focus of Solomon in Ecclesiastes. Throughout the Bible, the right side of the spectrum symbolizes good choices and the left, evil. In Latin, the word for "left–handed" means "sinister," while that for "right–handed" signifies dexterity.

The Latin labels are unfortunate. Bill Clinton and George Bush are both left–handed, as is my wife, Jo Beth. "Sinister" certainly would not describe her!

In Matthew 25, Jesus speaks of the last judgment and says the sheep, those blessed for eternity, are assigned to the right, while the "goats," destined for judgment, are to the left.

So get your heart right spiritually, and you won't be left behind!

> **SPIRITUAL HEART FOCUS**
> To get your heart right before God, you must make the choice to steer it toward Him in every situation. Pray for wisdom and strength to do that.

PHYSICAL HEART FOCUS

Instead of orange juice for breakfast, eat one whole orange. It is digested slower.

❤ Bottom Feeders

HEBREWS 13:9
Do not be carried about with various and strange doctrines.
For it is good that the heart be established by grace, not with foods
which have not profited those who have been occupied with them.

BOTTOM FEEDERS ARE SCAVENGERS who range the floor of a body of
water, looking for food from every unsavory source.

People in certain jobs are considered bottom feeders when they search
for profit in the mire of human life.

Spiritually, a bottom feeder gobbles up
strange teachings. No matter how contradictory to
truth an idea might be, the bottom–feeding heart
finds it tasty. Bottom feeders delight in the alien
and exotic, no matter how destructive those are.

SPIRITUAL HEART FOCUS
Ask for wisdom not to be attracted to ideas, concepts, and trends just because they are exotic or novel.

The bottom–feeding heart goes to
ever–darker levels, from depravity to sensuality
and from rationalization to rebellion. Finally,
it goes so deep into the murkiness that the
bottom–feeding heart gets stuck in the mud.

The opposite of the bottom–feeding heart is one
nourished by grace. The ingredients of grace include the bitterness of
acknowledging sin and the sweetness of God's forgiveness.

Grace is found down at the bottom of life, too, but it carries hearts to
the top!

PHYSICAL HEART FOCUS
Make changes in your resistance exercise program every six to eight weeks to stay
fresh and avoid boredom.

❤ Eager Heart

2 CORINTHIANS 8:16

But thanks be to God who puts the same earnest care
for you into the heart of Titus.

THE EARNEST HEART IS FULL OF ZEAL. Harness that eagerness, and God can do powerful things through you.

Eagerness alone actually can be misleading. Paul wrote about folks who had zeal without knowledge (Romans 10:2). They were the bulls in the spiritual china closet, wrecking themselves and everything in sight. Many a cultist has died over empty zeal.

The person zealous for God will see only one thing: pleasing God.

Some people are zealous for themselves. Years ago, I eagerly signed up for a golf tournament, wanting to play in the championship group, but I quickly found out my zeal for myself was overinflated.

> **SPIRITUAL HEART FOCUS**
> Set your heart through prayer to an eagerness to glorify God and serve others in Jesus' name.

God put a special eagerness of heart into Titus. This is the zeal of serving God through ministering to others. Empty eagerness causes you to be zealous for your own benefit, while God's zeal gets you directed toward Him and others.

PHYSICAL HEART FOCUS
Risk of heart disorder in women begins to increase in menopausal years.

❤ Focusing the Heart Outward

JOHN 4:35

"Do you not say, 'There are still four months and then comes the harvest'? Behold, I say to you, lift up your eyes and look at the fields, for they are already white for harvest!"

"WHY WOULD A CORPORATION pay this man $100,000 a year to look out the window?" read an ad depicting a man peering out his office window.

It's easy to turn a heart inward. Judas betrayed Jesus because the devil was able to manipulate Judas's personal agenda, the focus of his heart. Earlier, the hearts of some of the other disciples had gotten self–focused, and they quibbled over their positions beside Jesus' throne in Heaven.

SPIRITUAL HEART FOCUS
Repent of the sin of self–focus, and ask the Lord to fill your heart with vision for the needy world.

But their hearts returned to Jesus' agenda.

Jesus grabs self–absorbed hearts and holds them up to the window of the world. He shows these hearts the fields where they should focus. The fields are heavy with hurting people, seeking people, and confused people who all need Jesus.

The only antidote for the inwardly turned, self–absorbed, self–destructive heart is to focus outward.

Allow Jesus to show you the world as He sees it.

PHYSICAL HEART FOCUS
A no–brainer: Use a cup of skim milk rather than a cup of whole milk.

❤ The Hollow Heart

NAHUM 2:10

She is empty, desolate, and waste!
The heart melts, and the knees shake;
Much pain is in every side,
And all their faces are drained of color.

AFTER A HURRICANE RIPPED our city in 1983, I walked my neighborhood and looked at the many downed trees. I was surprised that pines I thought would snap still stood, while some big oaks I thought would stand had been destroyed. The oaks fell because insects had been eating at them for years, and they were hollowed out.

In the verse above, the Prophet Nahum considers the city of Nineveh, once so pumped up in her arrogance. But evil has eaten out her core, and she is hollow. She melts like a hollow wax form.

SPIRITUAL HEART FOCUS

Allow God's Spirit to reveal little things eating at your heart, and ask for Christ's blood to remove them.

This is a picture of the human heart that allows sin to snack on its interior. Gradually, small sins erode the substance, and the heart is an empty vessel with no strength to stand when the winds of testing come.

Get the bugs out of your heart. Fill it with God's truth and its inner strength will be restored.

PHYSICAL HEART FOCUS

Split your exercise routine rather than exercising your whole body every time.

♥ Lovingkindness

PSALM 69:16–17

Hear me, O LORD, for Your lovingkindness is good;
Turn to me according to the multitude of Your tender mercies.
And do not hide Your face from Your servant,
For I am in trouble;
Hear me speedily.

KINDNESS MAKES THE HEART HAPPY, but lovingkindness makes it celebrate! Salvation is the demonstration of lovingkindness. In Christ, God removes our guilt. But then He goes beyond that and gives us Christ's innocence. The guilt–cleansed heart is happy, but the innocence–given heart positively rejoices.

SPIRITUAL HEART FOCUS
Make a list of God's lovingkindnesses extended to you, then spend time celebrating. Praise Him for His specific mercies in your life.

When the Psalmist faced scary threats and passed through shaky times, he leaned on the lovingkindness of God. Long before the New Covenant of grace, the Holy Spirit lit the heart with the light of God's mercy.

That's what David relied on and it is why he could rejoice, although he had every human reason to be miserable.

Lovingkindness means God spreads on mercy when we fear that all we will get is justice.

PHYSICAL HEART FOCUS

Don't put anything in your pantry that tempts you to say, "I can't stop with just one!"

❤ On Your Back or Heart?

PHILIPPIANS 1:7

Just as it is right for me to think this of you all, because I have you in my heart, inasmuch as both in my chains and in the defense and confirmation of the gospel, you all are partakers with me of grace.

YOU CAN CARRY PEOPLE on your back or you can hold them in your heart.

Those on your shoulders are burdensome, but if God puts someone in your heart, the load is a blessing.

For example, Paul regarded the people he brought to Christ as his spiritual children. Like anybody's kids, they sometimes were burdens to him. Yet because God had placed Paul's spiritual children in his heart, he was still grateful for them.

People say occasionally, "I'm so burdened about this person. Would you visit them?" I always know when someone is carrying another person on their shoulders, because they will attempt to shift the burden.

But when God places someone in their heart, usually the individual will say, "Please, pray for me that I can really help this person."

We may try to offload the people on our shoulders, but we must be willing to carry the people God puts in our hearts.

SPIRITUAL HEART FOCUS

Think about the people for whom you are responsible or concerned. Ask God to take them off your shoulders and put them in your heart.

PHYSICAL HEART FOCUS

Be careful not to lock your joints while weight training.

♥ The Dry Heart

PSALM 143:6

I spread out my hands to You;
My soul longs for You like a thirsty land.

"MY PREACHER IS SO DRY I would be scared to strike a match around him," a man told me once.

Most of us, not just preachers, experience times when our souls are as parched as a desert floor under a summer sun on a cloudless day.

"Parched" means languid, dull, low in energy, full of weariness and boredom. When your passion is flat–lined, you're suffering from dry heart.

David said his cure was to "spread out my hands," meaning he prayed.

When our hearts are dry, praying is not high on our priority list. Neither does a thirsty person feel like digging a well, but the well is the way to the water that quenches the thirst.

When the heart is dry, don't try to dredge up a religious prayer. Set aside some time to wait in God's presence. Immerse yourself in worship of the Most High. Stretch yourself out before Him so you can get rained on!

SPIRITUAL
HEART FOCUS
Are you suffering the symptoms of a dry heart? Allow the Holy Spirit to water your heart through worshipful prayer.

PHYSICAL HEART FOCUS

Rather than ordering a side of beef when eating out, order the four–ounce to six–ounce cut of lean meat or try the fish.

❤ Waterholes in the Desert

ISAIAH 57:15

For thus says the High and Lofty One
Who inhabits eternity, whose name is Holy:
"I dwell in the high and holy place,
With him who has a contrite and humble spirit,
To revive the spirit of the humble
And to revive the heart of the contrite ones."

IN A PARCHED DESERT, the best chance for water is found in the low places.

This helps us understand better why Jesus congratulates "those who mourn" (Matthew 5:4). You don't get refreshed until you get low.

This is because God dwells both at the highest place and also in the lowest spot—the humbled human heart.

Down there in our depression and despair, God can fill us up at last.

> **SPIRITUAL HEART FOCUS**
> If you are broken or depressed, ask God to fill you up with His Spirit. Pray for others you may know who are broken and depressed.

For both the broken and depressed, God promises revival. When His children sink to the lowest place, their hearts become like waterholes in a desert, able to hold the refreshing rain of God's very being.

So if you're currently broken and depressed, you are to be congratulated. You're at the place where God can pour His life into you afresh.

PHYSICAL HEART FOCUS

An upper–body twist is a good stretch. Place your hands on your hips, slowly turn to the left and hold the stretch for 10 counts, then repeat to the right. Do this 5 times in sequence.

❤ Tap Dance

PROVERBS 14:13-14

Even in laughter the heart may sorrow,
And the end of mirth may be grief.
The backslider in heart will be filled with his own ways,
But a good man will be satisfied from above.

SOME PEOPLE TRY TO DANCE their way through life, concealing their hearts full of pain. Their laughter is meant to drown out the dirge playing in their hurting hearts.

Most often, suggests the proverb, the heart suffers pain because of backsliding. A backslider is someone who once knew God and His ways but turned and traveled back into a lifestyle of unbelief. He gets all he wants, only to find it's grief.

SPIRITUAL HEART FOCUS

If you are in a backslidden condition, repent and return to the Lord. If not, ask God to keep you on His straight path.

The person who stays faithful is satisfied. Rather than the tap dance that disguises the pain, the faithful man or woman waltzes from the joy that arises from the heart of peace.

Are you tap dancing to hide your pain, or waltzing from the joy inside?

PHYSICAL HEART FOCUS

If swimming is your workout choice, begin with 15 minutes twice weekly and gradually increase to 45 minutes two times a week.

❤ Repair Job

PSALM 147:3

He heals the brokenhearted
And binds up their wounds.

OUR HOME AIR–CONDITIONING SYSTEM went on the blink. The repair company sent two servicemen who came in a truck loaded with state–of–the–art equipment. But the repair guys discovered they didn't have the tools to fix our particular problem!

So it is with the broken heart. Philosophy tries a mend but can't get the repair to hold. Psychology lathers the broken heart with goo, but the lotion dries and cracks and reopens the heart–tear. Religion attempts the fix but fails to mend the heart.

The answer is not an idea, strategy, or program, but a Person. Jesus of Nazareth said He had come to heal the brokenhearted. His repair job stays fixed, as many happy customers can testify across time and eternity.

SPIRITUAL HEART FOCUS

Even if you are brokenhearted today, by faith give the Lord thanks and praise for the mending of the heart.

PHYSICAL HEART FOCUS

Substitute heart–healthy seasonings and spices for salt.

❤ The Ostentatious Heart

JAMES 5:4–5

Indeed the wages of the laborers who mowed your fields, which you kept back by fraud, cry out; and the cries of the reapers have reached the ears of the Lord of Sabaoth. You have lived on the earth in pleasure and luxury; you have fattened your hearts as in a day of slaughter.

THE PERSON WHO FATTENS HIMSELF through oppressing others is someone who lives luxuriously, strutting wealth flamboyantly even though the riches have come by denying fair wages to those who labor for them. The man or woman with an ostentatious heart experiences wanton pleasure, enjoyment that denies and ignores injustice.

Right in the middle of Edinburgh, Scotland, there is a lush green pasture. Sheep turned loose in that emerald expanse could romp in the delight of being in such a rich field. But the pasture actually is the waiting place for sheep to be slaughtered.

God's heart is stirred with indignation when people are unjust. They may think they are being fattened in a huge green pasture, but in truth they walk ostentatiously to judgment.

SPIRITUAL HEART FOCUS

Consider those for whose welfare you are responsible. Are you making sure they are treated fairly? Ask God to give you wisdom to know how best to care for them.

PHYSICAL HEART FOCUS

Work out your abdominal muscles at least three times a week.

❤ Chosen

COLOSSIANS 3:12–14

Therefore, as the elect of God, holy and beloved, put on tender mercies, kindness, humility, meekness, longsuffering; bearing with one another, and forgiving one another, if anyone has a complaint against another; even as Christ forgave you, so you also must do. But above all these things put on love, which is the bond of perfection.

IT'S AN AWESOME THING TO REALIZE God has chosen you to receive a new heart.

Mrs. L. G. Gates, my pastor's wife, led me to Christ at age 11. My mother insisted I go to Vacation Bible School. Mrs. Gates was our teacher. One day as I lined up with other kids, she pulled me aside and helped me receive Christ.

To be chosen of God means to be pulled out from the human mass to be given the heart of salvation.

God isn't exclusivist any more than Mrs. Gates. When she yanked me from the line, she was not rejecting all those other children. She simply saw my readiness to receive the Savior. God's choosing us is based on His foreknowledge (Romans 8:29). He knows those who will receive Him, so He leads them out of the crowd and gives them each the gift of a new heart.

> **SPIRITUAL HEART FOCUS**
> Thank God for choosing you. Thank Him that His choice of you was not because of your merit but because of His divine grace. Thank Him for giving you a willingness to respond to His call.

PHYSICAL HEART FOCUS

When dining out, choose steamed or grilled foods.

♥ The Magnanimous Heart

EXODUS 35:5

"'Take from among you an offering to the LORD. Whoever is of a willing heart, let him bring it as an offering to the LORD: gold, silver, and bronze.'"

THE MAGNANIMOUS HEART is one that gives lavishly and cheerfully, the kind described in Exodus 35:5. As Moses gathers resources for construction of the Tabernacle, he looks for people with extraordinarily generous hearts.

SPIRITUAL HEART FOCUS
How would you rate your giving? Ask the Lord to nurture a magnanimous heart within you.

The giving heart matures through grades like a child advancing in school. First comes miserly obligation, then dutiful faithfulness, followed by willing obedience, moving to happy generosity, arriving at the peak of cheerful magnanimity.

Few people are born with a magnanimous heart. This extraordinary heart develops and grows. Moses knew when he called for contributions that there would be some who would dash forward, wanting to be first to give to God's work.

Developing your heart to magnanimity is a worthy goal. It's an indication of spiritual growth.

PHYSICAL HEART FOCUS

Trim the visible fat from your meat before you cook or eat it.

❤ How to Deflate a Heart

COLOSSIANS 3:21

Fathers, do not provoke your children, lest they become discouraged.

A FRIEND OF MINE PLAYED on a college football team that challenged ex–professionals. The old pros ran up a score of 78–3. No one on the college team wanted to carry the ball.

Finally, the college players staggered to the scrimmage line, hunkered down in their stance, and began singing "Amazing Grace." They hoped the hulking ex–pros would back off and show them mercy!

If your spouse, kids, employees, associates, or friends need to beg you for mercy, it's a sign you are deflating their hearts. When that happens, they are robbed of all motivation and cast into hopelessness like a bunch of college boys playing against NFL warriors.

Don't deflate the hearts of the people you ought to be pumping up with encouragement.

SPIRITUAL HEART FOCUS
Ask the Lord to give you the wisdom and discernment to be an encourager, not an exasperator.

PHYSICAL HEART FOCUS
When you first use weights or exercise machines, have your trainer show you proper technique.

♥ In a Rut

ECCLESIASTES 11:9–10

Rejoice, O young man, in your youth,
And let your heart cheer you in the days of your youth;
Walk in the ways of your heart,
And in the sight of your eyes;
But know that for all these
God will bring you into judgment.
Therefore remove sorrow from your heart,
And put away evil from your flesh,
For childhood and youth are vanity.

"GET IT WHILE YOU CAN!" is the cynical advice of Ecclesiastes. Solomon looked at his life of prosperity, power, and prestige, and he declared it meaningless and valueless. So with vinegary sarcasm he says, "Live it up! You're going to die and face judgment anyway . . . Have fun while you can!"

A hedonist world does just that, and in old age it is bitter and regretful like Solomon.

Paul's philosophy was better. "For to me, to live is Christ, and to die is gain" (Philippians 1:21). Since Paul met Jesus Christ his heart had never known a rut. He knew he was a winner whether he lived or died, and that made his heart pulse with joy.

SPIRITUAL HEART FOCUS

If your heart is in a rut spiritually, it's time to move into new stages of growth and service for Christ and His Kingdom. Ask God to provide the opportunities, no matter what your age.

PHYSICAL HEART FOCUS

For variety, take time to research and plan healthy menus rather than just eating what's available.

♥ The Bold Heart

PROVERBS 28:1

The wicked flee when no one pursues,
But the righteous are bold as a lion.

A YOUNG MAN IN OUR CHURCH went up in a hot air balloon. Then, far above the ground, he leapt out at the end of a bungee rope. His heart sought adventure.

People whose hearts are bent on evil lose their boldness after awhile. They spend their lives looking over their shoulders. They jump at the slightest breeze.

But hearts increasingly conformed to God's character increase in their boldness. Jim DeLoach, one of my associates, fought in World War II and was a daring young man. But Jim, in his seventies as I write, has a spiritual faith that outstrips his youthful heart in valor.

Decades of trusting God, entering difficult situations with enlarging faith, has brought this old soldier of God to lionlike boldness.

SPIRITUAL HEART FOCUS
Venture for God into situations that will require enlarged faith and courage, and ask God for the increase of boldness.

PHYSICAL HEART FOCUS

Be bold: Try a Pilates class or yoga (combining meditation on the Bible).

❤ Watch for Deception

DEUTERONOMY 11:16
Take heed to yourselves, lest your heart be deceived,
and you turn aside and serve other gods and worship them.

THE FUNDAMENTAL TEMPTATION is power, to be king of your own life.

The adversary works feverishly at shoving God off the thrones of individual human lives, and he attacks devoted disciples by using stealth.

One tactic is allurement. The enemy knows how to snare people with ego, past hurts, resentments, and bitterness, which is why it's important to allow the Lord to cleanse our hearts.

SPIRITUAL HEART FOCUS
Pray for wisdom to discern the devil's subtle tactics to deceive you.

The adversary also loves using enticements. The devil convinces some people that he can offer a better deal, which is what he was trying to do with Jesus in the wilderness.

The enemy also will employ flattery. He will inflate our egos so we soar on our own puff to the heights, where we run out of fuel and plummet into disaster.

Stay on guard. As you journey with Christ, don't let the enemy snare your heart.

PHYSICAL HEART FOCUS

Have fun with your diet. Eat 90 percent healthy foods and 10 percent fun foods as you begin. To increase weight loss, reduce the percentage of fun foods. Check your weight and BMI.

September

Relationships are harmonized
when hearts are tuned to God.

❤ Variations of the Heart

PHILIPPIANS 4:2
I implore Euodia and I implore Syntyche to be of the same mind in the Lord.

RELATIONSHIPS ARE HARMONIZED when hearts are tuned.

Euodia meant "success," and *Syntyche* meant "lucky." These women not only had different names, but different hearts that sometimes collided.

All churches and groups have people whose hearts beat differently. There are "thinker" hearts that love contemplating and analyzing ideas. "Feeler" hearts like tenderness, tears, and hugs.

SPIRITUAL HEART FOCUS

Think of someone whose gifting and style is unlike yours. Pray God's blessing on that person, and ask the Lord to help you work in harmony with him or her.

Paul didn't ask Euodia and Syntyche to live in *uniformity*, but in *harmony*. We should not force everyone to be alike, but to work together to make the variations symphonic.

In an orchestra this is done not by making all the instruments a cello, but by all the musicians playing their various instruments and focusing on one conductor. Variations of the heart can make beautiful music by following the Lord as the Maestro!

PHYSICAL HEART FOCUS

Include a fitness break in your daily planner, and do simple exercises during the day.

❤ Bridge to Belief

ROMANS 10:10

*For with the heart one believes unto righteousness,
and with the mouth confession is made unto salvation.*

As a young man, I dreamed of building bridges. When God called me to preach the Gospel, my desire for bridge building didn't die, but changed.

The human heart is a bridge on which you move from no faith to great faith. Drive out on that bridge, and its sturdiness can hold you up.

The heart–bridge leads you to saving faith, the place where you begin your journey the moment you believe in Jesus Christ as your Savior.

That means the heart–bridge also leads you to progressive faith, resulting in righteousness. Once you cross the heart–bridge to belief, you are on a pilgrimage of growth in Christ, by which God can transform you into His very character.

SPIRITUAL HEART FOCUS

If you haven't crossed the bridge of belief, do so today by receiving Christ as your Savior. If you have crossed the bridge, ask the Lord for strength and direction to continue the journey of faith.

PHYSICAL HEART FOCUS

Examine your eating preferences and seek out behaviors that spark your craving for too much food.

♥ The Hijacked Heart

1 KINGS 11:3–5

And he had seven hundred wives, princesses, and three hundred concubines; and his wives turned away his heart. For it was so, when Solomon was old, that his wives turned his heart after other gods; and his heart was not loyal to the LORD his God, as was the heart of his father David. For Solomon went after Ashtoreth the goddess of the Sidonians, and after Milcom the abomination of the Ammonites.

THE CAPTAIN WAS WEARY from the long voyage and drained from trying to restrain a mutinous crew. He dozed off in the wheelhouse, and the rebellious sailors hijacked the ship.

Similarly, Solomon as a young man had walked in the best steps of his dad, David, but through the years he married wives with idolatrous mutiny in their hearts. As Solomon dozed spiritually, they were able to redirect his heart, his spiritual rudder.

SPIRITUAL HEART FOCUS
You may be slowing down physically, but ask the Lord to help you not to slow down in your devotion to Him.

There are mutinous influences around us that would hijack our hearts and redirect them toward gods who are no gods at all. Just as Solomon's wives gained entry to his house, rebellious factions invade our hearts through media, poorly chosen relationships, and selfish ambitions.

Stay on the alert throughout life. Don't come this far in faith only to have your heart turned away from the true and living God!

PHYSICAL HEART FOCUS

Procrastination gives time for weight to go up and fitness to go down. So if you haven't started the journey toward total heart health, begin today.

❤ The Squeezed Heart

PSALM 33:14–15

From the place of His dwelling He looks
On all the inhabitants of the earth;
He fashions their hearts individually;
He considers all their works.

WHEN GOD FASHIONS A HEART, He "squeezes" it into shape, which is the literal meaning of the Hebrew word in the Psalm.

As infants inside our mothers, we don't choose the design of our physical heart. But we do have to decide about the second formation of the heart.

The first forming is for temporal function, but the second is for the heart's eternal operation. We each choose freely whether or not we will allow the Lord to fashion our hearts spiritually.

The spiritual heart, as the physical, cannot function without God's squeezing. We cannot make it beat through our religious efforts, good deeds, or moral behavior. Like a surgeon reaching inside a person's chest and squeezing a heart until it beats on its own, God gets our spiritual heart going.

Squeezing is often uncomfortable, but there's no life without it!

SPIRITUAL HEART FOCUS
Ask God to continue to shape your heart according to His design and purpose.

PHYSICAL HEART FOCUS

You are God's property, put here for a mission. Don't let the enemy take you from the world before your work is done. Be a good steward of the body God's given you.

❤ The Whole Enchilada

PSALM 86:11–12

Teach me Your way, O LORD;
I will walk in Your truth;
Unite my heart to fear Your name.
I will praise You, O Lord my God, with all my heart,
And I will glorify Your name forevermore.

AT A SQUABBLING POLITICAL CONVENTION, factions plot to undo one another. They are all in the same party, but with radically different agendas. So it is with your heart and mine. One facet of the heart wants to do God's will, and another wants to resist it.

> **SPIRITUAL HEART FOCUS**
> Yield all the factions of your heart to God and bring them under the dominion of reverence for Him and His holiness.

David asks the Lord to unify all these vying factions for one mission, that of fearing the Lord. That means every agenda of the heart must be focused on honoring and reverencing God and His Word.

When that happens, the lust faction has to go, the doubt group is banished, the deceivers are kicked out, and the grudge–holders are silenced. The united heart is not fragmented. It experiences God's peace, which is true heart health.

PHYSICAL HEART FOCUS

If you feel you've stalled on a plateau, don't get discouraged. This is a natural part of your progress.

❤ Extreme Surgery

HEBREWS 4:12–13

*For the word of God is living and powerful, and sharper than any
two-edged sword, piercing even to the division of soul and spirit, and of
joints and marrow, and is a discerner of the thoughts and intents of the
heart. And there is no creature hidden from His sight, but all things are
naked and open to the eyes of Him to whom we must give account.*

IN OPEN-HEART SURGERY the heart is shut down, the blood
detoured, the chest laid open, and the heart cut.

Not all of us need a physical cardiac operation,
but we do all need spiritual heart surgery.

God's Word lays out the heart. The
Scripture says "all things are open and laid bare
to the eyes of Him with whom we have to do"
(Hebrews 4:13 NASB).

God's word also purifies and cauterizes.
"Is not My word like a fire?" God asks, rhetorically
(Jeremiah 23:29). Rationalizations leading to heart
sickness are burned away through the searing of His truth.

Allow God's Word to do spiritual heart surgery to you *daily*!

SPIRITUAL
HEART FOCUS
Ask God to help you apply His
Word to your heart daily.

PHYSICAL HEART FOCUS

Obesity is an epidemic, with 60 percent of Americans overweight or obese.
Extract yourself from that statistic.

❤ When God Takes Pleasure

PSALM 149:4

For the LORD takes pleasure in His people;
He will beautify the humble with salvation.

A COUPLE ADOPTED TWO ORPHANS. One child's face was marred by deformity, so corrective surgery was performed. It took time for the scars to disappear from the orphan's face, but her new mother saw beauty instantly.

The human heart was deformed and afflicted by sin. God's glory in us was marred. But the Psalmist says God "beautifies" the afflicted, restoring the glory through Christ. That beauty can only increase as we grow in Christ.

At this moment, if you have Christ's salvation, you are beautiful in God's eyes. Let that sink in, and your view of yourself will be transformed with new confidence.

SPIRITUAL
HEART FOCUS
Thank God for making your heart beautiful in His sight through Jesus Christ.

PHYSICAL HEART FOCUS
Make nuts part of your diet by adding them to salads or snacks.

♥ The Willing Heart

EXODUS 35:4–5

And Moses spoke to all the congregation of the children of Israel, saying, "This is the thing which the LORD commanded, saying: 'Take from among you an offering to the LORD. Whoever is of a willing heart, let him bring it as an offering to the LORD: gold, silver, and bronze.'"

I AM BLESSED TO HAVE A WIFE with a heart yielded to the Lord.

Jo Beth wholeheartedly has embraced my role as a pastor, and her role as a pastor's wife. When we've moved from one church to another, she's always supported my decision and followed willingly wherever God has led.

We always seemed to move from larger churches to smaller. "If God is calling you, I will go," Jo Beth has said.

The willing heart will make sacrifices to follow God's call. Jo Beth's heart has never questioned her Master's authority. Only that kind of heart will experience the joy along the journey of faith.

SPIRITUAL HEART FOCUS

Do you measure everything by material standards or by God's will? Commit yourself to trusting Him even when things seem not to make sense.

PHYSICAL HEART FOCUS

When you dine out, choose menu items that are broiled or roasted.

❤ 'Tank Oo'

1 THESSALONIANS 5:18

In everything give thanks; for this is the will of God in Christ Jesus for you.

It was a thrill each time one of our toddler grandchildren said, "Tank oo!"

God's heart takes pleasure in the gratitude of our hearts, not because He is petty and needs us to thank Him constantly, but because of what it does for us. We were happy to hear the gratitude of our grandchildren because we knew that attitude was essential for their wellbeing. The grateful person is a positive, healthy person.

Grateful people also are folks who receive blessings. Every good thing we have is a gift of God (James 1:17). The grateful heart is humble, and the humble heart is willing to receive God's gifts.

The real test of a grateful heart is when you don't feel thankful. Learn to say "Thank you, Lord" when things aren't going the way you want. The Bible doesn't say, "*feel* thankful," but "*give* thanks."

SPIRITUAL HEART FOCUS
Thank God for things for which you feel gratitude. Then thank Him by faith for those for which you don't yet have the feeling of gratefulness.

PHYSICAL HEART FOCUS

Eat more foods that are low on the glycemic index. For example, eat an apple rather than drinking apple juice.

❤ Cooperating with the Thief

JOHN 10:10

"The thief does not come except to steal, and to kill, and to destroy. I have come that they may have life, and that they may have it more abundantly."

IT MIGHT BE SMART to hand over your purse or wallet to a gun–toting thief, but it's sheer stupidity to cooperate with a known scammer.

The devil usually doesn't commit armed robbery; instead, he uses schemes (Ephesians 6:11). This thief wants to rob you of physical life. He is not only a robber, but a murderer also (John 8:44). You are born with purpose from God, and if the devil can kill you, he eliminates a key person who could have reached family, neighbors, and friends for God.

The devil will try to con the life out of you by tempting you to neglect your physical health. Overeating, lack of exercise, and other heart-killing pleasures are in his bag of tricks to murder you and terminate your purpose.

SPIRITUAL HEART FOCUS
Spend time in prayer and with your Bible and journal. Consider reordering your priorities.

Take care of yourself. You are important or God wouldn't have put you here. Don't fall for the devil's scams!

PHYSICAL HEART FOCUS

Repent if you are neglecting your physical health, and commit to a healthy lifestyle.

♥ Accomplices

PSALM 18:3–4

I will call upon the LORD, who is worthy to be praised;
So shall I be saved from my enemies.
The pangs of death surrounded me,
And the floods of ungodliness made me afraid.

IN HIS ASSAULT ON THE HEART, the devil has many accomplices, "floods of ungodliness."

Don't blame the devil and his demons when you fail to care for your physical and spiritual heart, because *you* decide whether or not to be taken in by such scams.

However, the devil and his accomplices are at the *root* of the theft of health and life.

SPIRITUAL HEART FOCUS
Call on the Lord to save you from the enemy and his "floods of ungodliness."

One accomplice is lust, the longing to please the flesh rather than God. James says lust births sin and sin brings death (James 1:14–15).

Another accomplice is fallen culture, the world system. This ally of the devil hits you in three ways: the lust of the flesh, lust of the eyes, and the pride of life. All this, writes John, is "of the world" (1 John 2:16).

If we open the door of our hearts to the con artist's accomplices, they will strip the heart of all its God–given riches.

PHYSICAL HEART FOCUS

Your need for protein intake is in direct proportion to body weight, not gender. It can be altered for exercise.

♥ How to Beat the Thief

JAMES 4:7

Therefore submit to God. Resist the devil and he will flee from you.

To STOP THE DEVIL'S RUN on your heart, first get serious about the threat and be alert to what the enemy is trying. In youth we think we are invincible, and we flirt with the destroyer's schemes. But Peter says we should stay alert because the old lion never stops prowling, watching for any sign he could snatch our lives (1 Peter 5:8).

Second, dress for success in the battle for your heart. Put on God's whole armor from head to toe "so that you will be able to stand firm against the schemes of the devil" (Ephesians 6:11 NASB). God hasn't left you defenseless. Dress for warfare!

Finally, send the cheater packing. "Resist" means to "stand against" and "oppose." If you are submitted to Christ, you have that authority. Order the thief who would rob your heart of its health and life to get lost!

SPIRITUAL HEART FOCUS

Repent if you have a victim attitude. Ask God for the insight, courage, and faith to take responsibility for resisting the devil's assaults on your health.

PHYSICAL HEART FOCUS

Drinking water has great benefits, like no calories and no caffeine.

♥ Risk Factors, Part 1

JAMES 4:8

Draw near to God and He will draw near to you. Cleanse your hands, you sinners; and purify your hearts, you double-minded.

DOUBLE-MINDEDNESS IS A CONDITION negatively impacting heart health. Conflict of values and desires brings stress to the heart physically, emotionally, and spiritually.

Heredity also can threaten the health of the spiritual heart as much as it threatens the physical. For example, you might have grown up in a home where you were robbed of parental approval, and your heart bears the scars. But whatever the damage done, your heart can be healed if you focus now on who you *are* in Christ, not who you *were*.

SPIRITUAL HEART FOCUS
Ask God to purify you of the risk factors listed today.

Spiritual neglect affects heart health. God never stops calling us, but life's activities and demands can distract us from His voice. God says, "I stretched out my hand and no one paid attention; and you neglected all my counsel and did not want my reproof" (Proverbs 1:24–25 NASB).

When you get rid of the risk factors, you secure the health of your heart.

PHYSICAL HEART FOCUS
Eat fish twice weekly.

❤ Risk Factors, Part 2

PROVERBS 7:10, 18–19

And there a woman met him,
With the attire of a harlot, and a crafty heart. . . .
"Come, let us take our fill of love until morning;
Let us delight ourselves with love.
For my husband is not at home;
He has gone on a long journey."

THE RISKS TO TOTAL HEART HEALTH are seducers, luring us into destructive behavior.

Poor spiritual diet seduces us. We need a balanced meal, not faith that we gulp down like fries from a drive–thru. We need "meat," not just "milk" (1 Corinthians 3:2).

SPIRITUAL HEART FOCUS
Ask God for strength to see through the devil's seductions and escape the risks.

Also risky is a spiritually sedentary lifestyle. The spiritual couch potato is a person who does not work out salvation through ministry (Philippians 2:12). The spiritual muscles aren't developed, leaving the heart weak and vulnerable to disease.

Fear of failure is a health risk. Even the Apostle Paul acknowledged he hadn't arrived spiritually; he wrote that he pressed on in the goal of God's call (Philippians 3:13–14). Don't let your imperfect behavior stop you from growing.

Silence the voice of the seducer. Get rid of the risks to your heart's health!

PHYSICAL HEART FOCUS

When you're at a Chinese restaurant, order the steamed entrées. Also, eating with chopsticks will slow you down and give you the chance to feel more satisfied.

❤ Codebreaker

PSALM 44:20–21
If we had forgotten the name of our God,
Or stretched out our hands to a foreign god,
Would not God search this out?
For He knows the secrets of the heart.

DURING WORLD WAR II the Allies unraveled German codes.

Human beings attempt to conceal idolatries and other sins in complex deceptions. Achan defied the ban on the spoils of Jericho and tried to hide his thievery (Joshua 7). Ananias and Sapphira attempted to conceal their holding back of a promised gift (Acts 5).

Achan brought defeat to Israel, and Ananias and Sapphira's deception led to their own deaths.

SPIRITUAL HEART FOCUS
Ask the Father to probe the depths of your heart, expose your secrets, and help you walk in truth.

God breaks our codes and reads our secret communications. He doesn't do this because He likes to catch us doing something wrong or because He wants to deny us privacy. Rather, God knows that the secrets we hide in our hearts will destroy us. He brings them to light, and in doing so He saves us from ourselves.

PHYSICAL HEART FOCUS
If you're a couch potato, move your stationary bike or treadmill into your TV room.

❤ What's Under the Hood?

1 CORINTHIANS 4:5

Therefore judge nothing before the time, until the Lord comes, who will both bring to light the hidden things of darkness and reveal the counsels of the hearts. Then each one's praise will come from God.

OUR CHURCH HAS A CAR REPAIR MINISTRY. Volunteers fix automobiles for people, such as single moms, who might not be able to afford service for their vehicles. A car may be running, but making an odd noise. The mechanic knows that even though the engine seems to be functioning, he must discover what's really going on under the hood.

When God searches our hearts, He lifts the hood and examines the motives that energize our actions. Outwardly, our lives may be running smoothly, but God can detect the early signs of dysfunction.

When God works on the engines in our hearts, He discovers the wrong reasons driving our behaviors and He transforms them into the right motives that produce excellent actions.

SPIRITUAL HEART FOCUS

As God continues examining your heart, ask Him to reveal your impure motives and cleanse you of them.

PHYSICAL HEART FOCUS

Keep a slice of orange and a glass of water beside your bed if you're a late-night muncher.

♥ Raising the Heart

EZRA 7:9–10

On the first day of the first month he began his journey from Babylon, and on the first day of the fifth month he came to Jerusalem, according to the good hand of his God upon him. For Ezra had prepared his heart to seek the Law of the Lord, and to do it, and to teach statutes and ordinances in Israel.

"PUT UP YOUR FLAG for Jesus!"

Once I gave that invitation and a Jewish man, one of our city's top chefs, responded. "All I know is I just wanted to put up my flag for Jesus," he said later.

Ultimately, he left the restaurant business and became a pastor in our church.

SPIRITUAL HEART FOCUS
What flag is raised in your heart? Seek God for the courage to let your banner wave everywhere for Christ and His Kingdom.

When Ezra set his heart to study God's word, the literal meaning is that he stood his heart in a perpendicular position. Ezra's heart was the pole flying the banner of God's truths.

Maybe it's difficult to think of your heart as a flagpole, but when you raise the banner of Christ in your heart, everyone will know what you're about!

PHYSICAL HEART FOCUS

Exercise can relieve some symptoms of mild depression and stress.

❤ The Heart–Robe

COLOSSIANS 3:12–13

*Therefore, as the elect of God, holy and beloved, put on tender mercies,
kindness, humility, meekness, longsuffering; bearing with one another,
and forgiving one another, if anyone has a complaint against another;
even as Christ forgave you, so you also must do.*

SINK INTO A SOFT WOOL ROBE on a winter's morning and you will grasp
what it means to put on the heart that reflects Christ and blesses others.

The weave of this heart–robe is of five strands.

Compassions, or tender mercies, are sincere,
heartfelt understandings of the suffering and need
of others.

Kindness is integrity in dealing with people.

Humility is modest behavior, not the
strangling chord of bravado and self–exaltation.

Gentleness, or meekness, is pure silk; it's both
strong and soft.

Patience, or longsuffering, holds up under stress
and stays steady under annoyance.

When you weave a heart–robe of this rich yarn, you'll be
warm and so will all the hearts you touch.

> **SPIRITUAL
> HEART FOCUS**
> After praying, jot down in your
> journal some situations that
> demand these five traits and
> your plans for dealing with the
> situation or person in a
> Christlike way.

PHYSICAL HEART FOCUS

Stop eating when you first begin to feel satisfied, not stuffed.

♥ Capacity to Grieve

LAMENTATIONS 2:19

"Arise, cry out in the night,
At the beginning of the watches;
Pour out your heart like water before the face of the Lord.
Lift your hands toward Him
For the life of your young children,
Who faint from hunger at the head of every street."

THE HEART WITH NO CAPACITY for grief is like a limb that can feel no pain. The heart that cannot grieve cannot be healed, nor will it desire to heal others, for it does not understand their hurt.

The heart that cannot grieve is limited in its praying. "Those who sow in tears shall reap with joyful shouting," writes the Psalmist (Psalm 126:5 NASB). When evil brings pain and destruction, we realign our grieving human hearts with the grieving Holy Spirit.

Loving is risky business. It exposes the heart to the possibility of grief. But without it, human personality is a barren plain unwatered by tears, a vast dryness in which nothing can grow.

SPIRITUAL HEART FOCUS
Have you been wounded in relationships so that you are reluctant to risk your heart in caring for others? Ask the Father to restore your capacity for grief.

PHYSICAL HEART FOCUS

Zooming toward the "fabulous 50s"? You need cardiovascular, resistance, and stretching exercises now to head off middle–age bulge, maintain bone mass, and stay flexible.

❤ Peace Force

PHILIPPIANS 4:6–7

Be anxious for nothing, but in everything by prayer and supplication, with thanksgiving, let your requests be made known to God; and the peace of God, which surpasses all understanding, will guard your hearts and minds through Christ Jesus.

IMAGINE YOU'RE A PIONEER LIVING on a frontier, surrounded by fierce enemies. The government builds a huge fort close to your spread and garrisons well–armed soldiers there. The enemy can rage outside the walls, but those inside have nothing to fear. The adversaries can't get in. If you live inside the fortress, you will be at peace because you dwell in security.

SPIRITUAL HEART FOCUS
List all your stressful concerns. Allow the Holy Spirit to lead you to pray for each. Thank God for the answers yet to be revealed.

God never gets uptight, anxious, or panicky. He's never surprised, worried, or bummed out about anything. He dwells in a steady state of peace. If you abide in Him, as Jesus put it in John 15, you reside in His peace.

The way you get this incomprehensible peace is to let every stress be a call to prayer, then couch your prayers in gratitude for the answers not yet seen.

PHYSICAL HEART FOCUS

If you're overweight, you have an increased risk of hypertension, diabetes, and heart disease.

♥ 'Overparenting'

ISAIAH 35:4

Say to those who are fearful–hearted,
"Be strong, do not fear!
Behold, your God will come with vengeance,
With the recompense of God;
He will come and save you."

MOMS AND DADS WITH OBSESSIVE HEARTS will overparent.

Obsessive fear makes you want to lock your kids in a closet and butt into their every decision. That's overparenting. It happens when you lose faith in God's capacity and willingness to take care of your children.

> **SPIRITUAL HEART FOCUS**
> If you have children, commit them afresh to God and His perfect will and care. If you don't have kids, pray for those in your extended family and their parents.

Anxious–hearted parents smother their kids and stunt their spiritual, mental, and emotional growth. Your children are never outside the Father's care, even when He allows one of them to fall by suffering consequences from their choices. That, by the way, is essential for their growth.

Balanced parenting is committing your children to God's care, preparing them for life as best as you can, and trusting the Father's care without fear.

PHYSICAL HEART FOCUS

Rowing machines are great fat–burners.

❤ How Not to Hate Yourself

1 SAMUEL 16:6–8

So it was, when they came, that he looked at Eliab and said, "Surely the LORD's anointed is before Him!" But the LORD said to Samuel, "Do not look at his appearance or at his physical stature, because I have refused him. For the LORD does not see as man sees; for man looks at the outward appearance, but the LORD looks at the heart." So Jesse called Abinadab, and made him pass before Samuel. And he said, "Neither has the LORD chosen this one."

IN 1997, ENGLAND'S GLAMOROUS PRINCESS DIANA died in a Paris car crash. On the day of her funeral, Mother Teresa died in Calcutta.

Which of these two women was more elegant in appearance? Diana, no doubt. Tall, stately, immaculate, she was a visual splendor. Mother Teresa was short, bent, and wrinkled. But that didn't stop her from being one of history's most beautiful women spiritually.

Keep God's purpose at the center of your heart, and your preoccupation with your physical appearance will fade from view.

SPIRITUAL
HEART FOCUS
Thank God for your body and appearance, recognizing it was He who designed you!

PHYSICAL HEART FOCUS
Consistent exercise helps you think more clearly.

❤ Door Ajar

PROVERBS 17:19

He who loves transgression loves strife,
And he who exalts his gate seeks destruction.

REGINA LEFT THE DOOR of her heart ajar, and ill winds blasted it fully open. She padded her sales reports a little because she had potential contacts. Regina fudged on vouchers and shaded the truth to close sales. Small compromises had opened the door of her heart to big ones. Regina had wanted to share Christ with her co–workers, but her integrity was gone.

Regina could stand it no longer. She confessed her sin to God, who forgave her, and her boss, who fired her. But she stayed in touch with a co–worker, Terri.

Finally, Regina told Terri what she had done.

"Why did you confess?" Terri asked. "It cost you your job!"

Regina walked through the open door of witness when she closed the door of compromise.

SPIRITUAL HEART FOCUS

What small compromises in your heart could lead to big ones? Confess your sin and commit to God to close the heart–door left ajar.

PHYSICAL HEART FOCUS

Increased fiber helps clean out your intestines.

❤ Energy In, Energy Out

PHILIPPIANS 2:12–13

Therefore, my beloved, as you have always obeyed, not as in my presence only, but now much more in my absence, work out your own salvation with fear and trembling; for it is God who works in you both to will and to do for His good pleasure.

NAN EIDSON HAD TUBERCULOSIS as a young woman. She was sent to a sanatorium to die, but instead, she got well. Grateful, Nan became a nurse.

She also took in needy people, gave away her possessions, and cared for people constantly. In her eighties, Nan still walked hospitals, every step pained by arthritis. Nan poured herself out for others.

Nan's secret was that she knew the importance of receiving spiritual energy. Prayer, Bible study, and worship were vital in launching her days. She got her heart filled before she emptied it in loving service.

Jesus began each day in personal communion with His Father. His energy for public ministry was in direct proportion to the energy He absorbed in His private moments.

SPIRITUAL HEART FOCUS
Commit to reordering your day with the top priorities being communing with God and receiving His strength.

PHYSICAL HEART FOCUS

Skipping meals and starving your body is not part of a Total Heart Health weight–loss plan.

❤ Be a Reporter

JOSHUA 5:1

So it was, when all the kings of the Amorites who were on the west side of the Jordan, and all the kings of the Canaanites who were by the sea, heard that the Lord had dried up the waters of the Jordan from before the children of Israel until we had crossed over, that their heart melted; and there was no spirit in them any longer because of the children of Israel.

THE DISCIPLES OF JOHN THE BAPTIST inquired on behalf of their master whether Jesus was the Messiah, and Jesus answered, "Go and *report* to John what you hear and see . . ." (Matthew 11:4–5 NASB, emphasis added).

The Apostle John opened a letter by writing, "What was from the beginning, what we have heard, what we have seen with our eyes, what we have looked at and touched with our hands, concerning the Word of Life . . . These things we write, so that our joy may be made complete" (1 John 1:1–4 NASB).

SPIRITUAL HEART FOCUS

Ask God to open opportunities for you to give your testimony to others and for you to continue composing your testimony through His works in your life.

Your testimony is your story of God giving you a new heart. An essay is dry and boring, but a first–person account is thrilling. When you tell others about Jesus, be a reporter, not an essayist.

Declare the transformation of your heart, and it will melt the enemy's heart!

PHYSICAL HEART FOCUS

Increased fiber in your diet helps lower cholesterol.

♥ Headwaters

2 KINGS 2:19–21

Then the men of the city said to Elisha, "Please notice, the situation of this city is pleasant, as my lord sees; but the water is bad, and the ground barren." And he said, "Bring me a new bowl, and put salt in it." So they brought it to him. Then he went out to the source of the water, and cast in the salt there, and said, "Thus says the LORD: 'I have healed this water; from it there shall be no more death or barrenness.'"

THE HEART IS THE HEADWATERS of the whole person, and what happens in the heart determines the wellbeing of the rest.

At Jericho, the water supply became polluted. Elisha purified the headwaters with salt, and the stream was restored to fruitfulness.

The purifying of a whole life begins when the heart is cleansed and pumps wholeness throughout the entire being.

This is true physically: Weak legs and wheezing lungs are the result of a bad heart. But it's especially true spiritually. When the spiritual heart is bad, strength for good works is sapped, zest is gone, and the person is unfruitful.

Salt symbolizes the Word of God in its purifying work. The more it penetrates to the heart—the headwaters of your life—the purer and more productive your whole life will be.

SPIRITUAL HEART FOCUS
Allow the Holy Spirit to reveal points at which your life is unfruitful. Find Scriptures relating to that issue, and use them as a guide for prayer.

PHYSICAL HEART FOCUS

Be careful taking soluble vitamins (A, D, K, E) because the body stores them. This can lead to toxicity.

❤ More Than Memorizing

PSALM 119:11
Your word I have hidden in my heart,
That I might not sin against You.

YEARS AGO I KNEW of an evangelist who had memorized the entire New Testament. However, he would be the first to say that memorization is not enough.

Had the salt Elisha poured on Jericho's polluted headwaters stayed merely on the surface, it would have been useless (2 Kings 2:21).

The Word of God poured on our hearts must penetrate. "Hidden" means something is hoarded like a treasure. It's the idea of gathering all you can and holding onto the collection like a reserve of gold or silver.

> **SPIRITUAL HEART FOCUS**
> Memorize key Scriptures you need for your current challenges, meditate on the passages by journaling your thoughts, and use the verses to form your prayer today.

When you treat God's Word like that, says the Scripture, it will keep you from sinning. People often make mistakes because, when glittery temptation presents itself, nothing outshines it in the person's mind.

If God's Word is the gold treasured in your heart, the best that temptation can offer is merely brass. It's a no-brainer; choose the treasure!

PHYSICAL HEART FOCUS

Heart disease can be present with no symptoms, so regular heart checkups are important.

❤ Question the Heart

1 CORINTHIANS 14:24–25

But if all prophesy, and an unbeliever or an uninformed person comes in,
he is convinced by all, he is convicted by all. And thus the secrets
of his heart are revealed; and so, falling down on his face,
he will worship God and report that God is truly among you.

"QUESTION EVERYTHING."

Sometimes people question everything but their own hearts.

Years ago I had a serious case of angina. The medical personnel took measures and readings, but they also questioned me. "How does it feel exactly?" "Where does it hurt?" "When did the pain start?"

Prophecy is a spiritual gift everyone should desire (1 Corinthians 14:39) because it will expose the secrets of people's hearts and provoke them to question afresh their spiritual wellbeing.

SPIRITUAL HEART FOCUS
Ask the Lord to sharpen your spiritual ears when you hear sermons or Bible teaching. Ask that the truths might prompt questions to expose your heart's secrets.

If not discovered, the secrets collecting in the physical heart, such as the unseen buildup of plaque, can kill a person. The secrets of the spiritual heart can be devastating as well.

Question everything . . . about your own heart!

PHYSICAL HEART FOCUS

In your meals today, add foods that are lower in saturated fats, such as fish, chicken, and olive oil.

❤ Placebo

JEREMIAH 6:14; 17:14

"They have also healed the hurt of My people slightly,
Saying, 'Peace, peace!'
When there is no peace. . . .
Heal me, O LORD, and I shall be healed;
Save me, and I shall be saved,
For You are my praise."

A WOMAN HAD A BAD HEADACHE. She fumbled in her bedside table drawer for analgesic. Finding a squeeze tube, she glazed the refreshing ointment over her forehead, and her headache faded. The next morning, however, she discovered she was smeared with toothpaste!

The best the world can offer for a sick heart is a placebo compared to the real thing. Empty words mark sham religion. James describes placebo religion when he writes of those who tell hungry, inadequately clothed people to be full and warm, but then give these poor ones no food or garments (James 2:14–15). God uses people to heal people—sometimes medical specialists, sometimes a praying person who lays hands on a sick person. But however healing comes, it's always God. Without Him, everything else is a placebo.

> **SPIRITUAL HEART FOCUS**
> Mind your physician and take your medicine, but acknowledge God as your ultimate Healer.

PHYSICAL HEART FOCUS

Set a goal of not piling mountains of food on your plate and not going back for seconds. Do this for 90 days and watch your eating behavior change.

❤ Existential 'Faith'

JEREMIAH 10:3–4, 7–8

"For the customs of the peoples are futile;
For one cuts a tree from the forest,
The work of the hands of the workman, with the ax.
They decorate it with silver and gold;
. . . And in all their kingdoms,
There is none like You.
But they are altogether dull–hearted and foolish;
A wooden idol is a worthless doctrine.

EXISTENTIALISM PREACHES that the experience of the moment is the only reality, and the values of the present are the only ones that count.

Jean–Paul Sartre was a prominent existentialist voice. A magazine photo showed Sartre standing on an ice floe, the only solid thing adrift in a cold sea. But the ice floe itself is tiny and melting away. In existentialism, the bare moment is all there is, and even that is always vanishing into meaninglessness.

The mantra of existential faith is, "You believe what you want and I'll believe what I want because it all leads to the same place."

Jeremiah's culture was awash with existential faith. One idol was as good as another. But it's all insecure delusion, said Jeremiah.

Existential faith is as unsafe a resting place for the heart as is a melting ice floe for a human body.

SPIRITUAL HEART FOCUS
Worship God as the Absolute One whose reality is objective and eternal, not a mere fantasy of deluded human hearts.

PHYSICAL HEART FOCUS
Concentrate on your goal, not the temptation or your limitation.

October

Let your head instruct your heart.
Take in God's truth, and let
your heart build its dreams around His Word.

❤ Believing Historical Fact

ROMANS 10:9

If you confess with your mouth the Lord Jesus and believe in your heart that God has raised Him from the dead, you will be saved.

SOME PEOPLE BELIEVE in Jesus' resurrection like they consider Zeus sitting atop Mount Olympus: a myth from which to draw important lessons.

But Scripture tells us to believe in the resurrection as a historical fact. It is the scrape of a huge rock moving away from a tomb door, the rustling of a burial cloth falling off, the patter of running feet and gasping voices.

Biblical heart–belief is different from the pantheism that says the unseen "All" is God, or the shaved–head Krishna cultist who says it's irrelevant if Krishna truly existed, that what counts is the legend.

Christ's resurrection is not something real for one heart and unreal for another. It is objective truth for every heart, but transforming truth only for the heart that believes it as accomplished history.

SPIRITUAL HEART FOCUS

Confess your heart–belief that Jesus Christ is the Son of God and Savior of all who trust Him. Declare that He physically died and rose again and ascended to the Father.

PHYSICAL HEART FOCUS

Walking or running a mile burns about 100 calories for most people.

❤ True Confession

MATTHEW 10:32

*"Therefore whoever confesses Me before men,
him I will also confess before My Father who is in heaven."*

CONFESSION MUST BE ALIGNED with belief, and it is to faith what the upper story of a building is to its foundation.

If you believe in your heart and do not make confession with your lips, that's cowardice.

If you make confession with your lips and do not believe in your heart, that's hypocrisy.

But when you believe in your heart and confess what you believe, that's harmony, integrity, credibility, and reality (Romans 10:9).

The confession of the believing heart is three words: "Jesus is Lord!" The human mind can confess religious belief, but only the heart can proclaim the Lordship of Christ.

SPIRITUAL
HEART FOCUS
Make the confession of faith
that reflects the totality of your
being and that brings together
your intellect, emotions,
conscience, and will.

PHYSICAL HEART FOCUS
When the food craving hits, hit the road. Walking will help curb your appetite.

❤ The Fallacy of 'Only Believe'

JAMES 2:18–19

But someone will say, "You have faith, and I have works."
Show me your faith without your works, and I will show you my faith
by my works. You believe that there is one God. You do well.
Even the demons believe—and tremble!"

As a child I was taught a misleading chorus: "Only believe . . . all things are possible . . . only believe."

Not so. We're not saved by beliefs. We're saved by the historical reality that Jesus Christ died on the cross in payment for our sins and rose again to give us His new resurrection life.

Because faith in Jesus Christ is based on events that really did happen in real time and space, when we believe in the Christ of history, we partake of His historical accomplishment.

Faith is entrusting your whole weight to something. Believing is not leaping out into the dark, but standing on the solid substance of historical fact.

The believing heart is a resting heart.

SPIRITUAL HEART FOCUS
Let the peace of God envelop your heart. This is the peace that comes because you stand on solid reality in Christ.

PHYSICAL HEART FOCUS
Heart disease is the number one killer of women.

❤ Singing Slaves

COLOSSIANS 3:16

*Let the word of Christ dwell in you richly in all wisdom, teaching
and admonishing one another in psalms and hymns and spiritual songs,
singing with grace in your hearts to the Lord.*

I WAS PASTOR of First Baptist Church, Columbia, South Carolina. In 1860, that historic church was where the Secession Convention first met regarding South Carolina's withdrawal from the Union. The rest is Civil War history.

In the pre–Civil War days, slaves filled the balcony, while the lower floor was crowded with people eager to hear the slaves sing.

Many slaves were people of great faith because they had learned to trust God for every morsel. Human masters sometimes crushed them with tyranny, but the singing slaves knew they had a Lord who was their brother, someone who had come to "proclaim liberty to the captives" (Luke 4:18).

Their songs were not the litany of ritual, but the gratitude of a thankful heart despite their slavery.

SPIRITUAL
HEART FOCUS
Do you worship from the overflow of thankfulness or from adherence to religious ritual?

PHYSICAL HEART FOCUS
Breathing properly during exercise is essential. Consider having a trainer instruct you how to breathe during various workout activities.

❤ 'Blow On It'

PROVERBS 17:27

He who has knowledge spares his words,
And a man of understanding is of a calm spirit.

I WAS A VENTURSOME KID, and my body bore the cuts and scars to prove it. I always dreaded Mother dousing my scrapes with alcohol or some other germ–killer, because it burned. "Blow on it!" I would cry. I needed immediate "coolness."

In Solomon's time, a cool–spirited person was one who had dignity, a quiet calmness while others were spewing mindless chatter.

The cool–spirited person isn't a block of ice, but someone who has firmness when others gush. Their discreet hearts know when to keep quiet. When the air is hot with verbal fire, cool–spirited people "blow on it" and bring calmness.

SPIRITUAL HEART FOCUS
Pray for the wisdom to know when to keep your mouth shut and the self–control to do it.

PHYSICAL HEART FOCUS
Plan your meals a week in advance to help you stick to your nutritional strategy.

❤ The Heart's Legacy

JOHN 14:27–28

"Peace I leave with you, My peace I give to you; not as the world gives do I give to you. Let not your heart be troubled, neither let it be afraid. You have heard Me say to you, 'I am going away and coming back to you.' If you loved Me, you would rejoice because I said, 'I am going to the Father,' for My Father is greater than I."

WHEN THE SNOW FELL on our neighbor's pristine yard, his little daughter feared being blamed for it. The green lawn was her father's idol, and now it was gone. "Tell Daddy I didn't do it," she said.

The fear of blame hovers ghostlike in the dark attic of the human heart. Ultimately, because God has written His Law in our hearts, we are gripped with the fear of being blamed eternally for breaking it.

But Jesus removes the guilt behind the blame. Every person receiving Him receives His righteousness. He shoos the spook of blame–fear from our hearts and replaces it with the Holy Spirit!

In doing so, Jesus Christ leaves our hearts the legacy of peace.

> SPIRITUAL HEART FOCUS
>
> Are you playing the blame game with others? Receive Christ's forgiveness for your sins and extend forgiveness to people you blame.

PHYSICAL HEART FOCUS

Divide your diet and exercise goals into daily and weekly objectives. For example, if your goal is to lose 25 pounds, the objective might be a pound a week, and this would determine your daily calorie intake and exercise objectives.

♥ Defeathering the Peacock Heart

MATTHEW 19:16

Now behold, one came and said to Him, "Good Teacher, what good thing shall I do that I may have eternal life?"

THE PEACOCK HEART FEARS defeathering, and it would rather die than lose its glorious plumage.

The peacock asks Jesus for salvation. "Keep the Law," Jesus says. "Been there, done that," replies the plumed one. The "imaginations" of the proud peacock heart "run riot" (Psalm 73:7 NASB). Peacocks think they can do anything. But Jesus keeps raising the bar, telling the peacock to pluck out his glory and give it to featherless birds.

SPIRITUAL HEART FOCUS
Recommit yourself to trusting Jesus alone for your salvation.

Peacock hearts are so blinded by their own splendor they don't get it. The peacock heart, able to attain whatever it wants, has a hard time understanding grace. That's why there are no peacocks in Heaven.

Ironically, had the peacock allowed himself to be defeathered, he would have received a glory far lovelier and more enduring than the plumage of his pride.

PHYSICAL HEART FOCUS

Aerobic exercise is good for your cardiovascular system and excellent for burning fat.

♥ Sunday Best

2 PETER 1:3–4

As His divine power has given to us all things that pertain to life and godliness, through the knowledge of Him who called us by glory and virtue, by which have been given to us exceedingly great and precious promises, that through these you may be partakers of the divine nature, having escaped the corruption that is in the world through lust.

AS A TEEN, my arms kept getting longer than my sleeves.

I couldn't afford to buy new shirts to keep up with my growth. Today, the concept of "Sunday best" has faded, but when I was a boy I strove to wear my best clothes, even if the shirt sleeves were too short.

God has called our hearts to excellence, which is our best effort or accomplishment. Jesus Christ demonstrated excellence of heart in His mission to win our salvation. He was so effective that His work endures forever and saves us to "the uttermost" (Hebrews 7:25).

A young man attends our church regularly wearing a white T-shirt every Sunday. He is economically disadvantaged, and it's likely the best he owns. But the young adult asks our pastors penetrating questions, revealing the hunger in his heart for moral excellence. He always shows up in his true "Sunday best"!

> SPIRITUAL
> HEART FOCUS
> As you consider dressing your best for today's activities, focus on dressing your moral heart with excellence.

PHYSICAL HEART FOCUS

In the United States, 300,000 deaths annually are related to obesity.

♥ Electrification!

For it is the God who commanded light to shine out of darkness, who has shone in our hearts to give the light of the knowledge of the glory of God in the face of Jesus Christ.

IN 1936, CONGRESS PASSED the Rural Electrification Act. Imagine the thrill of a family as they flipped the switch for the first time!

Salvation in Jesus Christ is the Spiritual Electrification Act. When you receive Jesus Christ, His Holy Spirit turns on the light of your heart to illuminate your whole being!

The light is the glory, the gleaming character of God, personified in Jesus Christ. Through that light, God makes known to you the "mystery of His will" (Ephesians 1:9). God shows you the sweeping plan for your life.

If Christ is the light of your life, you can walk into each "room," each stage, knowing the light will come on in that area just when you need it.

SPIRITUAL HEART FOCUS
Yield to God's will in every area of your life, whether or not you can see it all, and the "light" will come on!

PHYSICAL HEART FOCUS

If you lift weights as a resistance exercise, use a weight you can lift 10–15 repetitions before fatigue.

304   Young, Duncan & Leachman

❤ Stifled Heart

JEREMIAH 20:9

Then I said, "I will not make mention of Him,
Nor speak anymore in His name."
But His word was in my heart like a burning fire
Shut up in my bones;
I was weary of holding it back,
And I could not.

QUENCH THE SPIRIT and you stifle the heart . . . and pressure mounts like that in a hot boiler. The heart has to speak up or blow up!

The most miserable people in the world aren't the pagans and reprobates, but Christians trying to keep quiet about their faith. At some point, you will weary of trying to hold it in, and keeping silent will be unendurable.

I preached my first sermon at eighteen in Petal, Mississippi. The text was Matthew 5:41, in which Jesus said His disciples ought to be willing to go the second mile. Even now I remember my first line of that first sermon. I told the people that Jesus' words contain "enough dynamite to change the course of the entire world."

SPIRITUAL
HEART FOCUS
Who needs to hear your
testimony today?

All these decades later, I still believe it. You can't hold it in, or your heart will explode!

PHYSICAL HEART FOCUS
Increased fiber in your diet helps you feel full longer.

♥ When the Zeal Fades

GALATIANS 6:9

And let us not grow weary while doing good, for in due season we shall reap if we do not lose heart.

ONCE, WHILE SERVING A CHURCH in a small community, I was on the volunteer fire department. At two o'clock one Sunday morning, while I was still preparing my sermon, the fire alarm shrieked. We fought the blaze, and I was in bed again at four. An hour later, there was another alarm.

I was so tired when I preached a few hours later I almost put myself to sleep!

I've known people who started out in Christ with the thrill of a full run. But after a few "fires" tested their faith, the zeal faded.

Mature people have moved from being motivated by adventure to being driven by commitment. They keep going when the feeling fades.

SPIRITUAL HEART FOCUS
Are you still devoted to Christ and His Kingdom even if the initial zeal has faded?

PHYSICAL HEART FOCUS

"Forward" is the right direction both in spiritual growth and in physical fitness. Remind yourself that every small step forward brings you closer to a total heart healthy lifestyle.

❤ Wake Up!

ROMANS 13:11

And do this, knowing the time, that now it is high time to awake out of sleep; for now our salvation is nearer than when we first believed.

ONE EASTER I WAS INVITED to preach a sunrise service for forty thousand soldiers and their families at Fort Jackson, South Carolina. The service was to start at 5:15 a.m. At 5:30 a.m. Jo Beth shook me awake. "The alarm didn't go off," she said.

By God's grace I wasn't fired upon as I raced through the military post's gate. I arrived at the platform just as the music preceding my sermon was underway.

Many hearts are sleeping now. The hands of history's clocks are moving with the inevitability of our clock that Easter morning. The moment known to the Father alone, when the Son will rise over the world, is drawing near.

Don't let the moment catch you asleep. Awaken your heart to His truth this day. Don't miss the Big Event on the horizon!

SPIRITUAL HEART FOCUS
Is the greatest happening in history going to pass you by? Allow God to awaken your heart to spiritual truth.

PHYSICAL HEART FOCUS
If your job demands travel, stay at a hotel with a fitness center, and hang out there rather than the bar.

♥ Pursued Heart

1 TIMOTHY 2:3–4

For this is good and acceptable in the sight of God our Savior, who desires all men to be saved and to come to the knowledge of the truth.

ROMANCE GETS SERIOUS when you move from "dating" to "courting," the pursuit of the heart of the beloved.

God courts us, pursuing our hearts.

He woos us in many ways. Sometimes heartbreak leads us to give our broken hearts to Him for healing. In my years of experience as a pastor, I've concluded that many people come to God because they get the stuffing knocked out of them.

A pro football player called me, desperate. He had been living a godless life. "Would you come pray for me?" he asked. No one would have believed this athlete would have called out to a pastor for help. "Please come lay hands on my knee!" he begged. "If the Lord will heal my knee and let me run again, I'll get my act together!"

God's pursuit of our hearts brings us to our knees so that we can learn to run with Him, not against Him.

> **SPIRITUAL HEART FOCUS**
> Look over your shoulder and see that it's not an enemy pursuing you, but the One who loves you above all.

PHYSICAL HEART FOCUS

There's much emphasis on heart care for men, but women should take heed too, because they are more likely than men to die after a cardiac event.

❤ Smiling Power

PSALM 119:111

Your testimonies I have taken as a heritage forever,
For they are the rejoicing of my heart.

HE WAS THE UGLIEST MAN in the church. "Clark" honestly looked like a character off the old TV show *The Munsters.* But he had a smiling heart!

Clark worked a hard job, but his heart smiled because it had a story to tell of God's transforming power in his life. Each Sunday he handed out bulletins to people entering the church. Just as they wondered if he was going to mug them, Clark would smile hugely and say, "Welcome!"

One week Clark's pastor opened a note. "You don't know me," the woman said. "I came last Sunday as a visitor to your church. I awoke that morning with the determination to kill myself if someone didn't show me some care. Your usher's smile saved my life."

The smiling heart is a powerful witness of hope.

SPIRITUAL HEART FOCUS
If your heart were a face, would it be smiling right now?

PHYSICAL HEART FOCUS

The number of Americans with type-two diabetes has increased significantly over the past 30 years, paralleling the increase in the number of people overweight or obese.

❤ Identity Discovery

JAMES 1:23–24

For if anyone is a hearer of the word and not a doer, he is like a man observing his natural face in a mirror; for he observes himself, goes away, and immediately forgets what kind of man he was.

AN EAGLET FELL from its high nest and was adopted by a turkey family. It ate turkey food, because when you're hungry you'll eat anything available. The eaglet also behaved like turkeys, conforming to those who accepted it.

SPIRITUAL HEART FOCUS
In Christ, you are a new creation with a new family, citizenship in a new kingdom, and new purpose for living.

"I wish I could do that!" cried the eaglet, watching a high-soaring bird. "No you don't!" the mother turkey gobbled back. "That's a buzzard!"

The eaglet, confused, wandered away into the forest and leaned against a tree. "Whooo are you?" asked an owl. "A turkey," answered the eaglet. "A turkey? Who told you that? You're an eagle, the king of birds!"

Soon the eaglet was soaring far above the turkeys and the buzzards.

Jesus Christ came to show us who we really are. When our hearts hear the Gospel, we want to fly. When we receive Him, we discover our identity as children of the Most High—we're eagles!

PHYSICAL HEART FOCUS

When you intake more fuel energy (calories) than you can use immediately, the body stores it as fat.

❤ Penned on the Heart

2 CORINTHIANS 3:2–3

*You are our epistle written in our hearts, known and read by all men;
clearly you are an epistle of Christ, ministered by us, written not with ink
but by the Spirit of the living God, not on tablets of stone
but on tablets of flesh, that is, of the heart.*

THE LAW, THE "DEAD LETTER," was written on tablets of stone while Grace, the "living letter," is written on human hearts.

The Law is the diagnostician of the heart, but Grace is the physician. The Law says something's wrong with us, but Grace says we can be made right.

The Old Covenant is head religion, but the New Covenant is heart truth.

The Law on stone tablets taught us important things about doing, and the Grace written on heart tablets teaches us about being.

SPIRITUAL HEART FOCUS
Revere the law and rejoice in grace!

The Law is written on our hearts. It gives us an instinctive sense of right and wrong, and therefore we are accountable (Romans 2:15). But the Grace written as the living letter by the Holy Spirit overlays the Law letter!

PHYSICAL HEART FOCUS
Overweight is a body mass index (BMI) of 25 or greater.
Obesity is a body mass index (BMI) of 30 or greater.
Morbid obesity is a body mass index (BMI) of 40–plus.

♥ No False Teeth Allowed

ROMANS 3:20, 23–24

Therefore by the deeds of the law no flesh will be justified in His sight, for by the law is the knowledge of sin . . . for all have sinned and fall short of the glory of God, being justified freely by His grace through the redemption that is in Christ Jesus.

HOLY DEEDS ARISE FROM HEARTS devoted to God, while mere actions are just the work of busy hands.

The legal devotees of the Old Testament were busy bees. God said to keep the Sabbath Day holy. But the law fans built a hive of rules on the Commandment's core, layering on thirty–nine principles, then piling on thirty–nine more.

Finally, Grandmother couldn't even wear her false teeth on the Sabbath because that was a banned burden!

SPIRITUAL HEART FOCUS
Your truly good works are stimulated by a grace–blessed heart, so bless others with graceful deeds.

Jesus took all the law books and refined them back to the simple, sublime truths the Father had given for our orderly, happy living in the fallen world. He then fulfilled all the statutes and applied credit for His perfect obedience to everyone who would receive Him.

Because God looks on the heart and not ritualistic actions of the body, all believers in Christ are judged in full compliance with the law.

PHYSICAL HEART FOCUS

Next to smoking, your weight is the most important measure of your future health.

♥ Forget the All–Night Pizza

1 CORINTHIANS 13:11

When I was a child, I spoke as a child, I understood as a child, I thought as a child; but when I became a man, I put away childish things.

LOCK–INS ARE BIG FUN for youth groups. Hundreds of kids gather to spend all night at the church. But we don't do lock–ins for mature adults. Staying up all night eating pizza has little appeal.

Similarly, there's also a big difference between the adolescent spiritual heart and the adult spiritual heart.

This maturity has little to do with chronological age. I know teenagers who are more mature spiritually than adults who've claimed to be Christians for forty years!

Adolescence describes someone who's half adult and half child. Jesus said that to enter the Kingdom we must be child*like*, not child*ish* (Mark 10:15).

Growth is a process. Nurture your spiritual heart and you will see spiritual adolescence give way to spiritual adulthood.

SPIRITUAL HEART FOCUS

Being alive results in growth. Allow Christ's spiritual energy to thrive in your heart, and you will mature in Him.

PHYSICAL HEART FOCUS

Limiting daily calorie intake is the single most important strategy for controlling weight, but success won't come easily without adding consistent exercise.

❤ Enter at Your Own Risk

ACTS 8:35-37

Then Philip opened his mouth, and beginning at this Scripture, preached Jesus to him. Now as they went down the road, they came to some water. And the eunuch said, "See, here is water. What hinders me from being baptized?" Then Philip said, "If you believe with all your heart, you may." And he answered and said, "I believe that Jesus Christ is the Son of God."

IT'S RISKY TO GIVE someone your heart.

Suzy believes Bill's pledges of everlasting love, gives him her heart, then finds he's tossed that same bait to other women.

Philip tells the Ethiopian eunuch that to be Christ's disciple he must believe with his whole heart. Sounds like a risky venture.

SPIRITUAL HEART FOCUS

Stop trying to play it safe when it comes to serving others and witnessing to them in the name of Christ.

Giving Christ your whole heart means risking relationships and rejection. Following Christ with your heart means you take the risk to be open and transparent, communicating your whole heart to people so they may see the Christ who dwells there.

At the end of his life, the Ethiopian eunuch doubtless made the same discovery as all others who choose Christ: the heart believing in Him is in the safest place of all!

PHYSICAL HEART FOCUS

Basal metabolic rate (BMR) is the caloric requirement at rest. It changes as we age, so adults shouldn't consume as many calories as they did when they were teens.

❤ It Takes Lions to Build Hearts

1 SAMUEL 17:34–35

But David said to Saul, "Your servant used to keep his father's sheep, and when a lion or a bear came and took a lamb out of the flock, I went out after it and struck it, and delivered the lamb from its mouth; and when it arose against me, I caught it by its beard, and struck and killed it.

YOU DON'T GET A STRONG HEART without facing lions.

Young David had a master's degree in lion–killing, which was a credential vital for giant–slaying. In the sheepfold, God was building a heart of courage into the feisty teenager so he could face giants later in his life. The battle with Goliath was David's Ph.D. in heart–courage, a dissertation completed in a single afternoon.

SPIRITUAL HEART FOCUS
Recognize that the quiet places where you struggle are opportunities for you to grow in Christ.

If you're being stretched, your heart is in learning mode. If the lions are chasing you, in the words of James, "Count it all joy . . ." (James 1:2–4).

Don't go chasing after the lions, but when they come recognize them as God's means of building your heart and character.

PHYSICAL HEART HEALTH

There are 3,500 calories in a pound of fat, so to lose a pound of fat you need to burn 3,500 calories more than you consume.

❤ Anyone Can Know a Horse

JOHN 2:24–25

But Jesus did not commit Himself to them, because He knew all men, and had no need that anyone should testify of man, for He knew what was in man.

"I KNOW THAT HORSE, and I wouldn't advise you to ride him," says the wrangler at the dude ranch. The urban cowboy had better listen. The wrangler is saying he's handled and ridden the horse and knows its character and tendencies.

But anyone can know a horse. The real challenge is understanding a complex human heart.

Jesus knew what was in people. He didn't need any help understanding them.

SPIRITUAL HEART FOCUS
When no one else understands you and your deepest heartfelt feelings, Jesus does.

Jesus zeroed in on the heart, which explains some of His strange behavior, like forgiving a prostitute.

He still knows what's in each man or woman, and His responses are still based on what He sees in our hearts.

PHYSICAL HEART FOCUS

A reasonable goal for weight loss is to burn 1,000 calories a day more than you take in.

❤ Up Close to the President

*And He has made from one blood every nation of men to dwell
on all the face of the earth, and has determined their preappointed times
and the boundaries of their dwellings, so that they should seek the Lord,
in the hope that they might grope for Him and find Him,
though He is not far from each one of us.*

How WELL ANYBODY KNOWS the president of the United States depends on how much the president wants someone to know him.

God, however, wants everyone everywhere to know Him at His deepest, which means knowing His heart.

Paul is saddened as he sees the Athenians groping to know God. After deifying everything in sight, they'd erected a catchall statue to "the unknown god." Paul tells the Greek philosophers he's come to town especially to introduce them to the God eager for them to know Him.

Jesus knows what's in a person, and God wants us to also know what's in Him!

SPIRITUAL HEART FOCUS
When you get opportunities to learn about God through personal communion with Him or through learning, worshiping, and serving Him with others, don't waste those blessings.

PHYSICAL HEART FOCUS

If you see your weight increasing steadily, remember that stopping the increase is a successful beginning toward weight loss.

❤ Getting Back an Hour

HEBREWS 3:12–13

Beware, brethren, lest there be in any of you an evil heart of unbelief in departing from the living God; but exhort one another daily, while it is called "Today," lest any of you be hardened through the deceitfulness of sin.

IF YOU COULD HAVE BACK one hour of your past life, which would it be? A newspaper posed that question. One woman described her near–death agony in childbirth, and the hour she held her newborn daughter in her arms before the infant died. Despite all the suffering, that hour would be the one she would want to relive.

The heart that does not recognize the beauty and opportunity of the present moment becomes hardened. Focus on what God is doing in your life today.

Our hearts must not be so dull and insensitive that we miss the wonder of the time we have right now.

We can't get it back.

SPIRITUAL HEART FOCUS

Stop pining for the past and living only for the future. Instead, embrace the blessings and joys of this present moment.

PHYSICAL HEART FOCUS

Launching your day with a healthy diet of God's word plus a healthy breakfast helps lead to total heart health.

❤ Heart–Worthy Goals

EZEKIEL 33:31

*So they come to you as people do, they sit before you as My people,
and they hear your words, but they do not do them; for with their mouth
they show much love, but their hearts pursue their own gain.*

PHILIPPIANS 3:14

I press toward the goal for the prize of the upward call of God in Christ Jesus.

YOUR HEART WILL BE FRUSTRATED if you elevate a desire to the level of a goal.

A woman may say her goal is having a great relationship with her husband, happy kids, and a beautiful home. These are great desires, but they're improper goals. They are objectives another human being can block.

The lady's husband may reject her. Her children might make unhappy choices. There may not be sufficient money to decorate her house as she wants.

> SPIRITUAL
> HEART FOCUS
> Allow the Holy Spirit to
> guide you in rethinking your
> goals and to help you
> discern between
> desires and goals.

A goal worthy enough to be the focus of the heart is to aim for something only God can block, because no human or circumstance can obstruct it.

Don't aim for gain, but for God–given goals. They alone are heart–worthy.

PHYSICAL HEART FOCUS

Go forward with small, manageable objectives that you can really attain.
Losing 15–20 pounds and keeping the weight off is achievable for most people.

❤ Illusion Machine

PSALM 73:3-7

For I was envious of the boastful,
When I saw the prosperity of the wicked.
For there are no pangs in their death,
But their strength is firm.
They are not in trouble as other men,
Nor are they plagued like other men.
Therefore pride serves as their necklace;
Violence covers them like a garment.
Their eyes bulge with abundance;
They have more than heart could wish.

SPIRITUAL HEART FOCUS
Ask the Lord to establish His eternal Word as the basis of your dreams and hopes, rather than relying on fantasies created by a heart celebrating its own accomplishments.

THE HEART THAT PARADES its immoral victories is marching on a parade ground of illusion.

The boastful, arrogant people in the Psalm are those who make big deals of their scores and conquests.

These individuals have one creed: "Follow your heart!" But it's a deadly cycle. Their hearts produce fantasies, and their eyes can see only the mirage conjured by their wayward hearts. They are hapless dogs forever chasing their tails.

Let your head instruct your heart. Take in God's truth, and let your heart build its dreams around His Word.

PHYSICAL HEART FOCUS
Foods with a high glycemic index tend to be simple sugars, easily broken down and quickly absorbed.

♥ How Pure Must It Be?

MATTHEW 5:8

"Blessed are the pure in heart,
For they shall see God."

HOW PURE DOES A HEART have to be to live in the presence of God? Imagine that someone declares that the Baseball Hall of Fame is merely mediocre, so he creates the Universe Hall of Fame to honor true excellence. To be inducted, there are only two requirements: an honoree must have played every inning of every game without an error, and he must have gotten a hit every time at bat. An errorless career and a batting average of 1,000 are all it takes to get into the Universe Hall of Fame.

A perfect record is also what it takes to get into Heaven.

Impossible! Until Christ. He removes the errors of sin blotching the human heart. When it came to law-keeping, Jesus had a batting average of 1,000, and He applies that perfect score to everyone who will accept it.

All it takes is a perfect heart to dwell in the presence of God, and Jesus Christ makes this impossibility possible!

SPIRITUAL HEART FOCUS

If you have received Jesus Christ as your Savior, rejoice that your name is written in the Lamb's Book of Life—the Universe Hall of Fame.

PHYSICAL HEART FOCUS

Cardio exercise is always about progression—starting at a safe, comfortable level and periodically working up from there, using the FITT scale—frequency, intensity, type of exercise, time spent doing it.

❤ Fresh Oil

EXODUS 27:20

"And you shall command the children of Israel that they bring you pure oil of pressed olives for the light, to cause the lamp to burn continually."

IF THE HEART IS TO RADIATE CHRIST continually it must be infused with fresh oil daily.

The oil that fuels the light must be pure or the flame will be smoky. That means the sources from which we draw heart–strength must be pure, unmixed. Christ's followers don't seek power from a combination of the Holy Spirit *and* lucky charms.

The oil must be freshened daily. The Holy Spirit never runs dry, but our hearts do.

Every day we must designate time for spiritual refreshing. Through daily Bible study, worship, prayer, and service the flame in our heart–lamps leaps with new vitality.

Don't let your oil run low!

SPIRITUAL HEAR FOCUS
Pray today for a fresh infilling of the Holy Spirit.

PHYSICAL HEART FOCUS
The body needs a certain amount of fat; olive oil, fish, and walnuts are healthy sources.

❤ New Wine

"Nor do they put new wine into old wineskins, or else the wineskins break, the wine is spilled, and the wineskins are ruined. But they put new wine into new wineskins, and both are preserved."

GOD GIVES US A NEW HEART because Jesus fills us with new wine.

Goatskins were used for bottling wine in New Testament times. The chemical power of fermentation would explode old, cracked skins, but new containers were able to stretch and contain the energy that transformed grape juice into rich wine.

Christ makes us new creatures with new hearts that contain the new wine that is transforming us into new people!

This means if you have received Christ, His Holy Spirit is bringing special fermentation to your heart, and it's being stretched as transformation occurs.

You may feel conflict and frustration as your fallen flesh strives with your fresh spirit (Galatians 5:17). But don't worry, because the new wine is doing its work in your new heart.

SPIRITUAL HEART FOCUS
Drink in the new wine by allowing Christ to cleanse you and the Holy Spirit to invigorate you.

PHYSICAL HEART FOCUS
The average American diet is 3,500 calories a day, twice what most people need.

❤ The Honeymoon Heart

SONG OF SOLOMON 3:11
Go forth, O daughters of Zion,
And see King Solomon with the crown
With which his mother crowned him
On the day of his wedding,
The day of the gladness of his heart.

JO BETH AND I SNEAKED OUT the back door of the church after our wedding, outfoxing devious friends who wanted to detour us. I still remember the gladness of heart on our wedding day and the joyfulness of that honeymoon. We married on Sunday and had our brief honeymoon before driving to South Carolina, where I preached on the next Sunday.

SPIRITUAL HEART FOCUS
Ask the Lord to search your heart and determine if you are still trying to function at the honeymoon stage, or if maturity of faith is developing.

Reality soon smacked into our honeymoon hearts. But what followed was a new maturity and a new intimacy.

New believers in Christ often experience a honeymoon heart, boosted by the new awareness of freedom from sin and fire for God.

My hope always is that when the honeymoon heart gets hit with trials and testing it will not depend on emotions, but solid, mature faith that lasts a lifetime.

PHYSICAL HEART FOCUS

Exercise no more than one hour at a time, six days per week. God says rest every seventh day for good reason. Your muscles must replenish glycogen consumed in workouts.

❤ From Clatter to Clatter

LUKE 21:34-35

"But take heed to yourselves, lest your hearts be weighed down with carousing, drunkenness, and cares of this life, and that Day come on you unexpectedly. For it will come as a snare on all those who dwell on the face of the whole earth."

PEACE AND QUIET ARE RARE in today's audio–intensive world. Everywhere, it's noise, noise, noise.

So you seclude yourself in a secret room. There you find more clatter, the internal jangle of your heart's worries.

Maybe it's because we don't want to face the internal rumblings that we turn up the volume on the external racket. Sometimes we try to avoid our worries by dousing our minds with alcohol and drugs.

But we must deal with the din in our hearts caused by the worries of life, or we won't be ready for the day when all our secrets will be laid bare. Turn down the volume so you can hear what's really going on.

SPIRITUAL HEART FOCUS
Find some solitude and listen to your heart with God's guidance.

PHYSICAL HEART FOCUS
Successful weight loss is losing 10 percent of your initial body weight and not regaining it.

❤ Descent into Darkness

ROMANS 1:21

Because, although they knew God, they did not glorify Him as God, nor were thankful, but became futile in their thoughts, and their foolish hearts were darkened.

THE DARK HEART IS LIKE a spooky basement at the bottom of creaky stairs. A staircase leads down into the darkness of a rebellious heart.

The first step is ingratitude, where people enjoy God's bounty but don't thank Him for it. The next step downward is willful ignorance through empty reasonings that ignore the brilliant light of God and His truth.

SPIRITUAL HEART FOCUS
Look around you and consider God's miraculous creation. Thank Him for all He provides. On a day when the world celebrates darkness, meditate on the reality that "God is light, and in Him is no darkness at all" (1 John 1:5).

Finally is the darkest step of all— idolatry. Way down in the grim world of the unbelieving heart, we whistle in the dark by worshiping whatever we can find, hoping it will give us some light. But the darkness only deepens.

Get off the staircase plunging you into darkness. Thank God for His goodness, open your heart to His truth, smash your idols, and worship the true and living God. That will turn on the light!

PHYSICAL HEART FOCUS

Saturated fat tends to be found in red meat and dairy products.

November

The heart that does not worship,
is not grateful.

❤ Two–Hearted Mutant

GALATIANS 5:17
For the flesh lusts against the Spirit, and the Spirit against the flesh; and these are contrary to one another, so that you do not do the things that you wish.

COWS MAY HAVE TWO STOMACHS, but I've never heard of an animal with hearts on each side of its chest. That would be a mutant.

Yet some people try to operate with two spiritual hearts. One heart attempts to beat for God, and the other for the world. These mutants haven't learned the principle that being the ally of the world's values makes them automatically the enemy of God (James 4:4). To avoid spiritual and emotional breakdown, you need one heart guided by one passion.

SPIRITUAL HEART FOCUS
Nourish the spiritual heart and it will overcome the flesh–focused heart.

Recognize that if the flesh–focused heart wins, you still have a mess. Go with the heart alive with God's Spirit.

PHYSICAL HEART FOCUS
Studies show that people who take fish oil supplements are less likely to die of sudden death than those who don't.

❤ The Whatever Heart

REVELATION 3:15–16

*"I know your works, that you are neither cold nor hot.
I could wish you were cold or hot. So then, because you are lukewarm,
and neither cold nor hot, I will vomit you out of My mouth."*

"WHATEVER" HAS WORKED its way into our lingo as the expression of ultimate apathy.

The whatever heart cares for nothing. It is neither hot nor cold.

Some ancient Christians actually thought apathy could be positive. Extinguish the passions like the Stoics do, counseled Saint Marcarius and others. The doctrine of apathy actually became a creed of sorts.

The whatever mentality may be core doctrine in Zen Buddhism, but not in the faith of Jesus Christ. He calls us to engagement, involvement, and action on the front lines of human struggling and anguish.

The whatever heart is lukewarm and an abomination to God's heart.

SPIRITUAL HEART FOCUS
If you have fallen into apathy because of burnout or sheer laziness, ask the Lord to restore the passion to your heart.

PHYSICAL HEART FOCUS

Complex carbohydrates, like those in whole-grain bread and oatmeal, take longer to digest but provide more nutrients and help forestall hunger pangs.

❤ Cut the Ropes and Set Sail

2 PETER 1:19

*And so we have the prophetic word confirmed, which you do well
to heed as a light that shines in a dark place, until the day dawns and
the morning star rises in your hearts.*

YOU CAN'T APPRECIATE the morning star until you cut the ropes and sail out to sea.

SPIRITUAL HEART FOCUS
Energize your relationship with Jesus Christ by setting sail for the open seas of discipleship and service.

In the old days, sailors who ventured far from land relied on the stars for navigation. Landlubbers might have a passing interest in the stars, but mariners rely on them.

The Lord Jesus Christ is the Morning Star of the heart. Stay ashore and He won't seem important to you. But set sail for the high seas of discipleship and service, and He will be your everything!

PHYSICAL HEART FOCUS
HDL is good cholesterol increased by regular exercise.

❤ The Bedstead Heart

JOHN 16:33–17:1

"These things I have spoken to you, that in Me you may have peace.
In the world you will have tribulation; but be of good cheer,
I have overcome the world." Jesus spoke these words,
lifted up His eyes to heaven, and said: "Father, the hour has come.
Glorify Your Son, that Your Son also may glorify You."

THE BEDSTEAD HEART is like an old iron bed, firm on both ends but saggy in the middle.

The person with a bedstead heart is firm in receiving Christ as Savior. On the other end, he's firm too, confident he will go to Heaven when he dies.

But in the middle Mr. Bedstead Heart sags.

The mature spiritual heart is firm throughout. It is solid in its commitment to Christ and confident of eternity with Him. And in the middle, in this life, the individual is courageous, stable, steady, and firm.

SPIRITUAL HEART FOCUS
Are your spiritual springs creaking under temptation? Strengthen them by meditating on what it means that Christ has overcome the world.

Mature believers know that Christ overcame the world, that Christ is enthroned upon their hearts firmly, and that they won't sag under the weight of daily living.

PHYSICAL HEART FOCUS
Simple carbohydrates, like those in fruit juices, provide a quick rise in blood sugar and energy but tend to cause a quick rebound of hunger.

❤ Cruise Ship or Dreadnaught?

ISAIAH 13:6–7

"Wail, for the day of the LORD is at hand!
It will come as destruction from the Almighty.
Therefore all hands will be limp,
Every man's heart will melt."

JAMES 5:8

You also be patient. Establish your hearts, for the coming of the Lord is at hand.

THE GOOD SHIP ZION is not a luxury liner, but a battleship!

A recruit believes the posters, and signs up to see the world. He reports for duty on his Navy ship in a splashy Hawaiian shirt, open–toe sandals, and festive red Bermuda shorts. Too late he discovers he's on the wrong ship and should have worn battle dress.

SPIRITUAL HEART FOCUS
Ask the Lord to prepare you for battling the powers of darkness, not snorkeling the Caribbean.

People who embark on the Christian life believing it's a Caribbean cruise retreat when they see guns and ammo. There is indeed wonderful peace and joy in Christ, but it all comes in the midst of battle, not apart from it.

Prepare your heart by yanking off glad rags and putting on the battle dress! (Ephesians 6:13–17).

PHYSICAL HEART FOCUS

Your heart's about the size of your fist. In a normal lifetime it will beat about 3.5 billion times. Fuel it properly and keep it healthy with consistent exercise.

❤ Behind Closed Doors

PSALM 42:7

Deep calls unto deep at the noise of Your waterfalls;
All Your waves and billows have gone over me.

MATTHEW 14:23

And when He had sent the multitudes away, He went up on the mountain
by Himself to pray. Now when evening came, He was alone there.

"DEEP–TO–DEEP" TRANSACTIONS happen when you hide God's Word in your heart, draw aside to your "mountain," and get on your face before God. There, you find affirmation of His truth.
Other voices call out to us and try to distort the Voice of the Deep, so we need this quiet time with God to filter out the noise.

> **SPIRITUAL HEART FOCUS**
> Designate a day of silence, when you will spend significant time in quietness, meditating on God's Word, praying, and listening.

What we hear in these moments is filtered in two ways. First, through the sieve of Scripture. Everything we hear in subjectivity must be measured against the standard of objectivity. Second, everything we hear in our private times then should be assessed by wise and mature followers of Christ who know us in the community of faith. Once you make the deep–to–deep connection, confirm what you've heard by conferring with other believers, and then share it throughout your world!

PHYSICAL HEART FOCUS

The difficulty level for resistance exercise is measured on a continuum: challenge to fatigue to failure. The more fit you become, the further you can push yourself.

♥ Live from the Overflow

PSALM 36:9

For with You is the fountain of life;
In Your light we see light.

JOHN 7:38–39

"He who believes in Me, as the Scripture has said, out of his heart will flow rivers of living water." But this He spoke concerning the Spirit, whom those believing in Him would receive; for the Holy Spirit was not yet given, because Jesus was not yet glorified.

"PREACH FROM THE OVERFLOW!" a professor used to tell his students. People sometimes see my library, the tool of my trade, and ask, "Do you remember all you read?"

I tell them, "No. I fill up and pour it out, fill up and pour it out, fill up and pour it out . . ."

That's how we're all to live in Christ. We are to drink Him into our innermost beings, our hearts, and then live through the overflow. Overflow living is thriving from grace's prosperity, not from the poverty of compliance with the law. Overflow living is doing spontaneously the things that conform to the character of life.

Overflow living is the outpouring through our bodies of the One who is the fountain of life.

> **SPIRITUAL HEART FOCUS**
> Commit to turning aside from all the other fountains and drinking instead only from the one that leads to quality, overflow living.

PHYSICAL HEART FOCUS

Incorporate a stretching routine into your weekly exercise program.

❤ When God Says, 'It's Over'

GENESIS 6:3

And the LORD said, "My Spirit shall not strive with man forever, for he is indeed flesh . . ."

THE JUDGE LISTENS PATIENTLY as the testimony drones on, but there comes a moment when he gavels for silence, the unchangeable verdict is pronounced, and the judge exits.

What does it take for God to withdraw His Spirit from people's hearts? Jesus said the unforgivable sin is blaspheming the Holy Spirit (Matthew 12:31). It's not that God doesn't want to forgive, but when we repeatedly reject the Spirit, there is a point at which God recognizes the rejection is so thorough we no longer can hear the invitation.

Those who have received Christ in their hearts automatically receive His Spirit. God promises that He will never leave us nor forsake us (Matthew 28:20; Hebrews 13:5). If your heart is secure in Christ you can rest in the awareness that you will never lose God's Spirit.

SPIRITUAL HEART FOCUS
If you feel the Holy Spirit convicting you of sin, rejoice! This is proof that He continues to strive with you.

PHYSICAL HEART FOCUS

The key to the fuels (calories) you put into your body is getting the quality and quantity you need for optimum health, not for excess.

♥ Glued to Disobedience

EXODUS 14:5

Now it was told the king of Egypt that the people had fled, and the heart of Pharaoh and his servants was turned against the people; and they said, "Why have we done this, that we have let Israel go from serving us?"

A GUY REASSEMBLING some furniture got his fingers stuck with superglue, and he couldn't separate them.

Similarly, each time Pharaoh changed his mind about freeing God's people, his heart became a little more glued to disobedience. Ultimately, he couldn't get loose, and Egypt experienced disaster.

Having the liberty to wiggle your fingers is normal. So is obedience to God.

This is a paradox: Our freedom is in our enslavement to God. You're going to be glued to something inevitably, so glue your heart to God.

SPIRITUAL HEART FOCUS

You glue your heart to God by adhering to Him daily, both in your personal communion and in choices you make in the face of temptation.

PHYSICAL HEART FOCUS

Munch 8–10 raw almonds as a filling snack that adds fiber.

❤ Love Is Wanting to Say You're Sorry

JOEL 2:12–13

"Now, therefore," says the LORD,
"Turn to Me with all your heart,
With fasting, with weeping, and with mourning."
So rend your heart, and not your garments;
Return to the LORD your God,
For He is gracious and merciful,
Slow to anger, and of great kindness;
And He relents from doing harm.

THE HEART THAT LOVES GOD passionately knows when it has grieved the Spirit of God, and it can't apologize quickly enough.

This is the essence of the repentant heart. That's why God would rather see our tears than our rituals.

The repenting heart "re-turns" and moves back to the compassionate Father.

Regret can be expressed religiously, but real repentance flows from the weeping heart, one compelled by its deep love to say, "I'm sorry, Lord."

SPIRITUAL HEART FOCUS
Recognize the difference between the regretful heart and the repentant heart. When you ask God for forgiveness, let both your heart and your lips say, "I'm sorry."

PHYSICAL HEART FOCUS
Limit the amount of saturated fat and trans fat in your diet.

❤ Armistice Is Not Peace

PSALM 140:1–2

Deliver me, O LORD, from evil men;
Preserve me from violent men,
Who plan evil things in their hearts;
They continually gather together for war.

SOMETIMES WHAT WE CALL "PEACE" is nothing more than an armed truce.

On November 11, 1918, World War I halted through an armistice agreement. But there was no peace, and twenty–one years later the same nations were at war again.

> **SPIRITUAL HEART FOCUS**
> Never settle for an armistice with the powers of darkness when God's will for you is total peace.

On July 27, 1953, the United Nations forces signed an armistice agreement with the North Koreans, but a half-century later, the agreement is fragile. Papers signed; no peace.

Shalom means much more than a mere truce. It signifies the obliteration of the evil that would steal the peace.

Personal peace is not a cessation of hostilities against the devil, but a crushing defeat that makes it impossible for him to wage war against our souls. Jesus Christ accomplished that at the cross.

That's why our salvation is true peace, not a mere armistice.

PHYSICAL HEART FOCUS

Food fallacy: *All fats are bad.* Actually, you need the proper types of fat, like mono– and polyunsaturated fats.

❤ The Strength That Counts

GENESIS 3:1

Now the serpent was more cunning than any beast
of the field which the LORD God had made. . ."

MATTHEW 4:1

Then Jesus was led up by the Spirit into
the wilderness to be tempted by the devil . . .

THE STRENGTH OF THE SPIRITUAL HEART trumps that of the physical heart.

Eve was physically strong but spiritually weak when the serpent came. Jesus was spiritually strong but physically weak when the devil appeared. Eve succumbed to the allurement, but Jesus sent the devil scurrying for cover.

The world lives by the creed of the survival of the physically fittest. In the Kingdom of God, as Paul discovered, "when I am weak, then I am strong" (2 Corinthians 12:10).

This is not a call to gaunt asceticism. It's not a mandate to dress in hair shirts or lash our bodies with whips. To the contrary, we are stewards of our physical health and have a mandate to take care of our bodies.

But in the ultimate struggle it's not physical strength that wins, but spiritual power.

SPIRITUAL HEART FOCUS
Make sure there is time daily to exercise your spiritual heart.

PHYSICAL HEART FOCUS

Food fallacy: *All carbohydrates are good.* There may be times when you need a "sugar high," but focus on low glycemic index foods, like fruits, vegetables, and whole grains.

❤ Bewitched or Buttressed?

ACTS 8:9–11

But there was a certain man called Simon, who previously practiced sorcery in the city and astonished the people of Samaria, claiming that he was someone great, to whom they all gave heed, from the least to the greatest, saying, "This man is the great power of God." And they heeded him because he had astonished them with his sorceries for a long time.

THE RELIGION OF MAGIC bewitches the heart, but moral faith buttresses the heart.

> SPIRITUAL HEART FOCUS
> The immature heart goes after magic, but maturing followers of Christ embrace moral faith. Ask God for the discernment to know the difference and nurture your passion for the moral.

Jesus, who had enough power over nature to still storms, rejected magic. The devil wanted Jesus to twirl His wand in the wilderness and change the stones into bread and levitate off the temple parapet. But Jesus always refused.

Jesus rejected magic because He knew that although the people might have been impressed, they wouldn't have been improved.

The big question of magic religion is, "What will God do *for* me?" But the quest of moral faith is, "What will Almighty God do *in* and *through* me for His sake and that of others?"

Magic religion may bewitch your heart, but it can't buttress it with strength to stand and serve. Turn from Houdini and go after Jesus.

PHYSICAL HEART FOCUS

Food fallacy: *All proteins are the same.* Differentiate between good protein (like from vegetables or fish) and bad protein (red meat) because of the associated saturated fats.

❤ Heart Bait

1 PETER 5:8–9

Be sober, be vigilant; because your adversary the devil walks about like a roaring lion, seeking whom he may devour. Resist him, steadfast in the faith, knowing that the same sufferings are experienced by your brotherhood in the world.

THE DEVIL IS NOT OMNISCIENT. To know your heart he must study your behavior, so he prowls and seeks.

For my fishermen sons the key to a successful outing is the bait. They study the colors, sizes, shapes, and sounds of artificial lures. They want to use the right lure at the right time at the right place.

The devil watches our walk and studies our behavior so he can cast his bait into our hearts and catch us. The bait the devil uses matches the yearnings of our hearts as revealed in our external actions.

> SPIRITUAL
> HEART FOCUS
> Pray for discernment
> to distinguish the bait from
> the real thing.

Growing in Christ means learning to distinguish bait from real food. Heart–bait promises to fulfill the flesh's desires, but God's real food will feed our spirits.

PHYSICAL HEART FOCUS

Food fallacy: *Dairy products are essential to good health.* Too much can negatively impact your weight and overall health, so either use a calcium supplement rather than a big glass of whole milk or consider skim milk.

♥ Lining Up the Lights

MATTHEW 7:21

"Not everyone who says to Me, 'Lord, Lord,' shall enter the kingdom of heaven, but he who does the will of My Father in heaven."

A SHIP APPROACHED A NARROW HARBOR. "How can you know where and when to turn?" asked a passenger. "I run parallel to the land, and then I turn when the ship is aligned with those three lights on the shore," the captain answered.

The heart knows direction when it's lined up with God's three lights. The first is the beacon of the Bible, which gives the broad revelation of God's will.

Second is the light shining through doors that open and close. This illuminates our trust in God to open the right opportunities and close the wrong portals.

The third light is the witness of the Holy Spirit. If He lives in your heart, you will have inner direction, which should be confirmed by external witness.

Get the Word, the doors, and the Spirit's inner witness lined up and your heart will know where and when to turn.

SPIRITUAL HEART FOCUS
Determine to make no decisions until all the lights are lined up.

PHYSICAL HEART FOCUS

Food fallacy: *What you eat is the key determinant of your health.* It's vital to monitor your daily calorie intake, but also exercise and try to maintain your ideal weight.

♥ Intense Desire

ROMANS 10:1

*Brethren, my heart's desire and prayer to God for Israel is
that they may be saved.*

THERE CAN BE NO GREATER heart desire than the rescue of people—
especially those dearest to our hearts—from the horror of eternal
separation from God.

To intensify your heart's desire, consider what it
means to be lost. Existence outside the presence of
God is like lungs without oxygen, eyes without
light. It is to spend eternity without hope,
trying always to sate the desperate thirst for
which there is no water.

To be lost is to be on safari in a deep jungle
where there is perpetual midnight, and where
every turn in the path could lead to a pit of vipers.

If our hearts grasped the horror of lostness,
our passionate desire would be for rescuing others!

> **SPIRITUAL HEART FOCUS**
> Make a list and pray daily
> for specific people you know
> who need Christ, beginning
> with your loved ones, and
> for opportunities to tell them
> about Jesus and
> His salvation.

PHYSICAL HEART FOCUS

Stretching is especially beneficial after a workout, and it isn't just for warm–up.

❤ Keeping the Cheer

1 CHRONICLES 16:10
Glory in His holy name;
Let the hearts of those rejoice who seek the LORD!

I CAN STILL SEE THE OLD GENTS who spent Sunday afternoons kicking car tires on the used auto lot. But there's a big difference between kicking tires and seeking.

SPIRITUAL HEART FOCUS
Seek God, not just knowledge about Him.

"Seek," in the Hebrew used in today's text, refers especially to searching out the Lord through prayer. There are people who "kick tires" with regard to spiritual things, but the cheer is for those who seek earnestly and continually.

Seeking the Lord brings a heart–cheer that never fades.

PHYSICAL HEART FOCUS
B vitamins may have heart protection benefits.

❤ The Whining Heart

PSALM 13:1–2

How long, O LORD? Will You forget me forever?
How long will You hide Your face from me?
How long shall I take counsel in my soul,
Having sorrow in my heart daily?
How long will my enemy be exalted over me?

JUST BECAUSE YOU GET OLD doesn't mean you get sweeter. In fact, the longer you live the more you become what you always have been.

It's sheer whining to think God could forget His child or hole up in a side room when He hears His kid approaching.

I once visited an elderly woman who was a perpetual whiner. Finally I had enough, and I suggested names of people she should encourage. She contacted them and then called me. For the first time I heard excitement dancing on her voice.

We whine when our unbelief comes between us and the light. But when we return to God, we are again in the light, catching its beams, and able to bless others.

Shine, don't whine!

SPIRITUAL HEART FOCUS

When whining wants to well up from your soul, focus away from yourself, first by looking at the Lord, and second by encouraging others.

PHYSICAL HEART FOCUS

Increased fiber in your diet may decrease risk of colon cancer.

❤ Reunion

JOHN 16:5–6, 22

"But now I go away to Him who sent Me, and none of you asks Me, 'Where are You going?' But because I have said these things to you, sorrow has filled your heart. . . . Therefore you now have sorrow; but I will see you again and your heart will rejoice, and your joy no one will take from you."

FAMILY REUNIONS INVOLVE three things—fun, food, and a few tears—sometimes all wrapped up in tension or even outright conflict.

Just about now you might be thinking about all the family you will see over the holidays. Annually, my mother's family gathers in a metal building, the family tree is read, remembrances told. Jo Beth's family has grandchildren perform.

SPIRITUAL HEART FOCUS
Ask God to prepare you to minister to loved ones you will see over the holidays.

If we grasped the joy of reunion we could handle separation better. That's what Jesus was telling His grieving followers shortly before His death.

So a mom and dad weep as their daughter weds and moves in with her husband. But that sorrow leads to the joy of grandkids scampering through the house and big tables populated with laughing, loving people thanking God that although they are separated, they are together.

It all points to the grand heavenly reunion and the loss of "goodbye" from our vocabulary!

PHYSICAL HEART FOCUS

For most people, a diet of 1,300 to 2,000 calories daily will maintain ideal body weight.

❤ The Holiest Eucharist

2 CORINTHIANS 4:15

For all things are for your sakes, that grace, having spread through the many, may cause thanksgiving to abound to the glory of God.

THE HEART THAT DOES NOT WORSHIP is not grateful.

"Eucharist" is the term brought over into English to describe the Lord's Supper, or Holy Communion. Literally, the word is a combination of two Greek words—*eu*, "well" or "good," and *charis*, "grace" or "favor."

The focus of the word is thanksgiving. The theme of the Lord's Supper is to remember Christ's sacrifice for us with gratitude.

Annually, the United States sets aside a day to give thanks. However, the heart that has been touched by the grace of Christ and knows the favor of the Father lives in a perpetual Eucharist, in which every day is Thanksgiving.

God gifts us so we may share our blessings. When the giving of thanks abounding to the glory of God fills the world, the smog of depression, anxiety, conflict, and strife will dissipate on the winds of worship.

> SPIRITUAL
> HEART FOCUS
> Rather than rushing to say "Thanks," wait before the Lord and allow the Holy Spirit to lift up the gratitude from your heart. Then express your gratefulness from the heart, not just the mouth.

PHYSICAL HEART FOCUS

Decide now that in your holiday eating you will choose smaller portions of the foods you love. Sample, don't stuff.

♥ Thanksgiving Is . . .

EPHESIANS 5:20

Giving thanks always for all things to God the Father in the name of our Lord Jesus Christ.

THANKSGIVING IS THE GRATEFULNESS of the Pilgrims in 1623 for the blessings of God that sustained them.

Thanksgiving is John Wesley singing on his deathbed, "Let's praise . . ."

Thanksgiving is Abraham Lincoln in the darkness of the Civil War proclaiming a day of fasting followed by a day of giving thanks.

Thanksgiving is a friend who told me on the eve of open–heart surgery, "This has been the greatest day of my life, and I'm so thankful I'm here!"

Thanksgiving is my mother, dying from a malignancy, looking at me with pained eyes and a twisted smile, saying, "God has been so good to me."

Thanksgiving is unsinkable people facing the worst with hearts of unceasing gratitude.

SPIRITUAL HEART FOCUS
Let Thanksgiving Day remind you that Thanksgiving season should never end.

PHYSICAL HEART FOCUS

Enjoy holiday sweets with a loved one by splitting a portion.

♥ Three Men, Three Hearts

PROVERBS 15:11

Hell and Destruction are before the LORD;
So how much more the hearts of the sons of men.

THREE FAMOUS MEN DIED on this date in 1963—John F. Kennedy, C. S. Lewis, and Aldous Huxley. Their spiritual hearts beat differently, as Peter Kreeft shows in his book, *Between Heaven and Hell*.[14]

Lewis "took his Christianity straight, or 'mere,'" Kreeft writes. Kennedy was "a humanistic Christian" who believed in the broad strokes of the faith, although he was uncertain about other important beliefs. Huxley's was a stewpot heart in which biblical faith mingled with Oriental mysticism. He was a believer in the god–who–is–everything.

> **SPIRITUAL HEART FOCUS**
> Meditate on and embrace the "simplicity and purity of devotion to Christ" (2 Corinthians 11:3 NASB).

Almost a half–century later, the genuine heart is revealed by its fruit. Kennedy is wrapped in legend that combines power, tragedy, and immorality. Huxley is forgotten except for book reports and a few curious scholars. But Lewis's heart still radiates with the transforming Gospel. Lewis's heart still strongly pumps the gospel message.

Death does indeed lay our hearts out in the open.

PHYSICAL HEART FOCUS

Keep it simple and accurate by weighing yourself at the same time each day you weigh.

❤ Gratitude Cures the Anxious Heart

MATTHEW 15:36

And He took the seven loaves and the fish and gave thanks, broke them and gave them to His disciples; and the disciples gave to the multitude.

PHILIPPIANS 4:6

Be anxious for nothing, but in everything by prayer and supplication, with thanksgiving, let your requests be made known to God.

How MANY PEOPLE WILL DINE on your turkey this Thanksgiving? Imagine four thousand growling stomachs waiting for lunch!

Jesus faced such a challenge with calm serenity. The key was in giving thanks. Jesus was anxious for nothing because gratitude was the continual condition of His heart.

SPIRITUAL HEART FOCUS
Don't let the holidays drive up your anxiety; instead, take time to meditate on God's faithfulness.

Giving thanks before you distribute seven loaves and a few small fish is an act of faith. Jesus' heart was thankful because it was "thinkful." He meditated on God's sufficiency before He dealt with the people's insufficiency. His heart focused on the Father's faithfulness in the face of the mob's fearfulness.

Gratitude kept anxiety away from Jesus, and it will cure your heart of that affliction as well.

PHYSICAL HEART FOCUS

Enjoy your food by sitting down to eat. Don't rush, but focus on when you *begin* to get full and stop eating at that point.

❤ Thanksgiving with a Grudge

2 TIMOTHY 3:1–2

But know this, that in the last days perilous times will come:
For men will be lovers of themselves, lovers of money, boasters, proud,
blasphemers, disobedient to parents, unthankful, unholy.

"SUSAN, EAT ALL your spinach!"

"But Mommy, I don't like spinach."

"Eat it anyway, because it's good for you!"

Susan downs the green gunk and says, "May I be excused?"

"No," answers her mother. "You stay there until you think of something you're grateful for."

"Okay," the child replies. "I'm thankful that stuff hasn't made me sick yet. Now can I leave?"

Many people will sit around a table this week and grudgingly thank God. Begrudging thanks is no thanks. Ingratitude makes for difficult times because ungrateful people are thoughtless people.

If you think about God's goodness to you, you won't be reluctant to thank Him. Gratitude will gush from your heart like a geyser.

> **SPIRITUAL HEART FOCUS**
> Before you thank God, consider the specific blessings He's brought to your life. This will make your gratitude not a ceremonial prayer but an explosion of praise.

PHYSICAL HEART FOCUS

Nibble on healthy foods like fruits and nuts throughout the day, rather than gorging once or twice.

❤ No One to Thank

2 CORINTHIANS 9:15
Thanks be to God for His indescribable gift!

THERE ARE LAKES IN SWITZERLAND whose waters are the color of blue sapphire. Snow–bright mountains stretch to the sky, and when wispy clouds swizzle the sky, the beauty is more than the eye can celebrate.

One morning a woman staying in a hotel across from an alpine lake cast open her window. The lady, an atheist, was overwhelmed at the scene. She cried to herself, "I wish I had someone to thank for this!"

At Thanksgiving I feel sadness for those whose hearts are faithless. The joy of gratitude is being able to say, "Thank you." But if there is no one to thank, the gratitude can only be turned back inward, and the idolatry of self grows another foot or two.

Thanks be to *God*!

> **SPIRITUAL HEART FOCUS**
> Above all else, thank God for being God. Praise Him for His attributes of love, mercy, justice, eternal being, and for being "there" for you to thank.

PHYSICAL HEART FOCUS
During the holidays, resist the "see food" diet. Don't let feasting become the reason for the season.

♥ Stand Up for the Turkeys

1 CORINTHIANS 1:27-29

But God has chosen the foolish things of the world to put to shame the wise, and God has chosen the weak things of the world to put to shame the things which are mighty; and the base things of the world and the things which are despised God has chosen, and the things which are not, to bring to nothing the things that are, that no flesh should glory in His presence.

GOD BUILDS HIS KINGDOM by transforming simple, foolish "turkeys."

Simon Peter gobbled foolishly all over the landscape until Jesus made him an eloquent spokesman named "Rocky."

John Mark hopped off the trail when difficulty came, leaving Paul and Barnabas. Later, though, God transformed John Mark from a turkey to a tiger, someone Paul was eager to have as a partner in spreading the Gospel.

Mary Magdalene, who was stuffed with seven demons, was as "turkey" as you could get. But Jesus turned her into the bold woman who beat everybody else to the empty tomb.

There's hope for us all. Let's hear it for the turkeys!

SPIRITUAL HEART FOCUS
Rather than resenting who you are, rejoice that God uses the simple and foolish to do His greatest works.

PHYSICAL HEART FOCUS

It's better to lose 10 pounds and keep it off than lose 20 pounds and regain it, then lose it again, only to get it back.

❤ Five Grains

LUKE 17:12, 15–16

Then as He entered a certain village, there met Him ten men who were lepers, who stood afar off. . . . And one of them, when he saw that he was healed, returned, and with a loud voice glorified God, and fell down on his face at His feet, giving Him thanks. And he was a Samaritan.

THE PILGRIMS WERE SO DESPERATE Governor William Bradford rationed each person just five grains of corn a day. When things got better, Bradford didn't want the people to forget, so at every Thanksgiving meal he had five grains of corn laid at each plate.

Think about *your* "five grains" of thankfulness. For me, one would be the bell I ring when I have the flu and need something. Another would be a hammer, representing opportunity in our country for everyone to earn a living and advance. A third would be a light bulb, symbolizing our affluence. Fourth is the Bible, because without it I wouldn't know God and this free, prosperous nation would not exist. The fifth would be a cross because it makes sinners like us able to live forever before Holy God.

SPIRITUAL HEART FOCUS
Lay out your five grains and give God thanks for each.

Make your heart a Thanksgiving plate, put *your* five grains there, then thank your Father for every one of them!

PHYSICAL HEART FOCUS

Although breast cancer is a serious threat, it's cardiovascular disease that will kill one out of every two women. It's as vital for women as men to take care of their hearts.

❤ Potluck

1 CORINTHIANS 11:20–21, 33

Therefore when you come together in one place, it is not to eat the Lord's Supper. For in eating, each one takes his own supper ahead of others; and one is hungry and another is drunk . . . Therefore, my brethren, when you come together to eat, wait for one another.

FOR MANY FAMILIES the Thanksgiving feast is like a huge potluck meal with various households bringing their favorite dishes. But sometimes the most affluent people bring the skimpiest contributions.

Church potluck suppers grew out of the love feasts of the early church. The focus was to be on Jesus, and then others in the community of faith. Some of the Corinthians had greedy hearts, and the point was lost.

Don't lose the point of Thanksgiving from your heart. Look first to Jesus, and be grateful for and gracious to all at the table with you.

SPIRITUAL HEART FOCUS
Try to remember all the people with whom you've shared a Thanksgiving dinner through the years—including this one—and give God thanks for them.

PHYSICAL HEART FOCUS

Studies show that you are more likely to succeed in weight loss if you take small, steady steps.

❤ Turkey Sandwiches

LUKE 12:18–20

"So he said, 'I will do this: I will pull down my barns and build greater, and there I will store all my crops and my goods. And I will say to my soul, "Soul, you have many goods laid up for many years; take your ease; eat, drink, and be merry." ' But God said to him, 'Fool! This night your soul will be required of you; then whose will those things be which you have provided?'"

A THICK TURKEY SANDWICH, the aftermath of Thanksgiving, is in your hands, and your world looks pretty good.

> SPIRITUAL
> HEART FOCUS
> Go through your house and get rid of the bad spiritual and mental leftovers, including TV and movies that satisfy your entertainment desires but starve your spiritual heart.

Many people, like the man in Jesus' parable, want to have strong spiritual hearts, but they feed constantly off the spoiling leftovers. They party rather than seeking the stimulus of the Holy Spirit. The leftover–eaters munch on literary trash and consume every rotten morsel falling from the Hollywood garbage bin. They fill up on fried excess and lie down satisfied only to discover their spiritual heart was so weak it wasn't ready for the day of judgment.

Quit eating leftovers and get some healthy food in your diet—spiritually and physically.

PHYSIAL HEART FOCUS

Excuse for not dieting: "It's boring." Eat from all food groups. It's not a diet, but a *lifestyle*.

♥ The Seersucker Heart

DEUTERONOMY 1:28

"'Where can we go up? Our brethren have discouraged our hearts, saying, "The people are greater and taller than we; the cities are great and fortified up to heaven; moreover we have seen the sons of the Anakim there."'"

A SALESMAN IN MY COLLEGE DORM offered three–piece seersucker suits for twenty dollars. I wore my new seersucker to a football game. I felt stylish as I sat with my buddy and our dates. Then it began to rain. By the middle of the fourth quarter, I was wearing a short–sleeved coat and my pant–cuffs were somewhere between my ankles and knees!

Cheap suits shrink in the storm, and so do cheap hearts. "Melt" can also mean "dissolve." That's what my suit did that day, and that's what happens to hearts that cling to cheap salvation.

Dietrich Bonhoeffer, martyred by the Nazis, reminded us that grace isn't cheap. It was bought by the blood of Christ, and it doesn't shrink in the storm.

The good news—salvation is not for sale. It's a gift. Take it!

> SPIRITUAL HEART FOCUS
> Don't settle for cheap salvation that offers no cross, no pain, and no repentance. It will shrink in the storm.

PHYSICAL HEART FOCUS

Excuse for not dieting: "I always feel hungry." Schedule frequent small meals within your calorie limit and snack on fruits and raw vegetables. Check your weight and BMI.

December

The ultimate good news of Immanuel:
God's heart is with us!

❤ Captivated by the Glitter

PSALM 86:11–12

Teach me Your way, O LORD;
I will walk in Your truth;
Unite my heart to fear Your name.
I will praise You, O Lord my God, with all my heart,
And I will glorify Your name forevermore.

SPIRITUAL HEART FOCUS
Determine that you will not allow your heart to be drawn away from focusing on Christ, especially during the season that celebrates His birth

AT CHRISTMASTIME THERE ARE so many lights, decorations, parties, and pageants that our eyes don't know where to look. As we get captivated by the glitter we lose sight of the focus of Christmas: Jesus Christ. The devil, among whose disguises is an "angel of light" (2 Corinthians 11:14), diverts our gaze from Christ's glory to Christmas glitter.

King David understood what it was to be so captivated by beauty and blessings that he lost focus on the truly important Giver of those blessings. He cried out for God to pull all the pieces together so his heart would be a total heart offering of worship.

That's a great day–starter: *Lord, give me an undivided heart.*

PHYSICAL HEART FOCUS

Excuse for not dieting: "If there are sweets in the house I can't be trusted."
Self–control is a fruit of the Spirit, which is why you must focus on the total heart.

❤ More Than Mannequins

GENESIS 2:7

And the LORD God formed man of the dust of the ground, and breathed into his nostrils the breath of life; and man became a living being.

ONCE UPON A TIME, there were no sprawling malls; instead, people went to town, strolled past department store windows, and gazed at scenes and lavish decorations. Mannequins of Santa Claus and elves beckoned to passersby from every store window.

Had God not breathed into Adam's nostrils, he would have remained an inert human form, a mere mannequin. But there is more to us than bones, muscle, and other tissue. We have souls, the very breath of God. The soul is our capacity to think, feel, and choose. At its core is the spirit, the "wick" that is set ablaze by God's Spirit and gives light to our whole body (Proverbs 20:27).

Enjoy the technical marvel of the robotic mannequins, but rejoice that God made you something much more than anything you see in the department store window.

SPIRITUAL HEART FOCUS
Don't let Christmas activities rob you of time to nurture your spiritual heart.

PHYSICAL HEART FOCUS

Sustained, repetitive exercise elevates your heart rate, facilitates blood flow, delivers oxygen to your cells, and increases your metabolic rate.

♥ Keep It Ticking

EPHESIANS 6:6

Not with eyeservice, as men–pleasers, but as bondservants of Christ, doing the will of God from the heart.

THE TWO OBVIOUS WAYS to keep your ticker ticking strongly are diet and exercise.

During the holidays, it's tempting to drift from good diet and exercise. But heart health is always in season. Your body has no censor to cancel out Christmas calories and the negatives of neglecting exercise.

The healthy spiritual heart doesn't take off for the holidays either. The will of God is to be carried out during the merriment just as in routine times. The healthy heart maintains its focus on God's will "in season and out of season" (2 Timothy 4:2).

Enjoy the Christmas holidays, but don't neglect heart health. Keep doing the things that keep your physical ticker ticking, and keep doing the will of God from your spiritually healthy heart.

SPIRITUAL HEART FOCUS

List activities in which you will participate during Christmas, and find ways you can serve God through them.

PHYSICAL HEART FOCUS

Try whole–grain rice instead of instant rice. Whole–grain rice has a lower glycemic index, higher fiber, and more nutrients.

❤ People Who Need People

Since you have purified your souls in obeying the truth through the Spirit in sincere love of the brethren, love one another fervently with a pure heart.

"PEOPLE WHO NEED PEOPLE are the luckiest people in the world," goes Barbra Streisand's song.

Sometimes even hermits might not relish being alone, and Christmas is one of those seasons. A Christmas without other people is as wrong as a Fourth of July without the flag.

The best place to be during Christmas in addition to home and family is among a community of people in a Bible–believing church. But such involvement with other folks shouldn't end with Christmas.

One study showed that people who never attend church "are four times as likely to die from respiratory disease, diabetes, or infectious diseases."[15]

You need God's people at Christmas—and year–round!

SPIRITUAL HEART FOCUS
During the holidays focus on being with people who will encourage your spiritual heart rather than those who will tempt you into ungodly activities.

PHYSICAL HEART FOCUS

You get the benefits of soluble fiber from foods like oatmeal, barley, beans, lentils, apples, pears, bananas, citrus fruits, and Brussels sprouts.

♥ Don't Turn Back

PSALM 85:8

I will hear what God the LORD will speak,
For He will speak peace
To His people and to His saints;
But let them not turn back to folly.

HOW WOULD YOU FEEL ABOUT a heart transplant patient who went back to the behavior that killed his or her first heart?

"Folly" means silliness and stupidity, which is exactly what that would be! Imagine a person celebrating a new heart by buying a case of cigarettes, loading up on red meat and pastries, and deciding systematic exercise is no longer necessary because of the fresh, healthy heart.

Sheer folly.

If you have started down the road toward total heart health, you will encounter many temptations to turn back. But to return to unhealthy eating habits and a couch–potato lifestyle is stupidity. In fact, it is a flirtation with death.

Holidays are times for relaxing, but not for giving up. Stay with healthy habits. Don't turn back to folly.

SPIRITUAL HEART FOCUS

Prepare for the holidays by renewing your devotion to Christ and to the stewardship of the temple of your body.

PHYSICAL HEART FOCUS

Women, more often than men, will have atypical signs and symptoms of heart disease.

❤ The Need for the 'Upward'

LAMENTATIONS 3:40–41
Let us search out and examine our ways,
And turn back to the LORD;
Let us lift our hearts and hands
To God in heaven.

"OUR CHRISTIAN FRIENDS have awakened in us the need for transcendence." The communist philosopher talking to a group of Christians in the 1960s was acknowledging one of the human heart's basic needs.

"Transcendence" refers to that which is above the immanent material world and its limitations. The heart without God has no transcendent focus, no hope beyond materialism. The human heart must have transcendence.

Worship is one of the ways people lift their hearts and hands. The heart that does not praise is anemic, earthbound. Surrender is another means of lifting hearts and hands. Supplication is a form of lifting the heart and hands. When the heart cries its need to the Most High it brings the burdens of the immediate into the chambers of the transcendent, unlimited One.

The miracle of Christ's coming is that it is the Transcendent entering the immanent!

SPIRITUAL HEART FOCUS
Spend some time worshiping God for Himself, not focusing on what you need from Him.

PHYSICAL HEART FOCUS

Obesity is reaching epidemic proportions in adolescents. Teach your children to eat properly, and set a good example for them in your eating.

❤ Surprise!

ACTS 9:1–5

Then Saul, still breathing threats and murder against the disciples of the Lord, went to the high priest and asked letters from him to the synagogues . . . he came near Damascus, and suddenly a light shone around him from heaven. Then he fell to the ground, and heard a voice saying to him, "Saul, Saul, why are you persecuting Me?" And he said, "Who are You, Lord?" Then the Lord said, "I am Jesus, whom you are persecuting. . . ."

JAPANESE PLANES, led by fiery pilot Mitsuo Fuchida, flashed like lightning across the Hawaiian sky that December 7, leaving much of the American fleet in flames in their surprise attack. Later, Fuchida's heart got a surprise of its own.

SPIRITUAL HEART FOCUS
The unknown frightens us with potential surprises, but settle your heart with the truth that Jesus is the Lord of surprises and will use them for His glory and your good!

Fuchida heard about an American woman—whose missionary parents had been killed by Japanese soldiers—serving Japanese POWs to demonstrate forgiveness. Then Fuchida read the New Testament and saw that Jesus' forgiveness was unconditional. Fuchida wanted that kind of love, and he gave his life to Christ.

Later, Japanese people on Tokyo streets were surprised as they heard a voice blaring through a car–mounted loudspeaker: "I, Captain Fuchida, have become a Christian!"

The Pearl Harbor surprise was a disaster, but the bolt from the blue for Mitsuo Fuchida—and Saul of Tarsus—was a blessing!

PHYSICAL HEART FOCUS

Eat more coldwater fish to decrease your risk of sudden cardiac death, arrhythmia, triglyceride levels, and blood clots and to increase your intake of essential fatty acids.

❤ Missing Christmas

LUKE 2:7

*And she brought forth her firstborn Son, and wrapped Him in swaddling cloths,
and laid Him in a manger, because there was no room for them in the inn.*

MATTHEW 2:2–3

*"Where is He who has been born King of the Jews? For we have seen His
star in the East and have come to worship Him." When Herod the king
heard this, he was troubled, and all Jerusalem with him.*

TWO PEASANTS ARRIVE at the inn, but the manager tells them it's booked up. Three sages show up at Herod's palace looking for the King, and Herod quakes in his boots. The innkeeper missed Christmas because he was diverted by the mundane. Herod missed Christ's birth because of fear.

Perhaps such concerns rob you of the joy of Christ's coming. The mundane world of shopping and decorations sometimes means no room in our hearts for Jesus. The fear that someone might unseat the self from our heart–thrones also will cause us to miss the joy of Christmas, as with Herod. Indifference also will cause us to miss Christmas. The street crowds saw the young woman swollen with pregnancy, but they passed her by, indifferent to her pain.

Don't let mundane things, fear, or indifference rob your heart of the miracle of the incarnation of God in the person of Jesus Christ.

> **SPIRITUAL HEART FOCUS**
> Your holiday schedule may be busy. Carve out some time in the days ahead for solitude, meditation on the Incarnation, and communion with God.

PHYSICAL HEART FOCUS

Obesity is associated with arthritis, gout, gallstones, sleep apnea, and some cancers.

♥ Empty Chair

JOHN 16:5–7

"But now I go away to Him who sent Me, and none of you asks Me, 'Where are You going?' But because I have said these things to you, sorrow has filled your heart. Nevertheless I tell you the truth. It is to your advantage that I go away; for if I do not go away, the Helper will not come to you; but if I depart, I will send Him to you."

FOR MANY PEOPLE, this Christmas will be marked by an empty chair, and the season looms as a reminder of the depth of the loss. Whatever the reason, at the very time the heart ought to be leaping with joy, it limps with grief.

> **SPIRITUAL HEART FOCUS**
>
> If you're facing the empty chair this Christmas, pray for the grace and courage to focus on loved ones who will be there to share with you. Pray for all the people you know who will face empty chairs this Christmas.

If a chair is empty at your table, Christmas will be a season of adjustment. You may be thinking, "If I can just clear this hurdle . . ."

Jesus' disciples grieved as they thought of living without His physical presence. But He told them it was part of the process by which they would know Him in a new, more intimate way—in their own hearts. It would be a huge adjustment, but He would help them through His Spirit.

If a chair is empty for you this year, Christmas is a major adjustment. But the One who lifted the disciples from their grief and turned their mourning into joy also will walk you through these days of the empty chair.

PHYSICAL HEART FOCUS

Not gaining weight is a successful step toward losing weight.

❤ Whose Birthday Is It Anyway?

MATTHEW 2:7–8

Then Herod, when he had secretly called the wise men, determined from them what time the star appeared. And he sent them to Bethlehem and said, "Go and search carefully for the young Child, and when you have found Him, bring back word to me, that I may come and worship Him also."

THERE WAS ONCE a topsy–turvy kingdom. Flowers grew in wintry ice and lakes froze in the summer. Jason, who lived in that strange realm, celebrated his eighth birthday. His mother baked a cake, but he never saw it because she gave it to the mailman. When Jason's friends heard of his birthday, they gave one another presents, but nothing to Jason.

Finally, Jason had all he could take. He got a bike and rode the streets shouting at the top of his lungs, "Whose birthday is it anyway?"

As far as Herod was concerned, Christmas was all about him. Herod faked a desire to worship the Christ–child so he could carry out his heart's secret agenda and protect his throne.

Many of us get confused about whose birthday we mark at Christmas. We behave like it's ours, not Christ's.

"Whose birthday is it anyway?"

Good question for Herod, and for a lot of us.

> **SPIRITUAL HEART FOCUS**
> Think about how you will celebrate Jesus' birthday this year. Will it be more about you than Him?

PHYSICAL HEART FOCUS

A person whose physical activity is limited by age should plan for a slower weight–loss program, but take encouragement that as long as you operate in "calorie deficit mode," the pounds will come off.

❤ Wake–Up Call

MATTHEW 26:74–75

Then he began to curse and swear, saying, "I do not know the Man!" Immediately a rooster crowed. And Peter remembered the word of Jesus who had said to him, "Before the rooster crows, you will deny Me three times." So he went out and wept bitterly.

THE CROWING OF A ROOSTER broke Peter's heart because it brought him face to face with the gap between his profession and his practice.

At Easter, we celebrate Christ's resurrection. Like Simon Peter, we declare, "You are the Christ, the Son of the living God" (Matthew 16:16). But then comes that chilly night when Peter warms himself by the fire as Jesus is being tried. Then come the denials, the cock's crow, and the bitter tears.

> SPIRITUAL HEART FOCUS
> Reflect on your heart's belief and lifestyle between the celebrations of Easter and Christmas. Is there a void of faith and commitment, or are you consistent in your profession and practice throughout?

We leave church on Easter morning and spend the rest of the year warming ourselves at the world's fires. By our words and actions we behave as if we do not know Him.

Then comes Christmas, reminding us of our affirmations of the divinity of Christ and what we profess to believe.

Christmas is the cock crowing, the wake–up call to reconcile the beliefs of our heart with the words of our mouths, actions of our hands, and direction of our steps.

PHYSICAL HEART FOCUS

You can cover about two miles in 30 minutes of brisk walking, burn about 200 calories, and in a year lose 20 pounds just from eating right and walking two miles per day.

❤ Compass

MATTHEW 2:10–11

When they saw the star, they rejoiced with exceedingly great joy. And when they had come into the house, they saw the young Child with Mary His mother, and fell down and worshiped Him. And when they had opened their treasures, they presented gifts to Him: gold, frankincense, and myrrh.

CHRISTMAS IS A COMPASS, giving us a new sense of direction and guiding us back to the right path when we've lost it.

When I was a boy, we put on the same Christmas pageant every year. A rope would be strung high across the stage. A trio of elderly deacons wearing bathrobes and turbans would enter stage right. One of them would pull a string that tugged a cut-out star along the rope. It led to the same place every year—the manger. Frankly, the cardboard star was the only character in that pageant that never missed its line or cue.

SPIRITUAL HEART FOCUS
Regard this Christmas as an opportunity to renew your walk to and with Jesus Christ as Lord of your life.

The wise men had spent their lives studying the patterns of the stars. Among all the billions lavishing the night sky, there was one by which they knew they could set their paths to the birthplace of the world's Hope.

If you focus on it properly, Christmas can be your compass, guiding you to the Christ, who is your Hope.

PHYSICAL HEART FOCUS

Begin a cardio exercise activity with a warmup of four to five minutes and end with a cool-down of three to four minutes.

❤ Invitation

LUKE 2:10–14

*Then the angel said to them, "Do not be afraid, for behold, I bring you
good tidings of great joy which will be to all people. For there is born
to you this day in the city of David a Savior, who is Christ the Lord.
And this will be the sign to you: You will find a Babe wrapped in swaddling
cloths, lying in a manger." And suddenly there was with the angel a
multitude of the heavenly host praising God and saying:*

*"Glory to God in the highest,
And on earth peace, goodwill toward men!"*

**SPIRITUAL
HEART FOCUS**
Listen to the invitation the
Holy Spirit sends to your
heart during this
blessed season.

CHRISTMAS MAY SYMBOLIZE many things, but above all else it is an invitation to our hearts.

When you and I receive an invitation, there's often a map attached and a little star affixed over the destination. The shepherds had a detailed invitation. The sign they were at the right place would be a swaddled Baby lying in a manger. The field hands didn't get many invitations to important events, but they scampered to Bethlehem. Here was the biggest happening in history, and it was shepherds who got the invitation!

The Christmas invitation is still open to every heart that will recognize and receive it. This Christmas, the Christ of all seasons invites you to His side. Get up and go to Him—in a hurry.

PHYSICAL HEART FOCUS

You will begin to feel your body tightening at about age 40, and range of motion becomes crucial. Stretching exercises cause muscle fibers to get longer and ease the tightening.

❤ Christmas Diet

MATTHEW 24:37–38

"But as the days of Noah were, so also will the coming of the Son of Man be. For as in the days before the flood, they were eating and drinking, marrying and giving in marriage, until the day that Noah entered the ark."

AND SO HERE WE ARE at Christmastime, eating and drinking in celebration of Jesus' *first* coming, though His topic in Matthew 24 is the *second* coming. The average American gains six pounds between Thanksgiving and Christmas. Here are rules many follow during the holidays:

If you eat something and no one sees you eat it, there are no calories.

If you down a diet drink and munch a candy bar simultaneously, the calories in the candy bar are cancelled by the diet drink.

Cookie pieces have no calories because breaking leaks calories.

> **SPIRITUAL HEART FOCUS**
> Fortify yourself for Christmas feasting by committing to stay with a healthy diet for your spiritual and physical heart.

Well, not quite—on any of the above.

As you contemplate your Christmas feasting, don't fall back into unhealthy habits. Strangely, people run their lives with rationalizations much like the above "rules" that starve the spiritual heart during the season celebrating Christ's birth.

Don't let your Christmas feasting leave you hungry!

PHYSICAL HEART FOCUS

Determine that you will enjoy Christmas dinners, but that heaping your plate and having seconds is off your Christmas list.

❤ Home Is Where the Heart Is

GENESIS 46:30-31

And Israel said to Joseph, "Now let me die, since I have seen your face, because you are still alive." Then Joseph said to his brothers and to his father's household, "I will go up and tell Pharaoh, and say to him, 'My brothers and those of my father's house, who were in the land of Canaan, have come to me.'"

"I'LL BE HOME FOR CHRISTMAS," Bing Crosby crooned. The song was written in 1943, expressing the wish of troops far away from home at the most celebrated holiday of the year. Decades later, the song still tells of the inner pangs many people feel when they think of going home for Christmas.

If your heart is not right toward a loved one, you are separated from home in the deepest sense.

> SPIRITUAL HEART FOCUS
>
> Pray for the salvation, peace, and prosperity of all your loved ones. If restoration is needed, ask God for His guidance, His wisdom, and the opportunity to heal broken relationships.

But when the relationship is restored, home is wherever you are together. Joseph lost his home but found it again in a strange land when he was restored to his father and brothers. And because they were reconciled to Joseph, his brothers also were at home in an alien place.

If brokenness in your family keeps you or others from home, forgive those who have hurt you, ask forgiveness for pain you may have caused, and seek restoration.

This will restore your heart, and home is where the heart is.

PHYSICAL HEART FOCUS

A great Christmas gift: a nonstick skillet packed with a heart–healthy cookbook and spices.

♥ Immersing the Senses

JOHN 1:14

And the Word became flesh and dwelt among us, and we beheld His glory, the glory as of the only begotten of the Father, full of grace and truth.

GOD USES ALL OUR SENSES to show the reality of Christ's coming.

SIGHT: The shepherds saw the blinding flash. The three sages saw the bright star. Simeon saw the salvation of Israel, and Anna the fulfillment of a lifelong search.

SOUND: Spoken words stunned Mary and Joseph, and heavenly music amazed the shepherds. Ears resonated with the sound of God's arrival in the world.

SMELL: Fresh hay signaled the manger and the odor of animals in the stable. Frankincense and myrrh perfumed the air around Him who brings fragrance to the world.

TOUCH: Mary held the Baby. Loving Him makes us caress and embrace others, hold their hands, and lift up sagging arms.

TASTE: Yes, there are hams and turkeys and Christmas pies. But taste also means flavor to living, the rich elevation of culture so that it satisfies the spiritual palate with art. Without the savor of the Savior, the world would be coarse and vulgar.

When God reveals Himself to us, it is to our total heart and senses!

SPIRITUAL HEART FOCUS
Engage your total heart and senses in the wonder of Christ's Incarnation.

PHYSICAL HEART FOCUS
Weight loss involves a two-pronged attack consisting of healthy diet and regular exercise.

♥ How Odd of God

JOHN 6:55–56, 60, 66

"For My flesh is food indeed, and My blood is drink indeed. He who eats My flesh and drinks My blood abides in Me, and I in him." . . . Therefore many of His disciples, when they heard this, said, "This is a hard saying; who can understand it?" . . . From that time many of His disciples went back and walked with Him no more.

MOST THINGS GOD DOES in history seem odd to natural human beings. Nothing could be odder than God's plan of salvation, which included the Incarnation and Christ's atonement.

SPIRITUAL HEART FOCUS
Meditate on God's penchant for using the lowly to make the highest impact and the implications of that for your life purpose.

Imagine you were born in the Amazon jungles as part of a tribe still locked in the Stone Age. Suddenly, you are carried to the operating theater of a large teaching hospital. You watch in horror as a man slices open a human being. Your heart asks, "What kind of scary ritual is this? How can I escape?"

Then someone explains modern medicine to you. The discoveries of the greatest minds in medical science are disclosed, and it all makes sense.

God's ways may seem strange to our earthbound minds. But there's a much bigger picture, and Jesus has come to reveal it to our perplexed hearts.

PHYSICAL HEART FOCUS

When it comes to parties, "eat before you meet." Fill up with heart-healthy food so you will lessen the temptation to overindulge on party delights.

❤ Speaking to the Child's Heart

HEBREWS 1:1–3

God, who at various times and in various ways spoke in time past to the fathers by the prophets, has in these last days spoken to us by His Son, whom He has appointed heir of all things, through whom also He made the worlds; who being the brightness of His glory and the express image of His person, and upholding all things by the word of His power, when He had by Himself purged our sins, sat down at the right hand of the Majesty on high.

CHILDREN LOVED MR. ROGERS because he spoke straight to them. The camera was always angled, and his words were chosen so that he didn't talk down to his little viewers.

At the end of the program, Mr. Rogers would say, "I'll be here tomorrow . . . You are special because you are you."

Fred Rogers knew how to talk to a child's heart. Each day he would lay the groundwork for what he would say and do the next. It takes time and patience to speak to a child's heart.

The Father went to great lengths to get us ready for the message He was going to give us in Jesus Christ. The Lord taught us that the only way we can know the Kingdom is to become like little kids. God understands He's talking to spiritual toddlers, and He's willing to take eons to prepare our hearts.

What God said to us yesterday prepares us for His messages today.

> ### SPIRITUAL HEART FOCUS
> Meditate on the prophecies related to the coming of Jesus and how He so perfectly fulfilled them all.

PHYSICAL HEART FOCUS

The quantity of food you eat is the single most important determinant of your health.

❤ A Savior, Not Superman

ISAIAH 53:2–3

For He shall grow up before Him as a tender plant,
And as a root out of dry ground.
He has no form or comeliness;
And when we see Him,
There is no beauty that we should desire Him.
He is despised and rejected by men,
A Man of sorrows and acquainted with grief.
And we hid, as it were, our faces from Him;
He was despised, and we did not esteem Him.

SPIRITUAL HEART FOCUS
The model for your heart isn't Superman, but the Savior, and that means being humble, not arrogant, a person whose strength is mighty love, not muscular force.

ONE CONCEPT OF "SUPERMAN" was invented by Friedrich Nietzsche, and another concept was imaged on the screen by Christopher Reeve.

That's also how some try to depict Jesus. But the real Jesus came to fulfill the prophecies of Isaiah, not the philosophy of Nietzsche or the fantasy of comic book fans. Jesus didn't come to be Superman, but the Savior who could be pierced for our transgressions, crushed for our iniquities, chastened for our wellbeing, and scourged for our healing (Isaiah 53:4–6).

Kryptonite was the only thing that could weaken Superman's heart. Christ could save us only by allowing all our sin to break His heart.

That's why He came as Savior, not Superman.

PHYSICAL HEART FOCUS
Enjoy some holiday treats, but limit the quantity.

❤ Testing the Divine Heart

HEBREWS 4:15–16

For we do not have a High Priest who cannot sympathize with our weaknesses, but was in all points tempted as we are, yet without sin. Let us therefore come boldly to the throne of grace, that we may obtain mercy and find grace to help in time of need.

OUR CONFIDENCE AND HOPE is that Jesus *gets it.* He understands.

When we're confronted with sexual temptation, intense cravings in our hearts, and unthinkable thoughts teasing our brains, He gets it.

Not like your pastor, guru, or psychotherapist gets it, but exactly like you get it. Tell human counselors your inner struggles, and they will filter them through the sieves of their own conflicts. They'll say, "I understand." But they don't.

But He does. His great heart was stretched to the breaking point just like yours. Your counselors try to help you through *identification* with your problems, but Jesus saves you through *participation* in your personal struggles.

> **SPIRITUAL HEART FOCUS**
> When temptation stretches your heart to the breaking point, realize that now you have a new heart—Christ's unbreakable heart—which is not enslaved to sin.

But what's the point of Him getting it if He can't do anything about it? There's our hope: His heart was stretched but didn't snap so that we can replace our sin–broken heart with His unbreakable one!

You are not alone in your trials and temptations. He gets it.

PHYSICAL HEART FOCUS

The average woman must eat less and exercise more to achieve weight goals and overall health quality.

❤ A 'Materialistic' Faith

JOHN 1:14
And the Word became flesh and dwelt among us, and we beheld His glory, the glory as of the only begotten of the Father, full of grace and truth.

I AGREE WITH WILLIAM TEMPLE that Christianity is more materialistic than any religion, but not for the same reasons.

Most religious systems stress the metaphysical and "transnatural," the ethereal and the fantasy. But that the infinite God would wear a body that could hunger, thirst, and tire says everything. It tells us the time–space–matter world is not some second–rate place for God to avoid. The material world is part of the whole fabric of His creation, just as important as the immaterial.

Jesus didn't come in the grandeur and stillness of a concert hall where no one dares breathe for fear of disturbing a symphony. Instead, down in the straw an Infant sneezes during the angelic aria. Later, the Baby cries with achy gums as He cuts teeth.

In the sneeze and the tears is reality—the reality of the supernatural merging with the natural, of the timeless hooking up with the historical, of the eternal Word becoming a human voice.

That's the real "materialism" of Christmas.

SPIRITUAL HEART FOCUS
As you contemplate Christ's Incarnation, consider the places and people you may look down upon, and ask the Lord to stir you with love and willingness to serve them.

PHYSICAL HEART FOCUS
Grazing is for cattle. Place a healthy amount of food on your plate and don't graze the kitchen or table.

❤ Prince to Pauper

PHILIPPIANS 2:5–8

Let this mind be in you which was also in Christ Jesus, who, being in the form of God, did not consider it robbery to be equal with God, but made Himself of no reputation, taking the form of a bondservant, and coming in the likeness of men. And being found in appearance as a man, He humbled Himself and became obedient to the point of death, even the death of the cross.

A PRINCE LOOKING FOR A WIFE journeyed to a village to handle business for his father. He spotted a ravishing peasant girl, and it was love at first sight. How could he express his heart?

He could order her to marry him, but he wanted the girl to do so because she freely loved him. The prince could arrive at her door in palatial splendor. But would she marry him for riches or love?

Finally, the prince decided to leave the palace, move to the peasant girl's neighborhood, and become a carpenter. He would work all day and woo her at night. If she loved him as he loved her he would propose to her, then tell her who he was.

> SPIRITUAL
> HEART FOCUS
> Give the Lord the only worthy response to One who loves you so much that He was willing to lay aside all royal privilege to woo and win your heart.

Soren Kierkegaard says this is what God did in Jesus Christ. Jesus is how God showed us what is in His heart toward us.

PHYSICAL HEART FOCUS

Progression is important in cardio exercise. If you walk, for example, set a goal of increasing from 30 to 40 minutes, or shifting from moderate to fast walking.

❤ Immanuel

MATTHEW 1:22–23

So all this was done that it might be fulfilled which was spoken by the Lord through the prophet, saying: "Behold, the virgin shall be with child, and bear a Son, and they shall call His name Immanuel," which is translated, "God with us."

THE DRAMA OF CHRISTMAS is wrapped up in one word—*Immanuel.*

Eighteenth–century deists believed God to be disinterested and inaccessible. Twenty–first–century spiritualists believe God is a vaporous force adrift in nature.

SPIRITUAL HEART FOCUS
Read Matthew 28:20 and Hebrews 13:5 and meditate on the implications for you and your immediate situation and needs.

But *Immanuel* means God is near and approachable. He's not hostile.

You can be with someone on a trip. You also can be with a person by being on their side. But when Jesus Christ is with us, we get Him both ways: He's on our side, and He continues to live with us in the world through His Spirit.

While Christ was here physically, He was baptized, not because He had sin, but to show He was identifying with sinners. He is taking our side.

"My heart is with you," we say to a hurting person. We're saying that at the deepest part of our being we are concerned and willing to do whatever we can to help.

That's the ultimate good news of Immanuel: God's heart is with us!

PHYSICAL HEART FOCUS
Don't be afraid to leave food on your plate at the end of a meal.

♥ Breaking News

LUKE 2:16–18

And they came with haste and found Mary and Joseph, and the Babe lying in a manger. Now when they had seen Him, they made widely known the saying which was told them concerning this Child. And all those who heard it marveled at those things which were told them by the shepherds.

THE LAMBS IN THE BETHLEHEM HERDS would become sheep that would be sold, then given as offerings in Herod's big temple whose parapets the shepherds could see out in the distance.

No wonder the simple shepherds were among the first to hear the news heralding the coming of the Lamb of God who will be the once–for–all sacrifice for human sin.

Big stuff always happens in the crucible of the small in God's way, and He entrusts to the hearts of lowly shepherds history's biggest event: God coming to live in the world!

Has Christmas become routine to you? Go back to ground zero, Shepherd's Field, and contemplate the miracle. You will see again the extraordinary truth of Christmas.

SPIRITUAL HEART FOCUS
Focus your heart on the extraordinary coming of God to earth, and shake off the routine of Christmas.

PHYSICAL HEART FOCUS

Each gram of carbohydrates and protein contains four calories, but a gram of fat has nine. If you consume a lot of fat, even if you increase physical activity, it's difficult to achieve a calorie deficit.

❤ Stepping Out of the Portrait

JOHN 1:14
And the Word became flesh and dwelt among us, and we beheld His glory, the glory as of the only begotten of the Father, full of grace and truth.

COLOSSIANS 2:9
For in Him dwells all the fullness of the Godhead bodily.

"I WISH FATHER COULD STEP OUT of that picture," said an English boy as he studied a portrait of his missing dad.

That had been the longing of all thoughtful men and women for generations prior to the coming of Jesus Christ. "I wish God would step out of eternity, and enter time," was the plea of many a heart.

SPIRITUAL HEART FOCUS
On this special day let your heart dwell on the reality that you live in an era the patriarchs and prophets yearned to see: the season of the revelation of God through Christ.

All the great thinkers could see God in their logic and in nature. The ancient mystics knew God existed. Hebrew patriarchs and prophets sharpened their heart–focus as intently as possible, yearning for a full, clear view. But all they could see was the fuzziness of an impressionistic painting. They yearned for Rembrandt and got Van Gogh. The colors are lovely to look at, but they can only hint at the promise and hope of the real.

Jesus Christ is God stepping off the canvas of eternity, showing us the reality of God.

PHYSICAL HEART FOCUS
Your physical body is the temple for God's continued indwelling in the material world, so respect it as you would a glorious cathedral.

❤ Boxing Day

ACTS 6:2-5

Then the twelve summoned the multitude of the disciples and said, "It is not desirable that we should leave the word of God and serve tables. Therefore, brethren, seek out from among you seven men of good reputation, full of the Holy Spirit and wisdom, whom we may appoint over this business; but we will give ourselves continually to prayer and to the ministry of the word." And the saying pleased the whole multitude. And they chose Stephen, a man full of faith and the Holy Spirit, and Philip, Prochorus, Nicanor, Timon, Parmenas, and Nicolas, a proselyte from Antioch.

IN THE UNITED KINGDOM, the day after Christmas is called "Boxing Day." There are many theories about this holiday's origin, but all of them involve the giving of gifts to less fortunate people.

The coming of Jesus Christ results in actions that bless needy people. There is a change in heart in the world.

Jesus Christ motivates unparalleled generosity, and He moves human beings to give their hearts as servants to distribute His blessed bounty. Some individuals in churches will be selected for the office of deacon, which means "servant." But all Christ's followers are to have servant hearts in the spirit of their Master who said, "For even the Son of Man did not come to be served, but to serve, and to give His life a ransom for many" (Mark 10:45).

Boxing Day is the logical sequel to Christmas.

SPIRITUAL HEART FOCUS

Now that Christmas is over, focus on a major service project you will undertake this coming year.

PHYSICAL HEART FOCUS

Saturated fatty acids threaten total heart health. Avoid them by eating more fish, chicken, olive oil, and canola oil.

♥ When the Lights Come Down

ISAIAH 9:2

The people who walked in darkness
Have seen a great light;
Those who dwelt in the land of the shadow of death,
Upon them a light has shined.

NOW COMES THE HARD PART: taking down the decorations and unraveling the lights after a festive season.

But it also may be hard on your emotional heart. For some, the world seems darker without the Christmas lights. But in God's plan, the light is for those in darkness. In fact, the deeper the darkness, the brighter the light.

A friend on a night flight from Tokyo to Los Angeles kept peeking out the window of the darkened cabin, trying to spot the Pacific. Suddenly, he saw a sliver of orange and yellow brightness split the darkness between sky and sea. Dawn was coming!

My friend said his heart was so full of beauty and hope it was all he could do to keep from running up and down the aisles of the jumbo jet, shouting to the sleeping passengers, "Arise, shine; for your light has come!"

Post–Christmas isn't the sagging–heart season, but the time to shout that the Light of the world has come!

SPIRITUAL HEART FOCUS
If your heart is feeling the blahs, meditate on the words in Isaiah and the fact that the deeper the darkness, the brighter the light.

PHYSICAL HEART FOCUS
Hydrogenated and trans fat items should be left out of your grocery basket.

♥ Shedding the Swaddling Cloths

1 CORINTHIANS 13:11

*When I was a child, I spoke as a child, I understood as a child,
I thought as a child; but when I became a man, I put away childish things.*

FIGURINES OF BABY JESUS head back to the attic soon, and that's how a lot of people prefer the real Jesus—away from view and always in swaddling clothes. Some individuals are frightened of the Jesus who leaves the manger and walks in life's marketplace.

There's a time to celebrate the Baby, but that must lead to the season of receiving the Man. Your faith and mine must shed the swaddling clothes and put away childish things.

I'm no Scrooge opposing kids' enjoyment of Christmas traditions. We must not push children into adulthood before they're ready. But we have to let Jesus outgrow the manger. It takes time for a human heart to transition from the Baby to the Man.

We miss the point of the Baby in the manger if we don't see the Man in the marketplace, because then we will never comprehend the God–Man on the cross.

It's time to shed the swaddling cloths.

SPIRITUAL HEART FOCUS
The New Year is a few days away, so consider some goals for spiritual growth to pursue in the coming year.

PHYSICAL HEART FOCUS

Start planning your exercise regimen for next year by committing to three days a week of cardio and flexibility training, with some resistance exercise and extended resistance workouts on non–cardio days.

♥ Front Office

PROVERBS 16:1

The preparations of the heart belong to man,
But the answer of the tongue is from the LORD.

GOD MAKES MAN in His image; then man makes everything else in man's image. Even our work–world institutions are remakes of our inner lives.

A factory makes rubber balls. There's a hallway for research and development that plans new balls. The R and D corridor is the human will, where plans are hatched and choices made.

A computer room has big machines storing data, running numbers, and linking the enterprise with the rest of the cyberworld. In human beings, the computer room is the mind.

Down in the quality control center, experts squeeze randomly picked rubber balls, tossing aside the mushy ones. For you and me, the "feeler" is the emotions.

Every factory has a front office where people understand how to unite all the functions.

Your heart is the front office. Only the Lord has the big picture for next year. As you envision resolutions, make Him CEO and He will bring together all the plans and functions into a successful totality.

SPIRITUAL HEART FOCUS
The greatest preparation you can make for the coming year is to enthrone Christ in your heart as Lord of your life.

PHYSICAL HEART FOCUS

You can cut the risk of coronary heart disease in half by replacing a mere two percent of your energy intake with monounsaturated or polyunsaturated fats rather than trans fatty acids.

❤ New You

2 CORINTHIANS 5:17

Therefore, if anyone is in Christ, he is a new creation;
old things have passed away; behold, all things have become new.

MANY PEOPLE EMBRACE religious philosophy rather than a new heart.

A member of our family graduated from college and seminary, earning a Ph.D. But after all that, in a tent revival meeting, he realized he had not truly received Christ, and was born again.

The genius of the new birth is that you become a new creation. As in natural birth, spiritual birth launches us on a process of growth that encompasses the total heart—the spiritual and the physical.

SPIRITUAL HEART FOCUS

Commit to continue or renew your routine of personal Bible meditation, worship, and prayer for at least 30 minutes every day throughout the next year.

You might have launched a new lifestyle of good diet and exercise habits last January, and maybe you achieved weight–loss and fitness goals. Now you're at the end of the year. But you still must commit to continuing the process of healthy growth that doesn't stop until you're in Heaven.

Perhaps you failed, slipping off your diet, neglecting personal time with God, forgetting your exercise regimen. The miracle of grace is that there is always a time and place for beginning again.

Stay on the course of renewal in Christ for your total person. He gives new lives for old!

PHYSICAL HEART FOCUS

Commit yourself to continuing or restarting a total heart healthy lifestyle of good eating and consistent exercise in the year before you.

❤ Lifelong Pursuit

2 CORINTHIANS 4:16

Therefore we do not lose heart. Even though our outward man is perishing, yet the inward man is being renewed day by day.

JESUS DOESN'T DISAPPEAR when the crèche is re–boxed.

Once He is born in a human heart He launches that person on a lifelong pursuit.

SPIRITUAL HEART FOCUS
Meditate today on Philippians 3:12, journal your thoughts, and ask God for the strength and encouragement to press on.

The total health of your spiritual heart won't be attained until your physical heart stops beating. So there's a continual pressing on to grab hold of all the good things Christ had in mind for you when He laid hold of you, as Paul put it in Philippians 3:12.

For the Christian, death is the portal into life's fullness. Life to that point is a process of adventurous growth.

In the meantime, see both spiritual and physical heart health not as a fad, but as a lifelong pursuit to lay hold of everything for which you were laid hold.

PHYSICAL HEART FOCUS

Check your weight and BMI. Celebrate this past year's health successes and renew your commitment for the coming year.

1. *The New York Times*, 30 May 1986.

2. "Penny–Pinching Tyrant," <www.bible.org>, July 1, 2004.

3. "Mind Over Body," Jim Szatkowski, *Kent State Magazine*, Volume 3, Number 4, <www.kent.edu.magazine>, July 7, 2004.

4. Walter B. Knight, "What the Old Clock Needed," *Knight's Master Book of New Illustrations* (Grand Rapids: Wm. B. Eerdman's Publishing Company, 1956).

5. Cited in Willard Aldrich, *When God Was Taken Captive* (Sisters, Oregon: Multnomah, 1989).

6. Walter Willett and P.J. Skerrett, *Eat, Drink and Be Healthy* (New York: Simon & Schuster, 2001).

7. *Epistles of Julian* 49, cited in Alvin J. Schmidt, *Under the Influence* (Grand Rapids: Zondervan, 2001).

8. Gary Thomas, *Christianity Today*, October 3, 1994, page 26.

9. *Our Daily Bread,* April 17, 1995.

10. Rebecca Mead, "A Man–Child in Lotusland," *The New Yorker*, <www.rebeccamead.com>, August 9, 2004.

11. Jay C. Grelen, "Why Everyone Looks Up to David Robinson," *Christianity Today*, <www.christianitytoday.com>, August 9, 2004.

12. Bertrand Russell, *Has Man a Future* (Hammondsworth: Penguin Press, 1961).

13. Cited in Mark A. Beliles and Stephen K. McDowell, *America's Providential History,* (Charlottesville: Providence Foundation, 1989).

14. Kreeft, Peter, *Between Heaven and Hell*, (Downers Grove: InterVarsity Press, 1982).

15. Kerby Anderson, "Health and Church Attendance," <www.probe.org>, August 9, 2004.

DR. ED YOUNG is senior pastor at the 41,000–member Second Baptist Church of Houston, Texas. He is a prolific author whose weekly radio and television program, *The Winning Walk,* is seen throughout the United

States and overseas. Ed and Jo Beth have three sons, all serving in fulltime ministry, and nine grandchildren.

Jo BETH YOUNG is a seminar speaker and Bible study teacher at Second Baptist Church in Houston, Texas, where her husband, Dr. Ed Young, is senior pastor.

Dr. Michael Duncan is an Associate Surgeon at the Texas Heart Institute (THI), Houston, Texas, since 1980. Dr. Duncan is also Clinical Associate Professor, Department of Surgery, The University of Texas Medical School at Houston, and the Director of the Cardiovascular Fellowship Program at THI. Additionally, he has served as a Cardiovascular Surgical Consultant to the Federal Air Surgeon since 1986.

Dr. Richard Leachman earned his Doctor of Medicine degree with honors from the University of Texas Health Science Center in Dallas, Texas. Dr. Leachman trained in cardiology at Parkland Memorial Hospital in Dallas and is board certified in Internal Medicine and Cardiology. He is a fellow of the American College of Cardiology.

Pastor Ed Young and his wife, Jo Beth Young, team up with two of the country's leading physicians from the world–renown Texas Heart Institute, Dr. J. Michael Duncan and Dr. Richard Leachman, to bring you these additional resources and launch you on your journey to Total Heart Health.

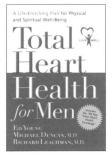

Total Heart Health for Men

An increasing body of research supports the link between physical and spiritual health. *Total Heart Health for Men* offers men the guidance they so desperately need to achieve total heart health in their lives. Men will be challenged to make practical changes toward a healthy heart, by honoring Christ both physically and spiritually, with their total hearts. 0849900131 $22.99

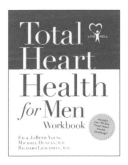

Total Heart Health for Men Workbook

It takes 21 days to break an existing behavior, 40 days to establish new behavior, and 90 days to transform the new behavior into a lifestyle. This workbook will guide, challenge, and motivate men through it all. 1418501263 $16.99

Total Heart Health for Women

Women have a unique set of pressures and expectations, and they're often urged to transform the outside in a vain attempt to heal the inside. *Total Heart Health for Women* brings women the guidance they so desperately need to achieve total heart health in their lives. The book includes practical health and fitness tips, smart recipes, and strategies for an authentic spiritual life. 0849900123 $22.99

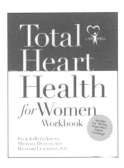

Total Heart Health for Women Workbook

This workbook presents practical steps for applying the truths of Scripture, and it encourages women as they replace unhealthy behavior patterns with healthy behaviors during the course of a 90-Day Challenge. 1418501271 $16.99

Total Heart Health Daily Living Software

The *Total Heart Health Daily Living Software* helps you achieve the goal of whole heart health. The software will actually track your progress through the 90–day program as it guides you through realistic, attainable goals for a healthier you. 141850128X $24.99

NOTES

NOTES

NOTES